The Primal Wound

SUNY Series in the Philosophy of Psychology
Michael Washburn, editor

The Primal Wound

A TRANSPERSONAL

VIEW OF TRAUMA,

ADDICTION, AND

GROWTH

John Firman and Ann Gila

State University of New York Press

Published by
State University of New York Press

© 1997 John Firman

Printed in the United States of America

For information, address the State University of New York Press,
State University Plaza, Albany, NY 12246

Production by Bernadine Dawes • Marketing by Nancy Farrell

Library of Congress Cataloging-in-Publication Data

Firman, John, 1945–
    The primal wound: a transpersonal view of trauma, addiction, and
growth / John Firman and Ann Gila.
        p.   cm. — ()SUNY series in the philosophy of psychology)
    Includes bibliographical references and index
    ISBN 0–7914–3293–9 (alk. paper). — ISBN 0–7914–3294–7 (pbk. :
alk. paper)
    1. Transpersonal psychology. 2. Self-destructive behavior.
3. Psychosynthesis. I. Gila, Ann. II. Title. III Series.
BF204.7.F57   1997
150.19'8—dc21   96–43767
                                                                          CIP

1   2   3   4   5   6   7   8   9   10

Dedicated to

Frank Haronian
(1922–1994)

and

S. K. N.
(1960–1969)

Contents

Acknowledgments

First of all we would like to thank our friend and colleague, Chris Meriam, who supported us, thought with us, and gave helpful advice and editing suggestions at all the many stages of writing. Through the convenience of e-mail, Chris was an abiding presence throughout this work, and we shall always be in his debt.

Our gratitude goes out as well to our friend and colleague, Philip Brooks, who gave us insightful feedback, especially at the formative stages of the book. Philip's ongoing support helped us persevere in this effort.

We are also grateful to Berget Jelane, Chuck Millar, and Sr. Carla Kovack for their friendship, encouragement, and insight, and to the people who made comments at various stages of writing (in alphabetical order): Mark Horowitz, Abby Seixas, Michael Washburn, Charles Whitfield, and Tom Yeomans. Many thanks as well to our students and clients over the years who have taught us about the human journey by sharing their lives with us.

Lastly, we would like to express our appreciation for the life and work of the late Frank Haronian, who deeply understood the meaning of the I-Thou relationship. He was a friend and mentor, encouraging and inspiring us for many years, and our world is a little less bright without him. We miss you, Frank.

In closing we would like to point out that Ann has resumed the use of her maiden name, Gila. Thus references to Ann Russell in the text are references to Ann Gila.

Introduction

The history of childhood is a nightmare
from which we have only recently begun to awaken.
—Lloyd deMause

Something is afoot which is bound to touch all our lives. There is a growing collective realization that much of the suffering found in life is not a necessary aspect of the human condition, but that it derives from a primal wounding to the core of our deepest humanity.

We may feel this wound as a sense of anxiety or impending doom underlying all we do; or as a sense of estrangement, falseness, and lack of meaning in our lives; or perhaps as a fear of intimacy and commit-ment in relationships. Although we may only dimly glimpse this hid-den wound, perhaps in the grips of a sleepless night, depressive mood, or personal crisis, this specter incessantly haunts us. Fleeing this wound, we desperately throw ourselves into addictions of all sorts—from sex, romance, and drugs to wealth, power, and violence—build-ing inauthentic lives that we know in our hearts are destined to crumble.

This primal wound is the result of a violation we all suffer in vari-ous ways. In this violation we are treated not as individual, unique human beings, but as objects. Our supportive milieu—whether early caregivers, peers, institutions, or society at large—does not see us as we truly are, and instead forces us to become the objects of its own purposes. In Martin Buber's (1958) terms, we are treated as "It's" rather than "Thou's." Here we are wrenched away from experiencing

1

ourselves as feeling, thinking subjects and thrust toward experiencing ourselves as soulless objects. Our intrinsic, authentic sense of self is plunged into the experience of annihilation and nonbeing. Child abuse and neglect, sexist and racist culture, and bonding to wounded caregivers are just some of the very many ways we receive the primal wounding.

However this wounding is inflicted, it is a break in the intricate web of relationships in which we live, move, and have our being. A fundamental trust and connection to the universe is betrayed, and we become strangers to ourselves and others, struggling for survival in a seemingly alien world. In psychological terms, our connection to our deeper Self is wounded. In religious and philosophical terms, it is our connection to Ultimate Reality, the Ground of Being, or the Divine that is broken. No matter how we elect to describe it, the fact remains that this wounding cuts us off from the deeper roots of our existence.

There are those who say that this alienation from self and other is intrinsic to human life, that this is fundamental to the human condition or a necessary evil in the course of evolution. However, it is becoming increasingly clear that this anxious estrangement is not integral to human life at all. Again, it is caused by *unnatural* experiences in which our fundamental relationship to other people, the world, and the Ground of Being has been violated.

From this point of view, the evils of the world may not then derive from powerful inner drives of sex, power, and survival; nor from a fundamentally "sinful" human nature; nor from collective archetypes or the narcissistic attachment to self; nor from the laws of spiritual involution, karma, or God. Rather, the pain and chaos of human existence may flow largely from this primal wounding to our essential selves. It is this wounded sense of self, this sense of emptiness and isolation, which underlies the violence, addiction, and greed disrupting our lives.

The growing collective realization of this primal wounding is manifesting in a number of ways. Since this violation begins in childhood, and there causes the most insidious devastation, our realization often revolves around the nature and effects of childhood wounding. This expansion of our collective consciousness has at least three obvious manifestations.

First, there is a strong grassroots movement—often called the "recovery movement"—in which people are realizing the many ways their lives are dominated by addictions, trauma, and self-destructive behaviors of all sorts. We find self-help groups for alcoholics and drug addicts; for compulsive gamblers, shoplifters, and overeaters; for sex and love addicts; for workaholics and chronic debtors; for sexual abuse survivors; and for those affected by another's addiction. One source estimates that as many as fifteen million people in North America alone belong to half a million support groups, and that there are two hundred different types of groups based on the recovery principles of Alcoholics Anonymous (Yoder 1990). Another source places the total membership of such groups at forty-five million (Dowd 1992).

This widespread phenomenon reflects our growing awareness that human life is pervaded by compulsivity, wounding, and the inauthenticity of our false selves. The recovery movement often plumbs the early childhood beginnings of the compulsive false self, seeking to uncover the core "true self," "child within," or "I am" that was lost in earlier psychological wounding. In other words, as people peel back the layers of their painful life situations, many discover the underlying primal wounding.

The recovery movement also involves a new appreciation for the centrality of spirituality in human life. As people work through the wounds of childhood, the true self can blossom, and they discover a new openness to prayer, meditation, and sacred ritual. This new openness can lead participants into a serious and committed spirituality as expressed in their recovery group, their religion-of-origin, or in spiritual practices beyond their own cultural context.

Second, within the field of psychotherapy there is a growing understanding of the unhealthy dynamics to be found in even the most normal of families, and so there is a deeper appreciation of the often hidden nature of childhood wounding. The normal family, even while perhaps offering healthy nurture at many levels, nevertheless can be pervaded by toxic nonempathic responsiveness, manipulation, and instability that later manifest in the compulsions, violence, and empty lives of the adult children. This pervasive wounding often remains hidden by the positive aspects of the family, leaving the adult children perplexed about the origin of feelings such as low self-worth, violation, and abandonment.

This focus on childhood wounding has been furthered by the recognition that Sigmund Freud—the father of modern psychotherapy—had seen initially that the symptoms of his patients derived from early abuse and neglect, but that he subsequently chose to interpret their reports as fantasy. Today, therapists from many schools are realizing that the underlying cause of most psychological problems is not so much childhood fantasies or conflictual drives, not so much collective archetypes or existential *angst*, but much more centrally, specific destructive events and relationships suffered in childhood. Harvard psychologist Gina O'Connell Higgins goes so far as to suggest that some version of posttraumatic stress disorder—a disorder caused by past trauma—may in fact be the "overarching rubric under which most other disorders are subordinated" (Higgins 1994, 13). In other words, it is not so much that we are sick or crazy, but that we have been *wounded*.

Third, this dawning realization of childhood wounding has gone hand in hand with an awareness of rampant child abuse and neglect. The various mass media are filled with reports of different types of child mistreatment, from overt physical and sexual abuse to the more hidden mental battering and emotional abandonment. Stringent laws have been passed that mandate many professionals to report even suspected child abuse, and there are organizations springing up that are dedicated to the advocacy of children.[1] This increased concern for children also is illustrated by interest in prenatal care, research into the sensitivity of the fetus, the heated abortion debate, and new childbirth procedures that respect the experience of the baby.

Empathy for children here means an appreciation for their inalienable rights, a new awareness that children are not "other than us" nor "defective adults" but sensing, feeling, volitional human beings with real legal standing. By the same token, it is a letting-go of the condescending, self-centered attitude by which adults maintain they always understand the child's needs better than the child. While not forgetting the important differences between adults and children, adults today are challenged to adopt a non-patronizing, non-matronizing, and respectful attitude toward children of all ages.

Of course, one might add to this list developments such as the women's movement, the men's movement, the gay and lesbian movement, or the civil rights movement, all of which are devoted to the struggle against dehumanizing elements in our culture. Such movements loudly proclaim the primal wound, revealing the tremendous suffering and injustice caused when people are seen as less than human beings.

Although much of what is happening in the above areas can be sensationalized and commercialized, and their extremes will cause inevitable backlashes, it nevertheless seems clear that there is something important happening in our collective psyche: there is a burgeoning awareness of psychological wounding through a collective empathic connection to the nature of childhood experience.

THE EVOLUTION OF EMPATHY

This increased empathy may represent a step forward in our collective evolution. The evolutionary scheme of parent-child relations, as presented by psychohistorian Lloyd deMause (1974), consists of six distinct historical modes:

1. Infanticidal Mode (antiquity to fourth century A.D.), characterized by infanticide and the sodomizing of children;
2. Abandonment Mode (fourth to thirteenth century A.D.), in which physical and emotional abandonment figure prominently;
3. Ambivalent Mode (fourteenth to seventeenth centuries), during which children "were seen as soft wax, plaster, or clay to be beaten into shape";
4. Intrusive Mode (eighteenth century), in which empathy began to appear, although there was great effort to dominate the mind, feelings, needs, and will of the child;

5. Socialization Mode (nineteenth to mid-twentieth centuries), which involved a movement away from domination to the socialization of children, as in Freud's "channeling of the impulses"; and

6. Helping Mode (beginning mid-twentieth century), which "fully involves both parents in the child's life as they work to empathize with and fulfill its expanding and particular needs."

This historical overview reveals a trail of murder, abandonment, and abuse—a collective assault on children caused by a lack of empathy. Children were considered objects, property, less than human, or small adults, and were not seen and respected as *children*, as unique human beings experiencing a particular phase of life. DeMause states that we have lacked the "psychic mechanism" necessary to empathize with children. Accordingly, he writes, "A very large percentage of the children born prior to the eighteenth century were what would today be termed 'battered children'" (p. 40).

Thus, as we mention later in this book, the primal wound seems to inhere in a broad river of abuse and neglect—often quite hidden as normal parenting practices and normal cultural beliefs—flowing down to us from ages past. At this level, the primal wound is a universal wound in our collective spirit.

We believe that the three currents of modern life noted earlier, among others, are part of a larger collective evolution. (Note that we are only commenting here upon Western civilization.) They are an expression of a developing human ability to empathize. A new "psychic mechanism" seems to be growing in our collective consciousness, and this empathic understanding embraces not only the actual children of today's world, but also the hidden childhood that is present and active within adults. As deMause notes, the evolving empathic connection to children derives from the ability of adults to engage their *own* childhood experience. The fate of the "outer child" and the fate of the "inner child" are one and the same.[2]

In sum, it seems we are drawing collectively toward the realization of a primal wound to our humanness, toward the healing of that wound, and finally, toward a deeper appreciation of the human spirit. Having said all of this, however, we would like to say that while this view of contemporary events is the context for this book as we see it, the material presented in the book itself does not hinge upon this broad evolutionary perspective. The book mentions this broader perspective only in passing, and focuses mainly upon the nature of the primal wound, the many ramifications of this wound, and the principles underlying any approach to the healing of this wound.

SEEKING A UNIFIED VIEW

In seeking to recognize and heal the many different effects of primal wounding, there is a need for a perspective that can embrace many dimensions of human being. Such a view would need to respect at least these main areas:

1. The current insights into the early relationships that impact the personality, and a focus on the nature of wounding as it occurs within these relationships—insights developed within family therapy, modern psychoanalytic theory, attachment theory, and contemporary infant research.
2. The existential psychologist's strong focus on the "I am" experience underpinning personal authenticity, courage, and choice. Here there is also a concern with fully engaging issues of nonbeing, meaning, and anxiety.
3. The approaches to human behavior developed in the field of cognitive-behavioral therapy, which provide clear conceptual models and practical methods for empowering the person to change problematic attitudes and behavior.
4. The appreciation for human psychological health, self-actualization, and "the farther reaches of human nature," found in humanistic psychology. Higher human functioning, as seen for example in "peak experiences," reveals a naturally resilient and joyous human self.

5. The realm of archetypal, paranormal, and spiritual experience studied by transpersonal psychology, psychosynthesis, and Jungian psychology. Here the sources of human selfhood are traced to dimensions that transcend the isolated ego, connecting the individual to a broader social, ecological, and even universal consciousness.

6. The healing that is taking place throughout the many self-help groups of the recovery movement, including such approaches as the Twelve Steps of Alcoholics Anonymous and "inner child work." Here too, there is an overarching concern for uncovering and healing the true self, as well as a commitment to practical, experiential spirituality.

A perspective that seeks to understand the primal wound, and to facilitate human growth beyond the effects of this wound, must be open to all the areas of the human being addressed by the above approaches. This is not to say that such a perspective would need to be a complete synthesis of all these approaches, but only that it respect the unique insights of each of them. But what sort of system could offer such a broad perspective? How might one view these widely varied views in a single gaze?

PSYCHOSYNTHESIS

This book attempts to move toward such an inclusive perspective by employing Roberto Assagioli's psychosynthesis. Assagioli was an Italian psychiatrist who in his 1910 doctoral dissertation rejected what he felt was the psychoanalytic overemphasis on psychopathology and underemphasis on the healthier aspects of the human person. Instead, he conceived *psychosynthesis*, emphasizing how the human being integrated or synthesized at ever-higher levels of functioning.

By developing psychosynthesis, Assagioli sought to address not only issues of psychological wounding and healing—work with what he called the *lower unconscious*—but, in addition, that area of the personality contacted in peak experiences, inspired creativity, and unitive states of consciousness, which he termed the *higher unconscious* (or *superconscious*). He sought to give each of these important dimensions of human experience its proper due, avoiding any reduction of one to the other. As we shall see, both of these dimensions are important in an understanding of the primal wound.

With this exploration of both the lower and higher unconscious, it becomes possible to move towards a synthesis of the personality that includes a very wide spectrum of human experience, taking into account both the heights and the depths of the personality. It is important to note, moreover, that this synthesis of the heights and depths is not simply a random coming together of these levels of the personality. Rather, the synthesis is guided by a relationship to a deeper source of being beyond the conscious personality—called *Transpersonal Self*, or simply, *Self*—which gives form and direction to the synthesis. This relationship to Self, or *Self-realization*, thus forms the context for this personal exploration and integration, providing direction and meaning not only for individual unfoldment, but for living out relationships with other people, nature, and the planet as a whole.

Psychosynthesis offers a broad outline of human being that includes the suffering of early wounding and trauma; the resulting defenses, compensations, and addictions; the confrontation with nonbeing and life meaning; the freedom and responsibility of self-actualization; the realms of paranormal, archetypal, and spiritual experience; and the challenge of Self-realization—all areas that may need to be addressed in the healing of primal wounding and in the healthy development of the whole human being.

As such a broad outline, psychosynthesis provides a workable orientation for the current work. However, while psychosynthesis does provide this wide perspective, it in no way pretends to possess all the vast knowledge contained in the many approaches listed above. Psychosynthesis here functions more as a broad sketch of the human being, a sketch that will need to be filled out and deepened by drawing on the insights from approaches specializing in the various areas of the human personality. Accordingly, this book draws a great deal upon aspects of modern psychoanalysis (object relations theory and self psychology), and many of the areas listed above as well (especially Jungian psychology, transpersonal psychology, and current infant research).

Finally, let us be very clear that this book attempts neither a comprehensive presentation of psychosynthesis nor an exhaustive point-by-point synthesis of the systems mentioned above. We concentrate instead upon the nature and effects of the primal wound, the healing of this wound, and the growth of the human spirit, and we draw upon various theoretical orientations only as they are relevant to these main themes. A focus on the human being—rather than upon the theory—thus becomes the true point of convergence for these many varied points of view.

Chapter 1 follows the participants at a workshop on addiction and abuse as they uncover the core experience of the primal wound—the plunge towards nonbeing—and the resulting compulsions and addictions. This provides an informal, experiential overview of the material covered more extensively in subsequent chapters.

Chapter 2 draws upon the insights of D. W. Winnicott, Heinz Kohut, C. G. Jung, Roberto Assagioli, and contemporary infant research in an exploration of the birth and development of human spirit. The source of personal selfhood is seen to be a connection to a deeper Self, a connection that is disturbed in primal wounding.

Chapter 3 is devoted to a careful examination of the nature of human selfhood as this endures through changing inner psychological experience. Here again the direct connection between personal being and the deeper being of Self is explored, and the damage to this connection from primal wounding becomes more evident.

Chapter 4 attempts to understand the natural pattern of human development as the unfoldment of personal selfhood within an interpersonal context. This discussion prepares the ground for understanding the ways this developmental pattern is affected when the interpersonal context is disrupted by primal wounding.

Chapter 5 reveals the nature of the primal wound of nonbeing and the manner in which this wound creates a fundamental splitting of the psyche into a negative sector and a positive sector—the lower unconscious and the higher unconscious.

Chapter 6 describes the higher and lower unconscious, two major sectors of the human personality. The separation between these two sectors is seen to be a function of traumatic disruptions in significant relationships —the primal wound.

Chapter 7 examines some of the major dynamics that result from the primal wounding and splitting of the human personality. These include the survival personality (or "false self"), the survival trance, rage, and the formation of subpersonalities.

Chapter 8 attempts to outline the larger path of Self-realization. This journey is seen as a lifetime process, one that may lead into the heights of spiritual experience and unitive consciousness, into the depths of wounding and healing, and to the discernment of a lifetime calling or vocation.

Chapter 9 presents psychosynthesis therapy as an approach that seeks to address the wide range of human experience encountered in Self-realization. The two stages of therapy are outlined and a clinical case is presented.

Chapter 10 focuses upon the person of the psychosynthesis therapist. This chapter describes the depths and heights from which a therapist operates in order to function as an empathic presence throughout a path of healing, growth, and Self-realization.

1
An Addiction/Abuse Workshop

*When our alive True Self goes into hiding, in order to please its parent figure
and to survive, a false, co-dependent self emerges to take its place. We thus lose
our awareness of our True Self to such an extent that we actually lose awareness
of its existence. We lose contact with who we really are. Gradually,
we begin to think we are that false self—so that it becomes
a habit, and finally an addiction.*
—Charles Whitfield

Over the past seven years, we have conducted workshops for professionals that address the issues of addiction and abuse. In these workshops, participants are invited to focus upon the inner experience of these two important mental health issues in order to learn about them from the inside, so to speak. What they discover is a wound that underlies not only addiction and abuse, but much of the human condition itself—the primal wound. The following is based on a typical workshop and provides a glimpse into the lived experience of the primal wound.

THE WOUNDED SPIRIT

At the beginning of the workshop, participants were asked to think of their own personal compulsions or addictions—behaviors or attitudes in which they found themselves involved against their will. Some thought of alcohol, drugs, sex, and food; others recalled obsessive relationships with lovers, spouses, or their children; still

13

others focused on compulsivity in their personal and professional lives. People seemed to have no trouble finding at least one of their addictions, whether to substances, people, or behaviors. Participants could elect to share or not share their addiction.

They were then invited to imagine themselves in a situation during which they were beginning to feel the urge to engage in their addiction. They were encouraged to allow themselves to feel this urge as much as they possibly could, but then to imagine they choose *not* to perform the addictive behavior. Instead of acting out the addiction in the usual way, they simply sat with this pressing urge as it cried out for expression.

Vividly feeling that unpleasant moment, they slowly and carefully examined their experience of this urge that sought to drive them into the addiction. They were asked to plumb the depths of the feeling, to look deeply into the experience and attempt to get to the very bottom of it. What was in the experience that was so profoundly unpleasant that it demanded the addictive behavior? Sit with it. Explore it. Get to the absolute core of it.

The room was filled with silent tension as people struggled to see into this experience of their addictive urge, to peel back the layers of restlessness, agitation, and irritation, and allow the core to be revealed. Then we stepped to the chalkboard and asked the participants to share what they found. Here is the list they made:

Disintegration

Worthlessness

Lost

Disconnection

Lack of existence

Invisible

Bad

Evil

Void

Vacuum

Abandoned

Alone

Powerless

Wimpy

Wrong

Tense

Paranoid

Not breathing, nonbeing

Humiliated

Shame

Unloved

The above experiences were in effect so terrible that these people were being forced, automatically and unconsciously, to avoid them in their lives. These are the experiences that trigger their powerful addictive behaviors, behaviors they could not control even though the addictions in many cases involved considerable discomfort and pain, and in some cases, posed a threat to life.

But what exactly is it that makes each of these experiences so terrible? What is the power here that drives us to addiction?

In looking for the common denominator or underlying theme of all these experiences, one can sense some core experience involving the extinction of individual selfhood. For example, if I feel "shameful" and "guilty," or "wimpy" and "powerless," I am in a vulnerable position that might eventually lead to my destruction. Or if I am feeling "worthless, unloved, and wrong," I feel like someone who can be eradicated. And of course, feeling "disintegration," "lack of existence," "invisibility," or "nonbeing" even more directly implies that I am passing out of existence. Such experiences suggest a threat to my existence, a threat to my being. In short, all these experiences imply the threat of nonbeing.

Part of the tremendous power of addictions is that they offer ways of avoiding the threat of nonbeing. Addictions are not simply habits and tastes casually gathered over the course of living; they are desperate strategies by which we attempt to avoid the unimaginable terror of nonexistence. This partially explains the perplexing tenacity of addictions even in the face of pain, illness, and physical death itself. Using three different random examples, we can diagram the relationship between nonbeing, these negative feelings, and addictions as shown in figure 1.1.

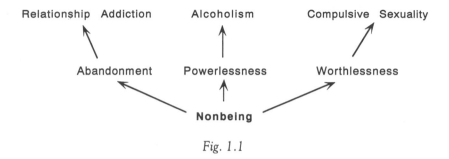

Fig. 1.1

The arrows illustrate a movement away from the negative experiences conditioned by nonbeing—abandonment, powerlessness, and worthlessness—into the apparent safety and comfort of the addictive process. These negative experiences or qualities embody the threat of nonbeing, and form the immediate foundation or "basement" of the addiction. We shall see in a moment that there is also an "attic" to the addictive structure, that is, positive experiences that are incorporated into the addiction.

By nonbeing we do not mean physical death. Although nonbeing and death often are confused, people prove daily that physical death is nothing compared to the dread of nonbeing: the betrayed lover feels so devastated that she or he commits suicide or homicide rather than live with the experience of a wounded self; the battered spouse returns time and again to the life-threatening relationship rather than ending the relationship and feeling profoundly lost and alone; alcohol and nicotine addicts ignore cirrhosis and cancer in pursuit of a habit that seems to offer some respite from underlying threatening experiences. All of these demonstrate a motivation beyond life and death. Given such empirical evidence, then, we speak here of something more terrible than death itself—nonbeing.

Participants in the workshop began at the top of the above diagram and moved down toward the hidden root of negative experiences beneath their addictions. (As we shall discuss later, this realm is what Roberto Assagioli termed the *lower unconscious*.) They found that addictions in effect seemed to offer some protection from the threat of personal annihilation. But this is only half of the picture. The addictive process involves not only this avoidance of nonbeing, but a quest for being as well.

THE ATTEMPTED REMEDY

After exploring the depths of nonbeing, the members of the group were asked to return to their imaginations and to that exact moment in which they first feel the urge to act out their addiction. This time, however, they were invited to imagine that they do not stop themselves, but that they instead freely engage in the addictive behavior.

As they fully experienced the addiction in fantasy, they were again asked to go to the core of the experience. What was the essential thing the addiction gave them? What was the positive experience they sought in their addiction, even though the addiction was destructive in many other ways? We again stepped to the chalkboard and asked the participants to share what they found. Here is their list:

I'm okay

Breath

Deep satisfaction

Completion

Allaying and release of anxiety

Peace

Approval, I'm okay

Security

Comfort

Being playful

Allowed to be my child

Self-discovery

A focus for my life

Meaning

Rebellion/power/anarchy

Self-directed

Surrender

Will

Spontaneity

Nonconformity

Illegality

Ritual

Normality

Acceptance by group

Feeling of being alive

Freedom

Acceptance of desire

Living in the flow of the moment

Identification with the group

Here they were discovering what might be called positive "kernels" or "nuclei" hidden within the addictive process. Such a positive nucleus is like a tiny glimmer of goodness buried in the destructiveness of the addiction. While engaging the addiction, these people reported feeling not the threat of nonbeing, but touches of acceptance, freedom, positive selfhood, and personal power. Even a feeling of oblivion or unconsciousness, which is experienced in many addictions, still holds the positive nuclei of peace or serenity—quite different from the gut-wrenching anxiety of facing true nonbeing.

Participants' compulsive behaviors served not only to avoid the negative experiences conditioned by nonbeing, but promised positive experiences also. Rather than feeling bad about themselves and life, empty and worthless, isolated and afraid, they could here feel good about themselves and about life, feel free and confident, feel connected to themselves and other people.

In short, rather than having a negative experience of self-and-world, of existence, of being, there is here a positive experience of self-and-world, of existence, of being. Participants discovered that their addictions were methods by which they attempted to climb out of a realm of negative experience into a realm of positive experience. Using our same three random examples above, we can add positive modes of being to the diagram.

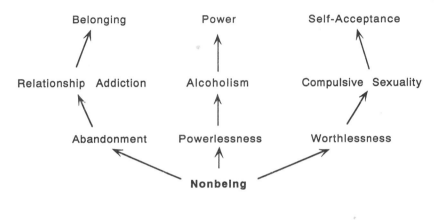

Fig. 1.2

This diagram shown in figure 1.2 depicts some positive modes of being—belonging, power, and self-acceptance—as forming the positive nuclei of the three addictions shown. In order to escape the feeling of abandonment, for example, I might become addicted to a particular relationship that gives me an experience of belonging. And however destructive this relationship is to myself or the other person, I will still remain in its thrall, pushed by the threat of abandonment and enticed by the promise of belonging.

Addiction embodies a powerful and destructive vicious circle in which we continually cycle through negative and positive modes of being. In abusive relationships, we are seduced by moments of peace and love and then are plunged into despair by the next round of abuse. In substance abuse, we feel the joy and well-being of the intoxication, but then the remorse and self-loathing of the morning after. Here is the closed system, the vicious circle, of the addictive process. Our drawing is more complete if we add the cycling between negative and positive modes shown in figure 1.3.

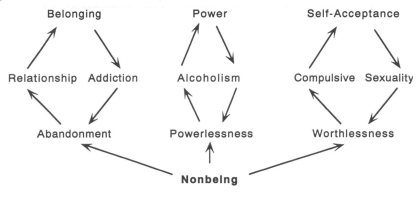

Fig. 1.3

The addictive process then juxtaposes these two powerful forces of positive and negative modes of being. We are like the proverbial donkey, threatened by the stick of the negative mode while being enticed by the carrot of the positive mode. We are trapped in a powerful energy field created by opposing negative and positive poles. The strong interplay between these poles, between what the Buddhists call "aversion and craving," pervades human existence.

We feel impotent and worthless beneath the desperate search for the right career, house, or stock portfolio that will give us some sense of power and self-worth. Or, feeling an undercurrent of meaninglessness and emptiness in our lives, we become addicted to sex and relationships, to children and family, or to fame and fortune, in order to feel fulfilled and purposeful. As we shall explore in another chapter, this dynamic also drives the formation of an entire *survival personality*, a presentable and even winning personality that hides the deeper experiences of isolation, low self-worth, and emptiness.

Virtually all dysfunctional human behavior seems conditioned to some extent by the threat of nonbeing and the resultant pushes and pulls of negative and positive modes of being. The twin dynamic between negative and positive modes of being drives our lives, while the still-deeper threat of nonbeing drives them both.

But now some final questions arise. Where does this threat of non-being come from in the first place? Is nonbeing intrinsic to the fabric of life, or does it represent a wound in that fabric? Is nonbeing a natural aspect of human existence, or is it the effect of some unnatural event?

The hypothesis here is that the threat of nonbeing is not intrinsic to human life, and that it indicates a primal wound to our sense of self caused by trauma. This position encourages one not to accept fatalis-tically the threat of nonbeing as an essential characteristic of nature, but to search for the root causes of this primal wound. Let us rejoin the workshop as participants do precisely this.

NEGLECT AND ABUSE

After some discussion of the preceding exercise, it became time to address the issues of neglect and abuse and their traumatic effect on the human personality. We did not define neglect or abuse at this point in the workshop, but simply moved toward exploring the par-ticipants' own sense of these.

People were asked if they wished to explore their own personal experiences of neglect and abuse, again with the intention of plumb-ing the experience to its core. Those who wished to do this were asked to close their eyes and to think of a time when they felt neglected or abused. They were asked to relive the experience in their imagina-tions to the extent to which this felt comfortable. If at any time they felt too uncomfortable during the exercise, they were to stop, open their eyes, and make contact with us. These experiences were disturb-ing to explore, so participants were encouraged to respect their own sense of whether to proceed or not at every point during the process. Too, there were bonds of trust among the group members that sup-ported this work.

After some time of experientially exploring what was for them the central experience of neglect or abuse, they were asked to open their eyes and again share what they had discovered. Here is their list:

I don't exist

Invaded (leading to dissociation and mistrust)

Overpowered

Impotent

You can't exist (leading to thoughts of rebellion, murder, suicide)

You can't exist, except as I say (causing withdrawal into fantasy)

I am worthless

Humiliation

Powerlessness

Betrayal (leading to rage)

Violation

Frustration, rage

Isolation

Denial of my existence

Trapped

Fearful

Loneliness

No one there to protect, to turn to

Feeling of being a bad person

During the discussion that followed, participants reported that while they were suffering neglect and abuse they did not feel like human beings. They did not in these moments experience themselves as feeling persons, but as mere objects with no freedom, dignity, or human identity. In Martin Buber's (1958) terms, they felt themselves not as "Thou's" but as "It's." They felt cut off from the life-giving communion of human relationship, and at the mercy of blind impersonal forces.

In moments of neglect, they felt unseen, unheard, and unacknowledged in their humanness. It was as if a lifeline had been cut, causing them to fall into a seemingly bottomless pit of isolation, loneliness, and worthlessness. And abuse added something more to this trauma of neglect: the active violation, betrayal, and destruction of humanness. In abuse we are not only treated as objects, but we are used in violent and humiliating ways.

The experiences listed above strongly resemble the experiences that participants had found earlier to trigger the addictive behaviors. But here is an even clearer focus on the primal wound of nonbeing: "I don't exist," "Denial of my existence," "You can't exist." Like the threatening experiences that triggered the addictions, the core experience of neglect and abuse tends towards nonbeing—the two lists are quite equivalent in this regard.

Thus it seems that this powerful threat of nonbeing, so central to self-destructive attachments, arises when we are treated as objects rather than as unique human persons. The wound of nonbeing is not like the accidental pain, fear, or injury we suffer in life; it is caused by the intentional or unintentional acts of those around us. As we shall see in the next chapter, the core experience of human being derives from our relationships in life, so it makes sense that the threat of nonbeing arises when these relationships are disturbed.

In Conclusion

In looking at the entire psychological terrain covered in the workshop, we are left with this hypothetical pattern:

1. Neglect or abuse, causing wounding, which creates
2. The threat of nonbeing, leading to
3. The powerful twin dynamism between negative and positive modes of being.

We have only to add the central element of wounding in order to complete our diagram (figure 1.4).

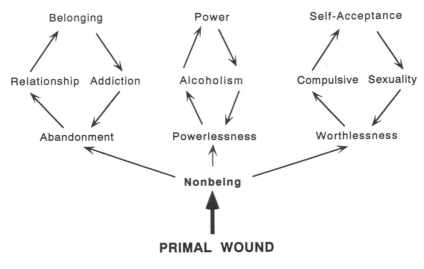

Fig. 1.4

What emerged during this workshop are core dynamics operating in human psychological dysfunction. The experiences of the participants support the view that human life is crippled—invisibly but powerfully—by the wound of nonbeing caused by neglect and abuse. This primal wound forces our lives to become dominated by the desperate unconscious avoidance of nonbeing, and the equally desperate search for a sense of being untouched by this wounding. While the sources of the wound may be hidden and difficult to recognize, it may well be worth searching for these sources when dealing with self-destructive addictions, compulsions, or attachments in our lives.

And as stated in the introduction, it is only in the past couple of decades that this hidden realm of wounding is fully revealing itself. There is today a strong and growing recovery movement, an explosion of different programs designed to heal the effects of childhood abuse and neglect. This movement is a collective grappling with the varied effects of childhood wounding, from codependence and workaholism to romance and sex addiction to alcohol and drug abuse. The list goes on and on, illuminating the many destructive ways we attempt to secure being in the face of nonbeing.

Indeed, the diagram above is quite similar to the "iceberg model" developed by a major thinker in the recovery movement, Charles Whitfield (1991). Whitfield's model points to dysfunction in family and society as the root cause of human wounding, but this wounding is submerged deeply in the unconscious in the same way an iceberg is submerged in water. According to Whitfield, from this hidden trauma there develop such feelings as abandonment, shame, and emptiness, which finally break into expression in such things as chemical dependence, eating disorders, and relationship addictions. These latter manifestations are more visible, and are thus the tip of the "iceberg" whose larger mass is hidden from view and whose core is early wounding.

We have then a model of human wounding and defense that is rooted in a primal wound of nonbeing and the resulting compulsive drive for being. We have found this model quite useful in our practice of psychotherapy, and it seems to clarify many important aspects of human psychological problems.[1]

Furthermore, the breadth of this point of view holds a possibility that many approaches to human health and healing can be seen addressing these same core issues of wounding, nonbeing, and being in different ways. In short, the nonbeing-being dynamic, focused as it is upon the core experience of human selfhood, can become one of the linchpins connecting many otherwise dissimilar approaches to human healing and growth.[2]

2

The Source of Human Spirit

And God created humankind in his image.
—Genesis 3:27

Your Self is a copy made in the image of God.
—Jalalud-din Rumi, Sufi

Before we can understand the powerful and destructive dynamic of
being-nonbeing outlined in the previous chapter, it is first necessary
to understand the genesis and development of human being, of the
human spirit, of the deepest "I" of personal identity. Only by understanding how human selfhood comes into existence can we see into
the essential nature of human being and thereby (a) recognize the disruptions to this being; (b) understand the desperate addictive compensations caused by these disruptions; and finally, (c) begin to apply
this knowledge in a comprehensive approach to psychological healing.

In this chapter we will explore the genesis of human being from
two different perspectives. The first is to examine briefly the primal
state of human existence, the state from which development proceeds.
We shall examine both the earlier view and the current view of this
primal state. The second approach will be to set aside any notions of
a primal state and instead study human being as it unfolds over the
course of time. Here we will trace the birth and development of the
human spirit within the nurture of empathic relationships.

27

The Early View of the Genesis of Human Being

At least since Freud, it was thought that the earliest states of human existence involved a fusion of self and other, an inability of the person to distinguish between self and environment. In Freud's words: "Originally the ego includes everything, later it separates off an external world from itself" (Freud 1961, 15–16). Freud saw the infant as immersed in a state characterized by "primary narcissism" and the "oceanic feeling," lost in instinctual drives and fantasy, and isolated from environmental realities. For the most part, the infant is seen here as not in active, meaningful, and reality-based relationship with others.

According to this view of early human development, the infant only gradually breaks out of this primitive undifferentiated state, learning over time to make the self-other distinction and thereby entering into meaningful relationship with the outside world. Margaret Mahler, Fred Pine, and Anni Bergman (1975) described this process as "separation-individuation" by which the infant emerged from a symbiotic fusion with the mother.

This same idea has been taken up by some thinkers in transpersonal psychology as well. Transpersonal theorist Ken Wilber called this supposed early fused state the "primary matrix": "The infant cannot differentiate self from other, subject from object, inside from outside but, rather, lives in a primary matrix where such distinctions are as yet absent (the pleroma)" (Wilber 1983, 233). In Wilber's system, this "subconscious, prepersonal, biomaterial fusion" precedes the climb upwards to the personal and transpersonal levels of development.

This model of early human life did not see the infant and child as actively and realistically relating to the world around them. Lost in the merged state, the young human being was presumed to be out of touch with reality, experiencing instead the distorted perceptions arising from this confusion of self and environment. It followed, of course, that any adult memories of past neglect and abuse must be the product of fantasy, because there could not have been any accurate perception of interpersonal realities when young.

The early trauma underlying psychopathology must not then arise from the actual events of life, it was thought, but instead from a struggle with the person's own inner world. This theory was not only effective in hiding early interpersonal wounding, it may even have encouraged it—if the infant and child were not conscious human beings, not conscious of reality, then why not do as one wishes with them? Here is author David Chamberlain, writing in the *Pre- and Perinatal Psychology Journal*, describing the effects of this "nineteenth-century view" of the baby:

> As long as parents and professionals continue to believe that babies are deaf, dumb, blind and mindless, babies will continue to be mistreated and the world will be robbed of the priceless opportunities afforded by each conception, each pregnancy, and each birth. (Chamberlain 1994, 11)[1]

According to this older view of human life, growth involved a movement up through developmental stages leading away from the supposed primary fused state. Psychopathology was seen as a regression or fixation along this path, a failure to wrest individuality from the undifferentiated matrix. With this theory, we had a tidy diagnostic typology in which those disorders closest to the undifferentiated state were the psychoses; a little further away, the borderline personalities; still further away, the narcissistic disorders; and finally, farthest along the developmental line, the neuroses (in transpersonal systems, this spectrum continues into transegoic development and perhaps an encounter with higher pathologies).

Psychological health and dysfunction therefore revolved around a struggle with this primordial undifferentiated unity presumed to exist at the root of our being. Terms such as archaic, primitive, and infantile were used to indicate these early states from which we were to free ourselves in a climb upwards through the stages of development. In short, the notions of regression or progression along a developmental timeline dominated the theory of psychotherapy.

But then came new infant research.

The Current View of the Genesis of Human Being

According to researcher and psychiatrist Daniel Stern in his landmark book, *The Interpersonal World of the Infant* (1985), contemporary experimental research into human infancy indicates that the foundation of human being is not a state of self-other fusion at all, but a state of self-other *relationship*.

Significantly, the research drawn upon by Stern is not based upon maintaining a psychoanalytic distance from infants, observing them "from the outside," so to speak (the major thrust of Mahler et al.). Instead this research entails an interactive relationship with infants and an emphathic inquiry into their subjective experience. This research—which Stern calls a revolution in infancy research—actively engages the infant, inviting him or her to respond to experimental situations through head-turning, sucking, and looking.

For example, infants are found to reliably turn their heads toward the smell of their mothers' milk versus the milk of another, indicating an ability to make this discrimination (MacFarlane 1975); infants have been found to have a preference for the human voice versus other sounds by teaching them to control these stimuli by sucking on an electronically bugged nipple (Friedlander 1970); and infant looking patterns have revealed their preference for looking at faces rather than other visual stimuli (Franz 1963). In effect, the infants *themselves* are here telling us about their experience.

The research Stern bases his work upon thereby represents a major breakthrough in our empathic connection to childhood, and by these methods the infant is revealed not as lost in a primal self-other fusion, but as a conscious, intentional being:

> The evidence . . . suggests that the capacity to have merger- or fusion-like experiences as described in psychoanalysis is secondary to and dependent upon *an already existing sense of self and other.* The newly suggested timetable pushes the emergence of the self earlier in time dramatically and reverses the sequencing of developmental tasks. *First comes the formation of self and other, and only then is the sense of merger-like experiences possible.* (P. 70, emphases added)

According to Stern, infants are not lost in a fantasy world distorted by instinctual drives, but are active and aware from the start, purposely engaged in the business of relating to the environment. In other words, the bedrock of human being is not undifferentiated unity, but relationship:

> Infants begin to experience a sense of an emergent self from birth. They are predesigned to be aware of self-organizing processes. They *never experience a period of total self/other undifferentiation*. There is *no confusion between self and other* in the beginning or at any point during infancy. They are also predesigned to be selectively responsive to external social events and *never experience an autistic-like phase*. (P. 10, emphases added)

But is it not true, as Freud maintained, that infants live in a world of fantasy, in the thrall of the "pleasure principle," only later to encounter the objectivity of the "reality principle"? According to Stern, apparently not:

> The position taken here is . . . that infants from the beginning mainly experience reality. Their subjective experiences suffer no distortion by virtue of wishes or defenses, but only those made inevitable by perceptual or cognitive immaturity or overgeneralization. . . . The views presented here suggest that the usual genetic sequence should be reversed and that *reality experience precedes fantasy distortions in development*. . . . It is the *actual shape of interpersonal reality*, specified by the interpersonal invariants that really exist, that helps determine the developmental course. (P. 255, emphases added)

Again, this new view of the infant as differentiated, relational, and volitional seems to be characteristic of current infant research in general. As Michael Washburn points out in his recent review of this research, "Contemporary opinion seems to favor the view that babies enter the world already differentiated, related to objects, and aware of themselves to some degree" (Washburn 1994, 33). See, too, the review of this research by Joseph D. Lichtenberg (1983), who attempts to adjust psychoanalytic theory to these new findings. And finally, note the growing body of knowledge concerning prenatal learning, communication with the prenate, and the effects of prenatal trauma documented in the *Pre- and Perinatal Psychology Journal.*

The current view seems then to be that human being arises not from an undifferentiated, unified source, but from a differentiated matrix of relationships, a *relational* source of being. There is not a primary state of self-other fusion that one must subdue in order to achieve individual selfhood, not an inborn autism that must be overcome to attain "object-relatedness." Rather, individual selfhood is meaningfully related to others from the beginning. At the deepest level, human being is relational.

Thus psychological disturbances are best understood not as regression or fixation vis-à-vis a fused primal state, but as damage to the primary state of relationship. It is the violation of this fundamental relational sense of being that can lead to painful experiences such as depression, anxiety, chaotic affective and cognitive states, dissociation, pathological narcissism, and self-other boundary problems. Such symptoms do not indicate a struggle with a primordial undifferentiated unity or narcissistic state, but a violation of relational bonds. States of fusion and alienation are not primary to human being—they are the effects of trauma.[2]

However, setting aside the question of a primal state, we can study the genesis of human being from another perspective as well—development over the course of time. Even though belief in an early fused state still seems subtly to condition much psychological thinking, there does seem to be a growing recognition that the human spirit arises and develops via the nurture of empathic relationships. From this point of view too, human being is seen as quintessentially relational.

We shall now turn our attention to several major thinkers who recognize this relational foundation of human being: D. W. Winnicott, Heinz Kohut, C. G. Jung, and Roberto Assagioli. For brevity's sake, we can of course only focus upon our current themes as these appear in their work. The final section will attempt to synthesize the relevant principles found in these four points of view.

D. W. WINNICOTT

The thinking of the British pediatrician and psychoanalyst D. W. Winnicott revolves around the insight that human being arises from an interpersonal context. Winnicott recognized a "true self" whose experience of existence evolves from a matrix of protective care beginning in the womb: "With 'the care that it receives from its mother' each infant is able to have a personal existence, and so begins to build up what might be called a *continuity of being* . . . If maternal care is not good enough then the infant does not really come into existence, since there is no continuity of being . . ." (Winnicott 1987, 54).

The experience of human being, of existence, develops from the relationship between the infant and the "good enough mother." Existence as an independent human being depends on relationship, on a relational source of being; here is a paradoxical synthesis of dependence and independence, of connection and freedom.

For Winnicott, even the ability to be alone is "based on the experience of being alone in the presence of someone" (p. 32). Whether that someone is the caregiver, the early supportive milieu, or the "internal environment" conditioned by these, the ability to be alone itself depends upon relationship to some other. Winnicott summed up his profoundly relational view in his famous statement, "There is no such thing as an infant" (p. 39). That is, the infant cannot be understood without reference to his or her relationship with the nurturing or "facilitating" environment.

The Empathic Connection

Central to good enough early caregiving is the empathic connection to the caregiver, which the caregiver helps establish by an attitude called "mirroring" by Winnicott and others (e.g. Kohut). Mirroring occurs as the caregiver can look at the infant and recognize the unique individual human being who exists there. As the infant experiences his or her self reflected in the caregiver's attitude, the infant is able to realize that she or he *is* indeed a unique, individual human being. Winnicott stated this in his profound and succinct phrase, "When I look I am seen, so I exist" (Winnicott 1988b, 134).

Of course, mirroring demands that caregivers not be projecting their own needs, fantasies, or demands on the infant, in which case the infant would not find "I" reflected, but find instead the caregivers' image of who the infant should be. Here is Alice Miller writing about Winnicott's notion of mirroring:

> The mother gazes at the baby in her arms, and baby gazes at his mother's face and finds himself therein . . . provided that the mother is really looking at the unique, small, helpless being and not project-ing her own introjects onto the child, nor her own expectations, fears, and plans for the child. In that case, the child would not find himself in his mother's face but rather the mother's own predica-ments. This child would remain without a mirror, and for the rest of his life would be seeking this mirror in vain. (Miller 1981, 32)

We might say the lack of mirroring leads to the reverse of Winnicott's statement quoted above, that is: "When I look I am *not* seen, so I *do not* exist." Under these unresponsive conditions the infant is given the choice of either not existing at all—nonbeing—or of developing what Winnicott called a "false self" in response to the caregivers' demands.

The Holding Environment

This empathic connection with the caregiver is not limited to the moments the caregiver is physically present, but comes to infuse the total environment—"the whole routine of care throughout the day and night" (Winnicott 1987, 49)—in which the infant lives, moves, and finds continuity of being. When the infant is at play, resting in the crib, or moving through "the minute day-to-day changes belong-ing to the infant's growth and development" (p. 49), there is the expe-rience of being held in empathic concern. These changing situations are in effect infused by the empathic connection with the caregiver, and become manifestations of this connection.

Winnicott called this broader empathic milieu the *holding environment* because the infant is held in being by this environment. This empathic holding, depicted in figure 2.1, is contrasted to a situation in which the empathic holding is broken—one is then "dropped" and "falls" so to speak—which gives the experience of *annihilation* or non-being.

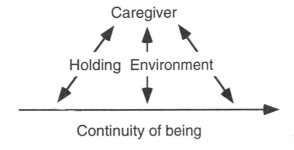

Fig. 2.1

The empathic mirroring connection seems then deeper than any of the child's particular sensations, different emotions and feelings, or various passing states of mind. For example, this connection is not to be confused with a contented state of discharged tension or satiated needs. Whether crying in soiled diapers or suckling at the breast, whether tired and upset or rested and calm, the baby can experience a continuity of being abiding through it all. Indeed, Winnicott points out that a converse dynamic is true as well—the infant can be annihilated by nonempathic response even while seemingly content at the breast.

The point is that this continuity of being abides through all experiences, pleasant or unpleasant, and through all the early developmental changes. A person here has the strength of selfhood to engage the widest possible range of human experience. Held in being, one finds the strength of self needed to feel fully the pain and joy, the anger and love, the defeats and triumphs, the dependence and independence, which make up the fabric of human existence.

Now let us outline how Heinz Kohut, working within a different psychoanalytic orientation and in another country, understood the source of human spirit in ways very similar to Winnicott.

HEINZ KOHUT AND SELF PSYCHOLOGY

Heinz Kohut, the American psychoanalyst who gave birth to the field of self psychology, was similar to Winnicott in understanding human being as founded in relationship (again, setting aside his belief in an earlier primitive fusion). Kohut believed that a person's sense of self is always dependent upon a connection to some other who is experienced as essential to that self.

This essential other functions not simply as an ordinary object vis-à-vis the self, but is so intimately connected to the self that Kohut called this other a *selfobject*. The human self is ever held within some self-selfobject relationship, is never to be found in isolation, is always dependent on this *selfobject function(s)*. Here Kohut describes the function of the self-selfobject relationship in a single remarkable sentence:

> Throughout his life a person will experience himself as a cohesive harmonious firm unit in time and space, connected with his past and pointing meaningfully into a creative-productive future, [but] only as long as, at each stage in his life, he experiences certain representatives of his human surrounding as joyfully responding to him, as available to him as sources of idealized strength and calmness, as being silently present but in essence like him, and, at any rate, able to grasp his inner life more or less accurately so that their responses are attuned to his needs and allow him to grasp their inner life when his is in need of such sustenance. (Kohut 1984, 51–52)

These "certain representatives of his human surrounding" are providing the selfobject function. They support the self through time via their mirroring empathic relatedness, that is, they "grasp his inner life more or less accurately so that their responses are attuned to his needs."

The Empathic Connection

As did Winnicott, Kohut saw that the healthy human environment is founded upon an empathic relationship to a significant other. The empathic connection is so essential to human selfhood that it is as "psychological oxygen . . . without which we cannot psychologically survive" (p. 18). This other, providing the selfobject function, allows the continuing experience of unique selfhood, of individual being. Kohut refers to this experience of continuing selfhood as the "cohesion of self in space and time," akin to Winnicott's notion of "continuity of being."

More than does Winnicott, Kohut emphasizes that these crucial empathic connections are not limited to childhood, but allow the unfoldment of a sense of self throughout the entire life span: "Self psychology holds that self-selfobject relationships form the essence of psychological life from birth to death, that a move from dependence (symbiosis) to independence (autonomy) in the psychological sphere is no more possible, let alone desirable, than a corresponding move from a life dependent on oxygen to a life independent of it in the biological sphere" (p. 47). The empathic selfobject function not only allows a cohesive self to abide through all life stages, but facilitates a meaningful sense of purpose and direction for that self—what Kohut calls the unfoldment of one's *nuclear program*, the unique path of the *nuclear self*. This idea is depicted in figure 2.2. As we shall see, this dynamic directionality in human growth is quite akin to Jung's notion of the ego responding to self, and Assagioli's concept of "I" responding to Self.

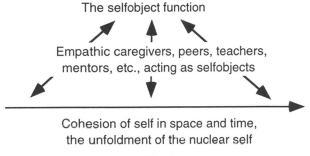

The selfobject function

Empathic caregivers, peers, teachers,
mentors, etc., acting as selfobjects

Cohesion of self in space and time,
the unfoldment of the nuclear self

Fig. 2.2

A Transpersonal Selfobject?

Kohut (1985) takes his relational view of the person farthest in describing how the self can remain intact even while facing the complete termination of life itself. Kohut studies human beings whose loyalty to the continuity of self and ideals becomes more important than biological survival. Here he finds a sense of self which is unbowed by physical annihilation, which in some way transcends even suffering and death.

This triumph of self over death is represented by those whom Kohut calls the "martyr-heroes" of history, such as Franz Jägerstätter and Hans and Sophie Scholl, who chose to face death under the Nazis, or Hamlet and Jesus who chose to confront death rather than betray who they were. Each of these people, according to Kohut, suffered death in what may have seemed like utter defeat, but this death was "actually a narcissistic triumph" (p. 44), that is, a triumph of deepest, nuclear self (Kohut uses "narcissism" to mean a sense of self). He describes the ability of such human beings to face death with qualities of the nuclear self intact—e.g., empathy, humor, and wisdom—and to choose even a painful death rather than lose their spirit.

Kohut sees this transcendence of death in a more common issue faced by us all: the existential task of coming to terms with our own personal limitations and mortality. In this regard, he writes that one can realize "a cosmic narcissism which has transcended the bounds of the individual" (p. 119). And he claims that this attainment is not a denial of individuality and mortality, but rather "a shift of the narcissistic cathexes, from the self to a concept of participation in a supraindividual and timeless existence" (p. 119). This very interesting notion of cosmic narcissism seems to imply a relationship to some cosmic or transpersonal selfobject—a supraindividual and timeless existence—which offers a continuity of being of such potency that it allows a victory over suffering and death. This type of transpersonal selfobject function is also recognized in Jungian psychology and psychosynthesis, where it is called "Self" (with a capital S).

JUNG AND ANALYTICAL PSYCHOLOGY

With Winnicott and Kohut, we have seen how the human spirit unfolds within the nurture of empathic relationships with other human beings. The next two thinkers trace the source of human being to a deeper Self that is encountered not only in relationships with other people but in relationships with symbols, dreams, archetypal patterns, and images of the Divine. The first thinker we shall discuss is C. G. Jung.

As Winnicott discerns personal existence arising within the empathic concern of the good enough caregiver, and Kohut within the empathic self-selfobject relationship, so Jungian psychology understands conscious personal existence—the ego—arising from an empathic self operating at a deeper level than the ego.

Note then the Jungian notion of self (or Self) is different from that of Winnicott and Kohut, whose concepts of self are more analogous to the Jungian concept of ego. For Jung, self is the deepest source of conscious personal identity or ego and represents a totality of the human personality including both the conscious and unconscious.

At first the Jungian concept can seem quite dissimilar to the relational approaches of Winnicott and Kohut. It would seem that self is not a "thou" to which one relates, but simply an aspect of the individual's own psyche. However, in Jungian thought self is not only an intrapersonal factor, but manifests interpersonally as well.

For example, according to Jungian thinker Erich Neumann, the self initially relates to the infant through the mother. Neumann writes, "Thus, paradoxically, the Self is that which is most our own, but at the same time it takes the form of a 'thou'" (Neumann 1973, 13). The Jungian psychiatrist Edward R. Edinger (1972) further points out that the authentic acceptance of a client by a therapist is an expression of the acceptance flowing from self to the client. That is, self is a source of empathic connection and selfobject function manifesting within human relationships. In short, the self functions as an other—a thou or a selfobject, both intrapersonally and interpersonally—and is the source of being for the conscious personality.[3]

The Empathic Connection

Although most often only implicit in Jung's thinking, the empathic connection nevertheless seems an important aspect of the ego-self relationship. For example, the conscious ego is embraced by the greater wholeness of self, a wholeness that comprises both the conscious and the unconscious. In this sense, as Jung says, the ego is a "content" or "exponent" of self, held within the broader field of self. It may be surmised that self is here completely empathic to the ego in that it includes the consciousness of the ego.

Also, the guiding influence of self over time can be experienced as personal and empathic. Jung characterized this influence as parental—"the relation of the ego to the self is like that of the son to the father" (Jung 1969a, 262)—while Neumann described this influence in terms of intimate friendship: "Engaged in a dialogue with the self and receiving guidance from the self, a guidance which the ego experiences as meaningful, the ego fashions anew its likeness to the self. This leads to a paradoxical form of intimacy which is often expressed in the symbols of friendship and kinship between the ego and the self and which compensates for the isolation of man in the cosmos" (Neumann 1973, 413–14).

This empathic ego-self connection can be seen most clearly in Jung's (1969a) discussion of the ego coming to know its limitations vis-à-vis self. Sensing the deeper movements of self, the ego faces the fact that it is not the ultimate center within the psyche, that it is not the captain of its own destiny. Self here invites the person to surrender the apparent primacy of the ego in order to then grow towards greater wholeness.

During this important transformative process, the person may experience that the ego is being sacrificed to a power greater than itself. This sense of being sacrificed, however, is not only the prerogative of the ego, but of the self—in empathic connection, the self experiences this sacrifice as its own as well: "We have seen that a sacrifice only takes place when we feel the self actually carrying it out on ourselves. We may also venture to surmise that insofar as the self stands to us in the relation of father to son, the self in some sort feels our sacrifice as a sacrifice of itself" (p. 262).

This sacrifice of the ego's primacy is but a recognition of a fundamental and paradoxical truth—that human spirit is dependent upon an empathic communion with Deeper Spirit, that our free will is dependent on a relationship with a Deeper Will. We shall return to this important point again.

Human Development

This deeper self is not only the source of the ego, but the central organizing principle behind the person's developing as an individual personality over the course of life. Here is Jungian writer Jolande Jacobi: "The Self is always there, it is the central, archetypal, structural element of the psyche, operating in us from the beginning as the organizer and director of the psychic processes. Its *a priori* teleological character, its striving to realize an aim, exist even without the participation of consciousness" (Jacobi 1967, 50).

Relating to this a priori center, the person experiences a directional force operating throughout life. This seems analogous to Kohut's concept of a self-selfobject relationship creating a directionality through life in the unfolding of the nuclear program.

Although Jung saw human development underpinned primarily by the self, he recognized also that this process was moderated by many collective patterns of development, which he called *archetypes* (self can also be considered an archetype, but the "archetype of archetypes"). For example, Jungians speak of encountering the archetypes of the *persona* (the public personality); the *shadow* (those contents repressed in forming the ego and persona); and the *animus/anima* (the feminine in the man, the masculine in the woman).

Archetypes, like self, do not act solely from within the person, but have an external, interpersonal dynamic associated with them. As Neumann writes, "The paradoxical truth about the evocation of human archetypes consists in the fact that their activation is dependent from the outset on the dimension of social relationship between human beings" (Neumann 1989, 85). Archetypes, like self, in some way operate through lived human relationships as well as within the individual psyche.

These archetypes mentioned above, among others, serve to facilitate the deeper relationship between ego and self. But throughout, self is distinct from these changing archetypes even though it is active through them.

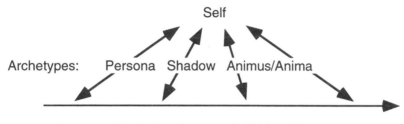

Fig. 2.3

Figure 2.3 illustrates that the ego-self relationship or *ego-self axis* (Neumann) is distinct from each particular archetypal development and social context, but is engaged in providing a directional, organizing principle throughout them all. In Neumann's words, the *self field* is at a deeper level than the *archetypal field*. This appears analogous to Winnicott's insight that the empathic holding of the caregiver gives a continuity of being through all the developmental changes inherent in early growth. Also, if we posit a transpersonal selfobject function in Kohut's system that is manifest in all selfobjects, this Jungian view may find an analogy in Kohut's work as well.

ASSAGIOLI'S PSYCHOSYNTHESIS

We have seen that the infant-caregiver (Winnicott), self-selfobject (Kohut), or ego-self (Jung) relationship is an empathic connection that allows the experience of personal existence. This type of relationship is the source of conscious, individual human being.

According to Roberto Assagioli (1965), the experience of personal existence—what he called the personal self or "I"—flows from a deeper Transpersonal Self, or simply, Self.[4] In his words, "I" is a "reflection" or "projection" of Self. Self as understood by Assagioli, like the self recognized by Jung, provides not only the source of personal being but a directionality for individual unfoldment and meaningful engagement with the world.[5]

Akin to the self seen by Jungians, Self can be experienced both internally and externally; the relationship between "I" and Self is moderated by different inner and outer facilitating contexts that Assagioli (1965) called *unifying centers*. Unifying centers can be either intrapersonal, such as inner symbols of significant others, a mandala, a wise person, the voice of conscience, or an inner light; or they may be interpersonal, as a caregiver, hero, community, social cause, or religious tradition. Thus other people, holding environments, selfobjects, and archetypes all function as unifying centers, as contexts that facilitate the flow of being from Self to "I." (Unifying centers will be discussed at length in a later chapter.)

The Empathic Connection

Assagioli clearly saw too that a central principle of the I-Self relationship is empathic connection. That is, Self is not a blind, impersonal totality; nor simply "the unconscious" (personal or collective); nor a state of unitive, cosmic consciousness; nor merely a higher organizing field or pattern of wholeness. Self, as the abiding source of being for conscious, willing, human I-amness, can only be deeper, conscious, willing, I-amness. Self is not an "It," but a "Thou."[6]

This "Thou-ness" means, among other things, that Self can have an intimate awareness of, and informed activity within, the specific unfolding life experience of the individual—Self is capable of profound and meaningful empathic relationship with the individual person. In Assagioli's words, one may think of Self as a "spiritual Self who already knows his problem, his crisis, his perplexity" (p. 204).

Assagioli (1973a) saw that Self is not simply a passive presence,

but continually acts via the *transpersonal will* to which we respond—
or do not respond—with the freedom of our own *personal will*. This
deeper will of Self is felt as an invitation to pursue particular directions in our lives. Such an invitation may be encountered in discovering an overall life direction as in the phenomena of "call,"
"vocation," and "dharma" (see Bogart 1995), or in sensing the more
here-and-now impulses to increased authenticity, more compassion,
greater wholeness, and better relationships with others. This ongoing interplay between "I" and Self is termed Self-realization by
Assagioli, and we will later devote an entire chapter to this central
subject.

The empathic I-Self relationship from which we receive our
being is distinct from any specific relationship in life, yet it is embedded in these relationships at the same time. Here is a fundamental
relationship that lies not solely at one end or the other of the personal timeline, but that transects this line at all points along the continuum (see figure 2.4). The I-Self relationship is ever present.

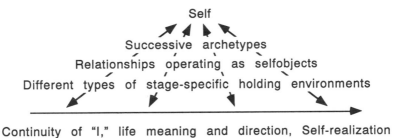

Fig. 2.4

It is this empathic relationship to Self that is expressed in each
unifying center, at each stage of life, and in each moment of our lives.
As we shall see too, this flow of being from Self to personal self or "I"
can be disrupted by problematic unifying centers; in such disruptions
of being we find the primal wound of nonbeing.

The next and final section will explore the nature of this I-Self
relationship in more detail. We shall focus on a psychosynthesis view

of this relationship, while drawing upon the thinkers we have reviewed. It will be proposed that Self is not an oceanic oneness or undifferentiated unity at odds with individuality, but the paradoxical source of both individuality and unity, independence and dependence.

THE I-SELF RELATIONSHIP

As outlined above, human individuality, personal being, personal self, or "I" is profoundly dependent upon an ongoing relationship to Self throughout all life contexts. This essential dependence of personal selfhood is reflected in these statements:

> "There is no such thing as an infant." (Winnicott)
> "A self can never exist outside a matrix of selfobjects." (Kohut)
> "The ego stands to the self as the moved to the mover." (Jung)
> "But in reality the isolated man does not exist." (Assagioli)

This abiding dependence of "I" upon Self amounts to an ontological union of "I" and Self; they are so fundamentally related that a true break in that relationship would mean personal annihilation, the non-being of "I." So complete is this union that it may be called "non-dual," a unity transcending any sense of duality, isolation, or separation. Assagioli puts it this way: "There are not really two selves, two independent and separate entities. The Self is one; it manifests in different degrees of awareness and self-realization. The reflection [of Self, "I"] appears to be self-existent but has, in reality, no autonomous substantiality. It is, in other words, not a new and different light but a projection of its luminous source" (Assagioli 1965, 20).

The I-Self union is not something one needs to forge, not a union to be attained, but a union that is ever present—if it were not present, you would not be here, because you have "no autonomous substantiality." In the words of the great mystic Meister Eckhart, "There is something in the soul so closely akin to God that it is already one with him and need never be united to him" (in Blakney 1941, 205).

If Assagioli drew upon Winnicott's phrase, "There is no such thing as an infant," he might say from this particular point of view, "There is no such thing as 'I.'" As an infant cannot be understood apart from the facilitating environment, so "I" cannot be understood apart from Self. However, this I-Self unity is obviously not the primary narcissism or oceanic feeling caused by a lack of differentiation between the individual and other.

This unity is the complete opposite of the elimination of selfhood, because it is by virtue of this I-Self union that individuality exists at all. From this relationship comes a sense of authentic personhood, of true individuality and freedom, of consciousness and will. Paradoxically, this dependence on relationship does not create passivity, but forms the very foundation of personal initiative and responsibility. So complete is the giving of Self here that "I" has even the freedom to disregard this relationship, and act in direct opposition to it (Assagioli 1973a).

This paradoxical synthesis of freedom and dependence at the root of personal selfhood also is recognized by Jung. He states that while the self "is an *a priori* existent out of which the ego evolves" (implying a profoundly conditioned and contingent ego), he says at the same time that "The existence of ego consciousness has meaning only if it is free and autonomous." Jung goes on to state clearly that this ego-self relationship embodies a paradox: "By stating these facts we have, it is true, established an antinomy [a contradiction], but we have at the same time given a picture of things as they are" (Jung 1969, 259).

Winnicott also describes this paradox of dependence and independence at the core of human being:

> What is the state of the human individual as the being emerges out of not being? What is the basis of human nature in terms of individual development? What is the fundamental state to which every individual, however old and with whatever experiences, can return in order to start again?
>
> A statement of this condition must involve a paradox. At the start is an *essential aloneness*. At the same time this aloneness can only take place under *maximum conditions of dependence*. (Winnicott 1988a, 132–33, emphases added)

According to Winnicott, what is fundamental to human being is a synthesis of aloneness—independent free-standing selfhood—and "absolute dependence." Here again we find the curious synthesis of independence and dependence.

This paradox, that our independent individuality is dependent on intimate, unitive, empathic relationship, can be called the *dependent-independent paradox* (Firman 1991). This principle can be observed in all healthy intimate relationships throughout the life span, from the infant-caregiver relationship to peer, mentor, and community relationships, and even to a spiritual relationship with Divinity or the Ultimate as described by many religions.

INDIVIDUALITY AND UNITY

In conclusion, we can say that the primal I-Self relationship is a union from which is born personal selfhood. This intimate relationship involves a unitive connection that not only respects individuality but constitutes the very source of individuality itself. Individuality does not then imply alienation, separation, or duality.

According to this view, human being does not arise by separating from an undifferentiated oceanic unity. "I" is not at first fused with Self, nor is "I" at first existing alone. "I" comes into existence already in relationship to Self. To lose that relationship is not to fall back into Self like a drop of water into the ocean, *but to cease to exist altogether.*

Another way to say this is that "I" is not "emanated" from the Self, is not an outflowing of the supposed substance of Self. We are not like waves on the ocean, an individualized form that, if lost, will return its borrowed substance to the ocean; nor are we like drops of water who have gained autonomy by virtue of borrowing our substance from the sea. Rather, we are like reflections in a mirror—we will completely cease to exist if we are cut off from the object reflected.

In agreement with the infant research outlined by Stern and others, we need not consider an oceanic self-other fusion as the foundation of human being, but can place meaningful, active relationship at the very beginning of, and throughout, human life. Here the I-Self relationship is not a primal fusion which must be overcome in order for individuality to blossom—the I-Self relationship is the very heart of individuality itself.

Thus, psychological symptoms are not caused by a struggle with a primordial fused state—the primal state is relational—but by real agents and events in the environment which have violated the bonds of relationship. We consider this view included in what child psychiatrist and trauma expert Lenore Terr (1990) called the "psychology of the external," embodying a focus on actual traumatic events and their psychological effects. Psychological disturbances are not most essentially caused by an inability to differentiate self and other out of a primordial unity; by regression or fixation vis-à-vis an archaic blissful state; by a battle between the regressive pull of a pleasure principle and the stern dictates of the reality principle; by difficulties in separation-individuation from a primary matrix. Rather, most psychological dysfunction is essentially the result of a disruption in the primary I-Self relationship owing to a failure of particular unifying centers. And this disruption is, of course, the primal wound.

The I-Self relationship is seldom realized in its fullness owing to failures in the various facilitating life contexts, in the various unifying centers. As we shall discuss later, these failures disrupt the fundamental relationship, causing the primal wound of nonbeing and, hence, psychological disturbances. But first let us look more closely at the precise nature of human spirit.

3

The Human Spirit

The individual self, or being, is an ultimate core of reality
which remains unchanged throughout changes of its qualities or states.
—Clark Moustakas

The "I," as I conceive it, is irreducibly a unity and invariably a subject.
It is, I postulate, the essential being.
—James Bugental

And we can observe the experience of an active "I":
either dissociated from the drive in self-observation,
or merged with the undischarged drive as the experience of a wish,
or fused with motoric discharge patterns as action.
—Heinz Kohut

In the sixteenth century, a heated theological debate raged over whether the native inhabitants of the New World were human or not. This was not merely an abstract academic debate affecting theologians alone, but was destined to affect the welfare of countless multitudes.

Through the efforts of the Catholic church and the heroic work of St. Bartolomé de las Casas, the humanity of the New World people was affirmed against the conquistadors' lust for conquest, slavery, and pillage. This moral stand caused a momentary pause in the tide of conquest, but it could in the end only temper a greed for land and wealth that demanded the dehumanizing of the New World peoples (see Boorstin 1983).

Such dehumanization—so essential to racism, slavery, war, and genocide—is the refusal to recognize the I-amness of other human beings. In other words, empathic failure characterizes not only childhood neglect and abuse, but much other human brutality as well.

Our shocking limitations in recognizing humanness can be seen historically in the failure to respect the personhood of infants and children, of the disabled and ill, of the poor or elderly, and indeed of entire genders (most notably women), nationalities, and races of human beings. The tendency to limit the title "human being" to specific physical characteristics, qualities of consciousness, cultural behaviors and beliefs, and any other *state* of human being, has led to dire consequences throughout history. It seems clear there is a crying need to understand human being as distinct from these different states of human being.

This chapter will present an understanding of the human spirit that can assist in recognizing and respecting this spirit in any situation—whether in sickness or health, ignorance or wisdom, poverty or wealth, and in whatever race, religion, or nationality. We will begin by a brief experiential interlude in which you are invited into your own personal exploration of "you."

AN EXERCISE IN DISIDENTIFICATION

As you read this sentence, be aware of the words printed on this page, the touch of the paper in your hands, and the sounds around you.

You immediately know something about who you are—you can be aware. Your awareness may vary in clarity depending on any number of factors, and you can even lose it completely in sleep, but awareness or consciousness is certainly an attribute closely related to your sense of personal self or "I." This might be illustrated in the manner shown in figure 3.1.

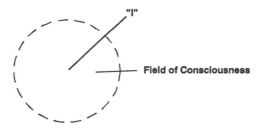

Fig. 3.1

Now be aware that the words on this page exist at some small distance away from you. You are distinct from these words. They are "out here" in front of you, while you remain "back there" observing them. You look out at them from a position in space that is distinct, though not completely separate, from their position in space.

Next gently rub your finger against this page. Again, notice there is a distance or distinction between your vantage point and where your finger is rubbing the paper. Again, you are "back there" whereas your finger is "out here."

Continuing to rub the paper, close your eyes a moment and note that this distinction between your vantage point and the sensation of rubbing the paper is the same with your eyes closed. Even with your eyes closed, you can be aware of yourself "back there," observing the sensation "out here." You are distinct from this page, and as well, from your tactile sensation of this page. Both the page and the sensations are contents of your field of consciousness. In figure 3.2 we add contents of consciousness to the drawing.

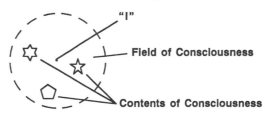

Fig. 3.2

And of course, if you stop rubbing the paper the sensation stops, but you are still there. So you *have* this sensation, but you *are distinct* from your sensation. The same holds true for all your other physical sensations. Whether you see or not, hear or not, taste or not, smell or not, you are still you—it is "I" who does or does not experience these things.

You are thus distinct from your sensations, or to put it another way, you are transcendent of your sensations. And although transcendent of sensations, you are at the same time present and engaged with sensations—that is, you are immanent within sensations. Since you are both transcendent of sensations yet immanent within sensations, it can be said that you are *transcendent-immanent* within the world of sensations.[1] This experience can be represented by the phrases:

I am distinct but not separate from my sensations.

I am transcendent-immanent within my sensations.

Now turn your attention inward again. Become aware of how you are feeling right now. Calm? Ruffled? Bored? Excited? Then close your eyes for a moment and imagine a scene that makes you sad, then one that makes you happy.

Again be aware of how your feelings come and go at some inner distance from you, while you remain. You experience one feeling and then the other, just as you can experience first one sensation and then another, yet you remain "you." You transcend your feelings, though you are immanent within them. These phrases might represent this experience of feelings:

I am distinct but not separate from my feelings.

I am transcendent-immanent within my feelings.

Finally become aware of what you are thinking right now. Take a moment to close your eyes and observe your thoughts as they pass through your consciousness like a river or stream. You can notice that one thought comes and goes, then another, then another, while you remain "back there" observing them.

Even though you may be caught up in your thoughts for a time (becoming "lost in thought"), you can return to your I-experience again and observe them passing by. You are transcendent of your thoughts, though immanent within them. Here we might use the phrases:

> I am distinct but not separate from my thoughts.

> I am transcendent-immanent within my thoughts.

So human I-amness—i.e., you—has a field of awareness through which different contents may pass. Sensations, feelings, thoughts, images, impulses, or intuitions all come and go in this field at varying distances from "I." And as illustrated in figure 3.3, "I" is able to know itself as distinct but not separate from these contents.

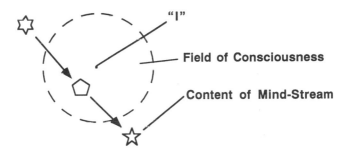

Fig. 3.3

Although we may be lost in intense physical sensation, over-whelmed by a feeling, caught up in a daydream, or obsessed by an idea, we are ultimately distinct but not separate from (transcendent-immanent within) such contents. Whether we are lifted to the heights of spiritual ecstasy or plunged into the depths of existential despair, we are distinct but not separate from (transcendent-immanent within) these experiences. We thus have the potential to

disidentify (Assagioli) from any and all possible contents of experience and to realize that the particular experience is not all that we
are. In such a *disidentification* (Assagioli), we realize we are distinct
from—and thus in relationship to—any particular content of experience.

On the other hand, when we become unwittingly identified with a
particular content such as a belief, feeling, or role, our entire experience
of reality is conditioned by that particular content alone. Here we lose
our sense of transcendence, and become wholly immanent, enmeshed
in the particular belief, feeling, or role. It is as if we see the world only
through the lens of the particular identification, and so our actions
become limited and controlled by that particular world view.

For example, if we are completely identified with our anger, we
feel, think, and act in an angry manner. If our anger impels us to
strike someone, we will strike, because there is no alternative inner
perspective from which to perceive and to act. Here we *are* our anger.
However, if we experience disidentification from the anger, we enter
into relationship with the anger, become aware of other inner
responses (hurt or sadness perhaps, or deeper values), and can make
choices which are not blindly controlled by the anger.[2]

OBSERVING VS. THINKING

Disidentification should not be confused with any sort of thinking
about contents of the inner world. Disidentification involves simply
observing events as they arise: the coldness of your hand, your feeling
of happiness, a memory. This is different from the thinking of thoughts
such as, "Now my hand feels cold; maybe I should turn up the heat,"
or "Now I am feeling happy; I guess that's because my friend wrote
me," or "Now I can see my childhood home in my mind's eye; I wonder why that occurred to me?"

Although valuable at times, this type of "thinking about" is different from a simple observation of inner states and, if this thinking
becomes chronic and habitual, it can amount to an identification with

cognitive functioning itself. Figure 3.4 shows how this type of mental identification might be diagrammed.

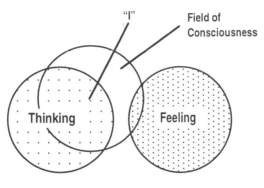

Fig. 3.4

This figure represents not an experience of pure observation, but instead an experience of thinking about that which is observed, in this case, feelings. Here we experience that we *are* our thoughts, and feelings only occupy the periphery of our consciousness. This identification then conditions our total awareness as if thinking were the lens through which we see. (And, too, we would here relate not only to the inner world via thinking, but to the outer world as well.)

Although such a mental identification is often referred to as "objectivity," it is clearly biased towards the thinking function, and operationally cuts off "I" from immediate experience of other dimensions of the personality, such as sensations, feelings, images, or intuition. If, for example, we are identified with thinking and become angry, we might say, "I *think* I'm angry." Inwardly we may be aware only of a vague discomfort, although our heart rate, blood pressure, and galvanic skin response are fluctuating wildly.

If, however, we are not identified with thinking, we are more apt to be in direct contact with the feeling, to own our feelings, to empathize with our own feelings. In this case we may say, "I feel angry," while vividly experiencing rapid breathing and a pounding heart. Here the energy of our feelings is not filtered, and that energy can be experienced directly. Only in this way can we truly take responsibility for our feelings; otherwise they remain "these alien things that happen to me."

So identification with thinking is very different from disidentification, different from simple, introspective, self-empathic witnessing. Such witnessing is founded in the transcendence-immanence of "I"— the ability of "I" to be distinct-but-not-separate from the contents of awareness. Identified with thinking, we are at least partially dissociated from any experience that is not thinking. Here we are only aware of thinking, and so are relatively unaware of feeling. Thought serves to mask the feeling, rendering the feeling experientially distant.

But "I" is transcendent of thoughts as well, and thus has the potential to disidentify from the thinking process. Such disidentification would initially entail witnessing the analytical thoughts, without becoming involved in their activity. The experience would then shift naturally from being actively immersed in thinking to the receptive experience of simply observing thoughts as they pass through awareness. Thoughts thereby gradually join other inner events as objects of awareness distinct from "I" who is aware. Figure 3.5 shows how this might be illustrated.

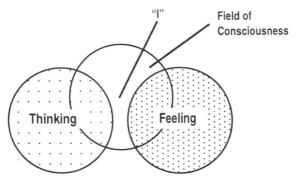

Fig. 3.5

This figure represents a person who experiences disidentification from thoughts, and thereby has become directly aware of not only thoughts, but now of feelings as well. This represents an intensification of "I" such that "I" now knows itself as transcendent of both feelings and thoughts, and thus can be immanent in both feelings and thoughts. Here the one-sided involvement in rational processes has yielded to a broader awareness of inner resources, a more complete self-empathy has occurred.

Such a disidentification might happen quickly in the moment, as for example when we break our concentration on a difficult problem in mathematics and suddenly become aware that we are feeling frustrated with the task. In this instance we have experienced disidentification from the single perspective of thinking and expanded our consciousness to include feelings as well.

But a shift in identification like this may also be seen in long-term transformations of the personality as a whole. For example, the thinking identification may represent not a momentary involvement in thought, but rather the aloof intellectual person who exhibits no empathy or warmth, approaching life only logically. Similarly, a feeling-identification might represent an impulsive romantic person devoted to a life of dramatic action and intense feeling, distrusting any rationality as cold and lifeless. In such all-encompassing identifications, figure 3.5 might then represent the results of a long-term process of personality change in which the person's entire experience of self and world is transformed. Perhaps facilitated by psychotherapy, here the "thinker" might have become more empathic and sensitive, or the "feeler" might have become less impulsive and more thoughtful.

Whatever the scale of change involved in the disidentification experience, disidentification allows a richer and more flexible experience of oneself. The transcendent nature of "I" allows the immanence of "I"—the inclusion of an ever-widening range of human experience.

DISIDENTIFICATION VS. DISSOCIATION

An identification with *any* mode of experience will render all other modes relatively inaccessible—one becomes dissociated from other modes. If we identify with analytic thought, we not only distance ourselves from feelings and sensations, but from other more synthetic and creative modes of mental functioning as well. Here we can do nothing but analyze, and we disown other cognitive modalities. This type of dissociation can be quite useful therefore in such things as focusing on an important task. It usually only becomes problematic when it is unconscious and chronic.

Similarly, if we identify with a particular feeling, we will not only distance ourselves from thought, but from other feelings. For example, we may become chronically identified with rage or grief, thus obscuring not only rationality, but the potential for any happier emotions as well. In the extreme, we may become what has been called a *rageaholic* who primarily relates to the world with rage, or develop a grief-stricken lifestyle with a view of the world as an endless struggle of pain and hardship.

In identifying with a particular role or life script, we become lost to all other dimensions of our personality. Ram Dass called this an identification with a constellation of thought that forms an "identity":

> You have at this moment many constellations of thought, each composing an identity: sexual, social, cultural, educational, economic, intellectual, historical, philosophical, spiritual, among others. One or another of these identities takes over as the situation demands. Usually you are lost into that identity when it dominates your thoughts. At the moment of being a mother, a father, a student, or a lover, the rest are lost. (Ram Dass 1980, 138)

Unfortunately, this state of moving unconsciously among different states of identification, different levels of dissociation, is perhaps the most common mode in which we live our lives. Here is transpersonal thinker Kathleen Riordan (Speeth):

> Identification is the opposite of self-consciousness. In a state of identification man does not remember himself. He is lost to himself. His attention is directed outward, and no awareness is left over for inner states. And ordinary life is almost totally spent in states of identification. (Riordan 1975, 303)

And economist E. F. Schumacher puts it this way:

> Most of our life is spent in some kind of thralldom; we are captivated
> by this or that, drift along in our captivity, and carry out programs
> which have been lodged in our machine, we do not know how,
> when, or by whom. (Schumacher 1977, 68)

This ongoing state of unconsciously shifting identifications has
been called "the trance of ordinary life" (Deikman), "consensus
trance: the sleep of everyday life" (Tart), "waking sleep" (DeRopp),
the "embedded unconscious" (Wilber), and "the primary infirmity of
man" (Assagioli). Disidentification marks the liberation from this
unconsciousness, a breaking of the trance, a waking up of "I." So
disidentification works not to reduce and dissociate awareness, but to
increase and expand awareness. We shall further discuss the nature of
this trance in a subsequent chapter.

By such work with disidentification, the thinking-identification
may yield to an awareness that includes sensations, feelings, and even
new modes of thinking. Or the feeling-identification may evolve
toward an awareness of sensations, thought processes, and other feelings as well. In disidentification the rageaholic would begin to realize
the control rage has over his or her life and begin to open to the fear
and helplessness beneath the rage. Or in the example of an identification with grief, the person would be more able to enter fully into,
and move through, this difficult healing work.

Note then that it is identification rather than disidentification
that is the dynamic underlying dissociation. It is an identification with
one particular mode of experience—sensation, feeling, thinking, intu-
iting, attitudes, life roles, etc.—that renders other modes remote.
Identification, not disidentification, is dissociative.

PERSONAL WILL

The ability to disidentify seems an essential aspect of what it is to be
human. We are not simply our desires and drives, our sensations and
feelings, our inner attitudes and outer roles, but can experience our-

selves as distinct from these contents of consciousness. However, human being is not simply passive consciousness, not simply an observing function. We also have the ability to act in relation to the contents of consciousness, to take responsibility for them in our lives. We even have the ability to affect our consciousness:

> I was hurt and furious with him for criticizing me like that, but instead of yelling at him like a part of me wanted to do, I suddenly could look deeper into him and see his pain, too. There I was, feeling my hurt, my anger, and also now my compassion for him. I said, "Sounds like you're really hurt, but don't take it out on me." He immediately softened and cried in my arms.

If the woman speaking above had been fully identified with her anger she probably would have had no option but to lash out at her friend. However, she experienced a disidentification from her anger and so found an ability to act with compassion as well. Note that her hurt and anger are not denied, but are included in the words, "but don't take it out on me." With this phrase she is respecting her own hurt and anger, while at the same time responding to the pain of the other with her own compassion. She was thus able to act gracefully, taking all of these factors into account, respecting both herself and her friend. This ability to act from a place disidentified from the many contents and modes of consciousness illuminates what Assagioli called *personal will* (as distinct from the *transpersonal* will, the will of Self). "I" has not only the function of consciousness, but of will: "The will . . . balances and constructively utilizes all the other activities and energies of the human being without repressing any of them" (Assagioli 1973a, 10).

This understanding of will is then quite different from a stern repressive "will-power" by which one forcibly dominates certain aspects of the personality. As would be predicted by the notion of a transcendent-immanent "I," the will of "I" has the potential to engage any and all personality contents, and therefore may work towards a harmonious relationship among them all.

For example, disidentification from the single modes of sensation, feeling, thinking, or intuition prevents us from becoming dominated by any one of these and gives us the freedom to draw upon them all. We are more able to experience and express the richness of our multiplicity rather than being limited to any single aspect of our personality.[3]

One can see here a central paradox of "I"—the more we are not immersed in any particular mode of consciousness, the more we can be open to, and enter into, all the many types of human experience. In other words, the more transcendent we know ourselves to be, the more we are capable of immanence.

Again, disidentification is not dissociation. Rather, it is moving naturally and easily from that alive sense of "I," from that "who" who is not limited to any single part of the personality and who can thus potentially connect empathically to all parts. Will is a graceful inner freedom and empowerment derived from an openness to all we are. In figure 3.6 we can add will to our diagram.

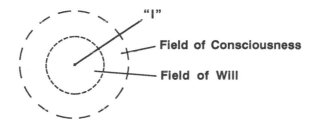

Fig. 3.6

The field of will is drawn as a concentric sphere because most often one is aware of far more content than one can directly affect. Of course the relative sizes of the fields would constantly fluctuate. During an intense concentrated action, for example, the fields of consciousness and will would nearly match. The point is that with disidentification often comes not only increased awareness, but increased potential to act on that awareness.

Having said all this about the freedom of will, it must be said, too,

that this freedom can include experiences of weakness and helplessness. There are times in life that call us to accept our very real human
limitations, to come to grips with the fact that we are far less in control of ourselves than we would like to think we are.

For example, many of the deeper layers of our psyche contain

He alone truly knows

himself, who knows

himself as nothing.

—St. John Chrysostom

wounds from traumatic experiences of helplessness and violation. Thus, when memories of
these experiences begin to reemerge and disrupt our lives, it is sometimes necessary to
enter into a full experiencing of the powerlessness characteristic of the original painful
events. Plumbing these depths may involve
disidentification from a sense of independence
and freedom in order to embrace and redeem wounded aspects of
ourselves.

If during these times we attempt to maintain an identification
with strength and invulnerability, we are in effect dissociating from
the depths of our own humanness. This is dissociation, not disidentification. If on the other hand one accepts such helplessness, one can
then disidentify from the need to be strong and move towards a deeper
experience of authentic I-amness—one "loses self to gain self."

There is a profound principle in this acceptance of our human
weakness and limitation. As we have seen, helplessness and dependence are not simply manifestations of early childhood experience,
but are actually at the very core of our being. The dependent-independent paradox describes the fact that our very existence is totally
dependent on a deeper Self. As many traditions say in different ways,
the core of human being is no-thingness.[4]

The process of Self-realization may thus involve the discovery and
acceptance of this ontological dependence, no-thingness, and helplessness. There may be times on this path when we are invited to experience the fact that we are severely limited creatures, perhaps even
that we have "no autonomous substantiality," in Assagioli's words.
There will be times when we are called to meet Self in experiences of
helplessness, disintegration, and loss of identity.

Paradoxically, the will of "I" is so very free that it can engage the experiences of helplessness, dependence, and emptiness. The transcendence-immanence of "I" is such that it allows an openness to freedom and helplessness, strength and weakness, somethingness and nothingness.

SUBPERSONALITIES AND HUMAN SPIRIT

This transcendence-immanence of human being can also be recognized in that sometimes disconcerting phenomenon in which one seems to become different people or different selves in response to different situations. As quoted earlier, these are what Ram Dass called the "many constellations of thought, each composing an identity," which take over as they are triggered by changing life circumstances.

Assagioli (1965) called these semi-independent aspects of the personality *subpersonalities*, and in an excellent comprehensive book on subpersonalities John Rowan (1990) vividly termed them "the people inside us." Rowan gives this definition: "My own working definition of a subpersonality is *a semi-permanent and semi-autonomous region of the personality capable of acting as a person*" (p. 8, emphasis in original). Kohut recognized this inner multiplicity as well: "We see these various selves fighting for ascendancy, one blocking out the other, forming compromises with each other, and acting inconsistently with each other at the same time" (Kohut 1985, 33)

An example of subpersonality activity would be the decisive business executive who begins to feel and act like a small child when visiting parents, or the easy-going young adult who transforms into a ferocious competitor while playing a sport, or the tough construction worker who becomes sensitive and vulnerable in love relationships. In such instances the person is disidentifying from one subpersonality and identifying with another subpersonality—a movement only possible if "I" is distinct but not separate from these different subsystems within the personality.

This transcendence-immanence of human being is also apparent in more global and long-term changes in the personality. For example, here is a paraphrase from a psychotherapy client who had been a workaholic, compulsively devoting so much time to his job that other spheres of his life were suffering:

> Now, when I feel pressure at work, I can actually feel the "Driver" part of me wanting to take over and push me, to prove myself, to impress my boss—to impress my dad, really. Before, I just *was* that part of me, so I was trapped by it, driven by it. Now it's like I *have* that part of me . . . it's not all I am, and so I can choose to work hard or not, to rest when I need to, to do other things in my leisure time. Before it didn't feel like I had the choice.

Over the course of psychotherapy, this person gradually realized that he had been emotionally neglected and abused by his father, leaving wounds of shame, worthlessness, and inadequacy. These feelings had been managed by developing this strong "Driver" subpersonality. Thus, as long as he was identified with the Driver, he did not feel the underlying inadequacy but could instead feel himself competent and worthwhile.

In uncovering his deeper feelings and working through the underlying trauma, he gradually learned to disidentify from the Driver. This allowed him to experience freedom from its control, and become open to alternative ways of being. He became more able to receive constructive criticism, to see and take responsibility for mistakes, to become less and less driven, and to begin to take an interest in developing areas of life other than his career. In short, an expansion of consciousness and will, of I-amness, was evident.

It seems clear in this case that this person's deeper identity or "I" was not identical to his chronic, compulsive way of being. He discovered that he was transcendent of his Driver subpersonality and could thereby be more deeply engaged in—more immanent within—all the varied areas of his life. This case and many others like it illustrate that transcendent-immanent I-amness can be recognized over longer time spans, and not only in moments of introspection.

So whether one is observing contents of consciousness pass by in quiet introspection, moving through various identifications over the course of a day, or even undergoing the often dramatic changes of major life transitions, it seems that "I" is somehow distinct from all these changes while immanent within them.

Since a person may disidentify from, and identify with, various inner contents and personality configurations, it seems reasonable to assume that human being is not completely identical with any particular content or formation of the personality. "I" is distinct from, though inextricably engaged within, the different identifications developed in life. This transcendence-immanence of human being gives us the potential to disidentify, to shift and/or transform these identifications in response to life changes, and to take responsibility for our lives.

In the section which follows, we shall see that this transcendence-immanence of the human spirit allows disidentification and identification within even larger structures of the human personality—body and soul.

BODY, SOUL, AND SPIRIT

As we have seen, it seems useful to understand the human spirit as distinct but not separate from contents of consciousness, consciousness and will, and subpersonalities. Continuing this examination of the nature of "I," it also seems that "I" is distinct but not separate from even the most encompassing structures of the personality as well. (Note that here we are discussing human spirit or "I" and not deeper Spirit or Self.)

Two of these major structures that make up the human personality are: (a) the objective dimension of the physical body and outward behavior, called *soma* or *body*, and (b) the subjective dimension of desires and sensations, feelings and thoughts, intuitions and images, called *psyche*, *soul*, or sometimes *mind* (as in the term body-mind connection). "I" also would be distinct but not separate from both these aspects of human being. We thus have what philosophy calls a trichotomous model of the human person: a trichotomy of spirit ("I"), psyche, and soma.[5]

In accord with our above discussion of "I," the trichotomy does not hold the human being as a soul with a body, nor as a body with a soul, but as a living spirit transcendent-immanent within both the body and soul. "I" thus experiences the objective outer world of physical existence as well as the subjective inner world of feelings, thoughts, and images. Human being is one and the same event with two aspects or dimensions: body and soul.

Let us take a simple example of the practical, experiential interplay of spirit, psyche, and soma. Say that a woman goes to the cinema and becomes bored with the film. She becomes restless, finding herself acutely aware of the temperature in the theater, the sounds made by the audience, and the uncomfortable hardness of the seat. At this point, she is for the most part focused on the dimension of soma—the physical experience of herself and her surroundings.

But then she begins to take more interest in the film, and begins to enjoy it. She shifts her awareness away from the somatic and toward her feelings and thoughts—soul experience—generated in her by the film. She becomes relatively unaware of her physical surroundings and increasingly engrossed in her experience of the story unfolding before her. Finally, she completely forgets the people around her, the temperature of the room, and the hardness of the seat, and becomes absorbed in the powerful feelings, meaningful associations, and vivid images generated in her by the film. She has here shifted from the relatively somatic to the relatively psychic. Although the objective sights and sounds of the film impinge upon her in the same way, these simple sensations now trigger a far greater immensity of soul experience. It may even be that such an experience is transformative, revealing to her new aspects of herself and her life.

Given such shifts in consciousness between soul and body, "I" obviously must to some extent be distinct from these two dimensions. She may even experience disidentification from both dimensions, suddenly becoming aware of her objective surroundings *as well as* her subjective responses to the film. In this case, she is experiencing transcendence of both objective and subjective dimensions, and ipso facto immanence in them both.

Note that any position of "I" can be appropriate—we may *want* to become absorbed in a film or *want* to attend solely to the physical environment. The point is that, because of the nature of who we are, we have the potential ability to identify or disidentify as we wish—we have freedom and responsibility (i.e., will).

The trichotomy of spirit, soul, and body not only illuminates the transcendent-immanent nature of "I," but describes human health as involving the intimate connection between psyche and soma, moderated by "I." This intimate union of psyche and soma is a function of core human I-amness and, conversely, the realization of I-amness is supported by an intimate psyche-soma unity. In Winnicott's terms, the state of psyche-soma cohesion is facilitated by the mirroring other, a cohesion that he calls *in-dwelling* or "the achievement of a close and easy relationship between the psyche and the body" (Winnicott 1987, 68).

By the same token, wounding to the human being can be recognized in a disturbed relationship between psyche and soma. For example, Winnicott maintains that a failure in the holding environment will create "unthinkable anxiety," one of whose forms is "having no relationship to the body" (p. 58). Here a wounding from the facilitating environment translates into alienation from physical experience.

Intersubjective psychologists Robert Stolorow and George Atwood also point out psyche-soma disturbances caused by empathic failures in the relational environment. Although self remains implicit in their discussion, they do clearly state the trichotomy: "The inquiry centers instead on mind and body as poles or elements of self experience" (Stolorow and Atwood 1992, 41). This statement is quite in accord with the idea of mind and body as two dimensions of I-experience.[6]

The blossoming of human spirit seems to imply an intimate union between body and soul and, conversely, wounding to the spirit seems to disturb that union. And once again human I-amness reveals itself as not separate from, nor identical to, the subjective and objective dimensions of experience. Our deepest core is essentially transcendent-immanent within the psyche-soma, deeply spiritual, and ultimately a profound mystery. Any of our conceptualizations of this elusive spirit are doomed to be limited, and we will always be left in awe about ourselves and the deeper Self from which we arise.

THE TRANSCENDENCE-IMMANENCE OF HUMAN SPIRIT

The human ability to observe and act in relationship to the immediate contents of consciousness, to subpersonalities, and to the psyche-soma may be conceptualized in different ways—psychological, philosophical, or religious—but the empirical reality seems clear: human being cannot be completely equated with the content of experience, and neither can human being be seen as separate from this. In other words, the human spirit is transcendent-immanent within the contents and structures of experience.

In fact, the entire endeavor of psychotherapy is based on precisely the implicit assumption that the human spirit is transcendent-immanent within the content of experience:

- The psychoanalyst and depth psychologist expect us to be able to observe and report upon our inner flow of experience.
- The cognitive-behaviorist teaches us to study our behavior and uncover the cognitive and affective underpinnings of our actions.
- The existential-humanist invites us to experience the here-and-now of our personal existence, take responsibility for this, and make choices regarding this.
- The transpersonal therapist understands the human being as capable of moving among a stunning variety of states and levels of consciousness.

All of the above approaches assume human being is not to be equated with the contents or states of consciousness, and that we can therefore observe, reflect, and act upon these.[7]

Furthermore, many spiritual practices of both East and West

assume this same distinction between the essential person and the contents and states of consciousness. Many such practices involve sitting quietly and simply observing the flow of experience without becoming caught up in this flow. This ability to assume a stance of inner observation is for example fundamental to Western contemplative prayer, as well as to Eastern approaches such as vipassana meditation and zazen.

From the discussion in this chapter it should be clear that we are not here proposing a monistic idea of human being. That is, we are not suggesting that "I" is completely identical to the passing stream of psyche-soma experience, and therefore that "I" is an irrelevant or illusory mapping of human experience. This would be to lose sight of the transcendence of "I," leaving only immanence.

But neither are we proposing a dualistic understanding in which human being would be seen as separate from psyche-soma experience. This would be to lose sight of the immanence of "I," leaving only transcendence. The transcendence of "I" does not in any way imply another, other worldly domain, a transcendent order disconnected from the world. Rather, transcendence *is* immanence—the transcendence of particular phenomena is identical to an enduring engaged presence within a greater range of phenomena.[8]

It is not even that transcendence and immanence are two different principles which are to be unified into some sort of monism-dualism synthesis. Transcendence and immanence are here understood as fundamentally inseparable because they are simply two descriptions of the same subject—"I."

Having looked at some depth into the ontogenesis and nature of transcendent-immanent "I," we now can entertain the question: "How does this sense of self grow and develop over a lifetime?"

4

The Development of Spirit

The wealth of a spirit is measured by how
much it can feel; its poverty by how little.
—William Rounseville Alger

As outlined in chapter 2, the unfoldment of the human spirit depends upon empathic relationship. Whether we see this empathic relationship as that with a good enough caregiver, a selfobject, or deeper self, it seems clear that when we are deeply understood and accepted our being blossoms:

> My grandmother used to look at me in a way that really let me know she saw me. I felt connected to her, accepted by her unconditionally. She was my beacon of hope growing up, and even now I feel her inside of me, being with me in that same way. I don't know. She gives me the heart to get up and keep going, to live life.

From a psychosynthesis point of view all empathic relationships embody the relationship between "I" or personal self and Self. The empathic other in effect channels the flow of being from Self to "I," becoming a medium through which Self projects or reflects "I." It is as if the light of Self shines through the various lenses of empathic relationships to create a reflection or image of Self—the personal self or "I."

This chapter explores how this I-Self relationship functions in the unfoldment of the human spirit through time. The focus here is upon

healthy development, while chapter 5 will take up the disturbance of
this development by the primal wound.

EXTERNAL UNIFYING CENTERS

The I-Self relationship is that essential empathic connection by which
we experience a continuity of being in our lives. At each stage of life
we experience this connection manifest in different empathic, validating, mirroring contexts. Each stage of growth would have an attendant *external unifying center* that is, some external other who serves to
act as the facilitating medium for the I-Self relationship. Such an
external center comprises, "an indirect but true link, a point of connection between the personal man and his higher Self, which is
reflected and symbolized in that object . . . (Assagioli 1965, 25).

Thus the optimum external unifying center of early childhood
would be the matrix of empathic connections with parents and the
larger family system. This early unifying center would form a stage-
appropriate I-Self relationship, allowing the experience of healthy
personal selfhood, a sense that "I exist as a unique, worthy, and volitional person." Later, this sense of personal self might be facilitated by
school teachers, peers, and other validating and mirroring contexts
such as social, cultural, and religious milieus. At each point in growth,
one would be experiencing a sense of self within the different
empathic connections one had at that time in life.

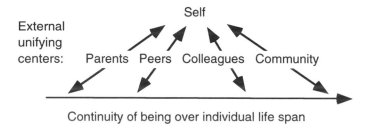

Fig. 4.1

The external unifying centers listed in the figure 4.1 are only a few examples of many possible supportive life contexts. Although we are not here proposing a specific number or order of unifying centers, there have been attempts to elaborate them. One such scheme of external unifying centers can be found in the work of transpersonal psychologist Dwight Judy (1991).

Following the work of Baker Brownell, Judy posits four levels of community—four major external unifying centers—each of which is important in the development of the whole human being. Here is our understanding of the Brownell-Judy levels as outlined by Judy:

(1) The first is the phyletic community which is "that stream of family through which we have been born" (p. 61). This includes not only our immediate family of origin, but past and future generations as well. Here one's identity blossoms (or not) within the context of parents and siblings, as well as in relationship to intergenerational family patterns. Assagioli (1965) emphasizes that therapy should include an exploration of just such ancestral relationships, showing his belief that this level of community has important psychological meaning. Furthermore, this level of external unifying center includes, "the claims of unborn future generations asking us to be responsible for our moment of human life, to honor the earth, and to leave her refreshed rather than depleted" (p. 61). The power of this level can be seen in the growing sense of identity that occurs in researching family roots or in the crises of identity caused by uncovering the hidden side of the family. Through a felt connection to the phyletic community, one comes to sense one's unique place within a larger evolutionary family moving through spacetime.

(2) The nature community is the second level of community according to Brownell and Judy. Here the external unifying center is the natural world, which mirrors our sense of physical identity, our connection to the earth, and our physical belongingness in the cosmos. As psychotherapists, we have found this tremendously important level often overlooked by clients and therapists alike. We have worked with people whose most profound unifying center was the ocean, the mountains, or a special place; or who survived childhood with a bond

to animals, a blanket, or teddy bear (Winnicott's *transitional objects*);
or who found themselves embarrassed by grieving their dead pet far
more deeply than they did the deaths of their parents. But again, such
bonds to nature embody an important aspect of
our relationship to Self, from which we receive
our being. A growing appreciation for this level
of community is clearly apparent in the contemporary concern for ecology, animal rights, and
earth-centered spiritualities.[1]

The eyes of seals are spirits that call out to certain souls.

—Marine Mammal Center, Sausalito, California

(3) The third level of community as external
unifying center is the mystic community. This
comprises those people who mirror our spiritual-
ity, who are felt to be most deeply bonded to ourselves at the level of
ultimate meaning. This level might include one's church community,
religion, or other spiritual group, but as well "that body of individuals,
living and dead, to whom we look for inspiration" (p. 62). So as well
as "mentors, teachers, and heroes" whom we know personally, this
level might also comprise a sense of inner connection to historical
personages and groups, as well as a relationship to inner figures of spiritual support and guidance. (Such figures, when felt as inner presences, are what we will explore shortly as internal unifying centers.)
This external unifying center forms a holding environment for spiritual development, operating as a supportive and guiding influence for
that development.

(4) The fourth and last level comprises "the communities of the
neighborhood and expanding circles of political and geographic communities that lead us through the city, to the state, the nation, the
hemisphere, and the world social-political community" (p. 62). If this
community is a healthy one, we find ourselves mirrored, our sense of
I-amness held, within the larger socio-political contexts of which we
are a part. Again, our sense of personal identity flows to us from such
contexts, forming deep strata of our personalities. In therapy, this level
is addressed in attitudes towards the accomplishments and mistakes of
one's national group; in struggles with cultural and racial prejudice; in
First, Second, and Third World individuals seeking right relationship;

or in an attempt to move beyond one's national identity to become a planetary citizen.

Each level above is an external unifying center from which we derive a different aspect of our being—they are "true links" and "points of connection" that allow the flow of being from Self to "I." The perspective offered by these four levels begins to illuminate the vast relational world in which we find our being.

Again, we are not here putting forth any particular number or types of external unifying centers, and it may be that we may continually discover new and unique centers. The point for the current discussion is that there are a series of relational systems or communities, selfobject matrices, or holding environments—external unifying centers—that are crucial to the development of human being along different dimensions of the personality. Each in a different way moderates the I-Self relationship, supporting the ontogenesis of transcendent-immanent "I."

And Self is distinct from these multiple life contexts, allowing a continuity among them all. As the source of transcendent-immanent I-amness, Self can only be deeper transcendent-immanent I-amness. Self is transcendent in that it is not to be identified with any one of these forms of relationship nor with a simple summation of them, but it is at the same time immanent in these forms in that it is present within them all. Wilber states this transcendent-immanence of Self throughout all life stages:

> Since the Self was both the *ground* of every stage of development and the *goal* of every stage of development, it is perfectly acceptable to say that the Self was present all along, "guiding," "pulling," and "directing" development, so that *every* stage of development is drawn closer and closer to Self-realization . . . (Wilber 1983, 225–6).

The I-Self relationship is not then to be equated with any particular stage of life or relational matrix, but is to be seen as present and active throughout them all, "guiding, pulling, and directing development," and abiding through "every change or transformation of the individual." There is here a single axis, akin to the Jungian "ego-self axis," persisting through all the multiple stages of the life cycle. If the I-Self axis were not transcendent in this way, one would never have been able to leave the first infant-mother relationship, and would have been forced to remain in it in order to maintain one's being. We would not be able to shift among different types of unifying centers in order to develop new dimensions of our personalities.

At the same time the transcendence of the axis is apparent, so too is its immanence—if the I-Self relationship were not immanent, embedded within all the facilitating relationships, these unifying centers would have no power to nurture human being at all.

In a very real way, then, Self is profoundly singular. Self is a "unity in multiplicity" because Self represents a single relationship that takes on a wide variety of forms throughout life. The I-Self relationship is not, however, singular in the sense of one despotic relationship that wields a dominating and repressive authority over all other relationships; the I-Self relationship is singular only in the sense that it is distinct from all the multiple forms of relationship. And it is precisely this singular distinctness from any one of the multiple life relationships that allows Self to be present within all relationships. As we shall see, this unity-in-multiplicity is reflected in the developing sense of personal identity as well.

INTERNAL UNIFYING CENTERS

As each stage of life is supported and held by the appropriate empathic external unifying center, active interaction with that external unifying center conditions the formation of an inner representation or model of that center, which can be called an *internal unifying center.*[2] That is, the experience with the external center conditions the development of an inner center capable of serving many of the same functions fulfilled by the external one:

> She was my beacon of hope growing up, and even now I feel her inside of me, being with me in that same way.

In object-relations parlance, the internal unifying center comprises internalized objects or object representations that develop an abiding inner presence through interaction with the outer environment.

In Winnicott's terms, the development of such an inner center could be described as the outer holding environment conditioning the formation of a similar internal environment (Winnicott 1987, 34). This process would also amount to what Kohut called transmuting internalization—"the acquisition of permanent psychological structures which continue, endopsychically, the functions which the idealizing self-object had previously fulfilled" (Kohut 1971, 45). This internalization of relationship would also include the type of phenomenon called *schemata* (Piaget), *internal working models* (Bowlby), and *Representations of Interactions that have been Generalized* (Stern). However one chooses to conceptualize this dynamic, the outer relational context conditions the formation of an inner relational context.

The internal unifying center may be experienced as actual inner presences, as when one inwardly "hears" the encouragement and advice of a parent or mentor. But these internal centers include also more abstract beliefs, values, and worldviews developed in relationship to external centers over one's lifetime. As such, they constitute a context or matrix, an internal holding environment, within which one derives a sense of individual selfhood, personal meaning, and life direction. These internal unifying centers (see figure 4.2) are then also "indirect but true links," points of connection between "I" and Self.

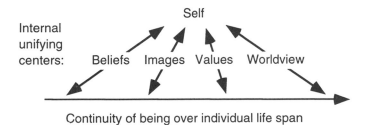

Fig. 4.2

Here again, we can see the unity-in-multiplicity of Self. Self is not
to be equated with any particular internal unifying center. Self is distinct from them all, yet present in them all. Self can appear inwardly
as an image of a wise person or mandala; as a masculine or feminine
God-image; as a sense of responsibility, values, and conscience; or as a
philosophical stance towards the world.

As has often been noted, the development of internal unifying
centers is not a matter of passively taking in the whole image or complete values of the empathic other, e.g., the primary caregiver.[3] In
infancy, this inner center is formed out of the specific relationship
between a unique infant and a unique caregiver, and thus the inner
matrix is partially formed by the activity of the infant as well. What
is internalized is not the caregiver, but the relationship with the caregiver, so the person and activity of the infant is ipso facto included.

It follows, too, that the infant can condition unifying centers, as
when the baby's unique character elicits innovative responses from
the caregiver. As Chamberlain writes, "Using their communication
skills they [babies] engage you in dialog, establish intimate relationships, and, without your realizing it, they begin teaching you how to
be a parent" (Chamberlain 1988, xx).

In some ways, then, the infant functions as a unifying center for
the caregiver, as the caregiver's sense of self blossoms in relationship
to the knowing gaze of the child. This type of developmental interaction between self and other has been called *mutual influence* and has
been observed even in the very earliest stages of infancy—stages
thought by Freud and others to be nonrelational, self-absorbed, narcissistic, and even autistic.[4] This principle of mutual influence per-
tains to all external and internal unifying centers throughout the life
span.

THE UNFOLDMENT OF THE PERSONALITY

The I-Self relationship is embodied in different internal and external
unifying centers at each phase of life. In the beginning there is the

bond with the primary caregivers, giving a first sense of continuity of being. But this connection to another is not limited to infancy, and is essential throughout life. True, we shift our infant dependency from the physical mother to our inner representation of the relationship with mother, or internal unifying center, thus reducing our need for direct physical contact with her. But as we grow, we are continuously relating to others who give us our sense of existence as individual human beings, and we never become completely independent of the environment.

Our sense of self continuously flows to us from friends, lovers, and family; from educational, professional, religious, and political milieus; and from all who embody our values and ideals, both living and dead. As psychoanalyst W. Ronald D. Fairbairn (1986) states, we only move from infantile dependence to mature dependence. Or in Kohut's words quoted earlier, self-selfobject relationships form the essence of psychological life from birth to death (Kohut 1984, 47). *We never in fact become purely independent—we simply shift our dependencies.* The fundamental dependence of "I" on Self shifts and moves among the various unifying centers, giving us our sense of independent individuality—the dependent-independent paradox.

As the I-Self connection abides through all life stages, so too can "I" abide through them all, and is able to experience and include the gifts and abilities that unfold over time. For example, if our developing independence, or sexuality, or cognitive abilities are mirrored, we will be able to recognize these as valid aspects of our identity: "I am my own person," "I am a sexual person," "I am a thinker"—that is, these unfolding developmental abilities become expressions of one's authentic existence, one's I-amness. Here are some brief examples of unfoldment within empathic unifying centers:

> My dad would always wrestle with us. We'd have "roughhouse" time. We kids would gleefully jump on him while he got on all fours and pretended to be a monster. I got a real sense of okayness in my body from this, I think. I always felt secure physically, capable, and pretty much unafraid that anything bad would happen to me in sports.

As a child I felt very connected to music. I'd listen to it for hours, feeling all kinds of things. I learned to play the guitar and used to sing songs which would actually make me cry. I had a whole feeling world wrapped up in my music. I did this mostly in relationship to my mother. She really liked to hear me play and didn't make too big a deal about it, which would have embarrassed me.

I remember spending time with my grandfather reading books and talking about them with him. He loved that as much as I did. I can hear him deep down in me saying my mind is okay and I can learn anything if I stick with it.

Even with all the problems I had with my mother, she was at least able to be with me in my spirituality. She'd always be willing to talk with me about my questions about God and about life. She was interested, not preachy. She seemed to know God in some way beyond all the stuff of the church—not theory but experience—and that rubbed off on me. I've almost always taken my relationship to God seriously.

It seems clear that when we are seen, understood, and respected, our sense of being expands as the riches of human development unfold. We are able to include all of ourselves as we grow. In effect, the empathy of the other allows us to develop self-empathy. That is, receiving understanding and acceptance from the other allows us to adopt this attitude inwardly towards all the many spheres of personal experience, whether physical, affective, cognitive, or spiritual. By this means, the sense of personhood grows harmoniously in a process of ongoing inclusion of the unfolding structures, abilities, and perspectives from all the different ages of life, and one experiences a continuity of being throughout the entire life span.

Conversely, if the person encounters a nonempathic unifying center, this will be reflected in the personality as well. For example, if the caregivers' personalities exclude their emotional life, the child's feelings will not be mirrored, and so emotions will not be recognized or included in the child's ongoing experience. In this case the child will develop an emotional blind spot, a "hole" in the personality, as it were, where feelings should have been. Here self-empathy has been truncated by the lack of empathy from the environment. These holes of nonbeing can later be reclaimed by subsequent relationships that provide mirroring for the rejected aspects—a prime function of psychotherapy, as we shall see.

Human development then involves both inner and outer experiences of a facilitating other or *essential other* (Galatzer-Levy and Cohler 1993), with whom the growing sense of individuality interacts. Together these experiences amount to an internal and external unifying center that manifests the I-Self connection. In the ideal case, one is held and mirrored at each stage of life by such an empathic inner-outer environment, and the experience of being expands smoothly through the life stages.

Authentic Personality

Assagioli (1973b) called this empathic communion with all one's psychological ages the *psychosynthesis of the ages*. Here are some verbal comments spoken to John Firman by Assagioli that elucidate this process:

> But "outgrowing" does not mean "losing." You can and should keep the child in yourself—not killing the child. You see, the child remains, the adolescent remains, and so on. Outgrowing does not mean eliminating. Of course that is the ideal process, but we are too stupid and try to kill or repress the past ages. There is the notion that one has to kill the child in order to become mature, or to repress the previous stages. (Assagioli 1973c, edited from audio tape)

Based in part upon a sketch John made during the above conversation, this model of the person might be diagrammed as shown in figure 4.3.

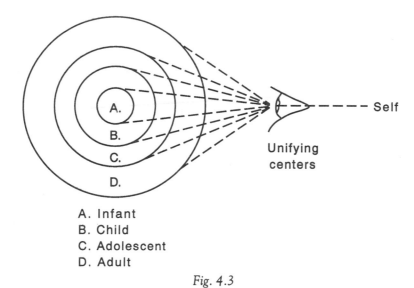

A. Infant
B. Child
C. Adolescent
D. Adult

Fig. 4.3

The concentric rings in the diagram represent the growing personality as expanding harmoniously outward through the various life stages, accumulating the human potential unfolding at each stage (the number of stages and their labels above are arbitrary). This expansion occurs via the empathic "gaze" of various stage-appropriate unifying centers that embody the flow of being from Self. This type of ring model can be seen in the work of Harvard psychologist Gina O'Connell Higgins: "Like an extensive set of Ukrainian nesting dolls, we are a collection of selves, simultaneously encompassing all of our previous versions . . ." (Higgins 1994, 70).

Here blossoms a sense of enduring, cohesive, initiating selfhood; one's sense of self or "I" expands through time, including all the multiple perspectives and abilities of the different ages in an ongoing way. This is what creates the experience of "continuity of being" (Winnicott) and "cohesiveness in space and continuity in time" (Kohut).

The developmental movement pictured above can be called the unfolding of *authentic personality*. Forming around the axis of a healthy I-Self relationship, authentic personality is a dynamic, ongoing, self-empathic inclusion of the developmental structures unfolding at the various ages of life. At each stage, unifying center(s) facilitate the I-Self relationship, and so personal being is supported at each point on the way.

The continuity of unifying centers amounts to a continuous relationship to Self, and thus facilitates the experience of continuity in personal being. To say it another way, authentic personality is the authentic expression of I-amness, in union with Self, conditioned by the person's unique genetic endowment and facilitating environment. See figure 4.4.

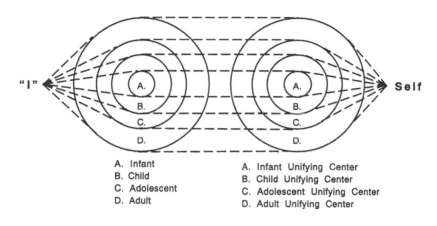

A. Infant
B. Child
C. Adolescent
D. Adult

A. Infant Unifying Center
B. Child Unifying Center
C. Adolescent Unifying Center
D. Adult Unifying Center

Fig. 4.4

And as shall be discussed later, a disturbed I-Self connection creates a personality that is not an expression of unique individual potential, but is instead a reflection of the needs and demands of the environment—what will be called *survival personality* (akin to Winnicott's "false self"). In this case, the unifying centers fail to mirror the unique I-amness of the person, and the unfoldment of authentic personality is truncated.

In optimum conditions however, authentic personality forms one's sense of ongoing identity, while the stage-appropriate empathic unifying centers (both external and internal) form the ongoing holding environment. One will always find this dialectic of ego and object (object relations); or self and selfobject (self psychology); ego and archetypes (Jungian psychology); or personality and unifying center (psychosynthesis); all of which are reflective of the I-Self relationship. The I-Self relationship itself, however, is ever distinct though not separate from all such dyads.

Multiplicity and Unity

As authentic personality continues to unfold uninterrupted through time, one would find it effortless and natural to shift among, for example, the wonder and playfulness of childhood, the assertion and adventure of adolescence, and the wisdom and responsibility of the adult. Having all of these perspectives available in ongoing daily living is the fruit of authentic personality. There is here a paradoxical experience of unity and multiplicity, as all the many aspects of the personality become expressions of a single, unique, human life.

This conception of distinct perspectives coexisting within the personality again agrees in principle with some of the more recent research into human infancy. Stern (1985) concludes that infancy entails the development of different senses of self or domains of relatedness, each valid unto themselves, which all remain available to the person throughout life. Stern does not portray healthy adult functioning as a renunciation of these earlier senses of self, but as an inclusion of them all in what he calls a "simultaneity of senses of self." All these senses of self, these domains of relatedness, remain available every moment, even though the person might be more acutely aware of one or another in any particular moment.

Note carefully, then, that we are not talking here about some sort of integration or synthesis in which the various aspects of the personality are fused into a unified, seamless whole. It is not, for example, that the outer adult layer in the ring model subsumes the material found in the inner rings of infant, child, and adolescent. Rather, each ring remains a distinct sphere of experience available to the person. Over the course of a day, one might shift among these different perspectives, perhaps expressing adult rationality and decisiveness in the workplace, then enjoying adolescent flirtation with one's spouse, and then becoming childlike in playing with one's children. We may, of course, move effortlessly and seamlessly among these perspectives, even drawing upon several of them simultaneously; however, the aliveness and unity of such expression flows not from an undifferentiated fusion of these perspectives into a larger whole, but from a sense of self able to engage the full diversified range of this multiplicity, i.e., a self-empathy. *The principle of personality integration is here not so much that of unity as of relationship*. This is what would be expected if the foundation and axis of this development is relational—the I-Self relationship.

Both Stern and Assagioli posit a sense of personal self that can engage the emerging multiplicities of experience over the course of development. Stern's emergent sense of self, Assagioli's "I," and too, Kohut's nuclear self, all refer to a subjective perspective that to some extent can experience, and thereby give continuity to, quite different and even conflicting spheres of psychological life.

This maintenance of differentiation in healthy human development is also affirmed by Rowan's study of subpersonalities. He indicates that the many subpersonalities within the personality are not to be fused into a oneness: "To be integrated is not to lose or to play down or to be superior to the subpersonalities. To be integrated is to be more in touch with more of one's subpersonalities, particularly the ones which have been feared, hated, and denied. And this enlarges the realm of our consciousness" (Rowan 1990, 188).

We can clearly see transcendence-immanence in Rowan's concept: as the sense of self is not identified with any particular subpersonality, so one is able to engage all the subpersonalities. Gestalt therapist Erving Polster agrees, presenting a notion of personality synthesis "characterized not by fusion but by the retention of dissonant selves" (Polster 1995, 15). Douglas Richards (1990) goes further still, suggesting that multiplicity in the personality is not only psychologically healthy, but may be an important factor in spiritual development as well.

Thus differentiation and multiplicity seem to be conserved, not eliminated, in healthy human growth. To draw a political simile, the human personality is much more like a pluralistic, democratic society than an oppressive monarchy or totalitarian state.

This unity-in-multiplicity of "I" reflects the unity-in-multiplicity that characterizes the presence of Self. Just as Self is not to be identified with the multiple internal and external unifying centers, so "I" is not to be equated with any of the multiple structures within the personality nor with any particular formation of the personality—not even authentic personality. As with Self, personal self or "I" is singular in the sense of being distinct from multiplicity yet completely engaged in multiplicity. "I," as does Self, endures throughout the changing contents and contexts of experience.

I-Self Relationship as Developmental Axis

In psychosynthesis terms, then, the central organizing principle within the personality is not an integrated pattern of wholeness, not a fusion of the different parts, but the I-Self relationship. This relationship is transcendent-immanent within the "pluralistic society" of the personality, persisting within all the changes in our immediate experience as well as throughout the larger transitions of life. Through all the changing unifying centers, and through all the transformations of the personality, the I-Self connection remains the abiding axis of human growth.

This I-Self relationship also thus represents an overall direction through time, lending meaning and purpose to the continually changing circumstances of human life. Assagioli (1973) understood this unfolding life direction as a function of the interplay—in mutual influence—between the personal will (the will of "I") and the transpersonal will (the will of Self). This notion seems quite in keeping with Kohut's (1977) concept that a person's nuclear program unfolds throughout life as energy flowing between the two poles of the nuclear self: between the pole of nuclear ambitions and the pole of nuclear idealized goals. Furthermore, both Assagioli and Kohut seem here to echo Jung, who saw personal development (individuation) as the response of conscious moral decision to the law of one's being or vocation emanating from deep within the psyche. In Jung's words, "Only the man who can consciously assent to the power of the inner voice becomes a personality" (Jung 1954180).

So each of these thinkers in his own way envisions an axis, formed by the interplay of some type of self-other relationship, which creates a meaningful direction or purpose unfolding throughout human life. And this axis itself constitutes a unity in multiplicity because it is a single direction, transcendent of all specific life circumstances, yet immanent within them all. The response to this direction in life is what in chapter 8 will be elaborated as *Self-realization*.

In conclusion, we can say that the hallmark of healthy psychological development—the flowering of authentic personality in a psychosynthesis of the ages—seems to revolve around an empathic, mirroring connection between "I" and Self throughout the life span. This relationship, facilitated by internal and external unifying centers, allows an experience of personal being that can fully engage all the rich variety found in the diverse spheres of human experience.

As stated at the beginning of this chapter, this has been largely a study of the optimum pattern of human development. But this smooth inclusive unfoldment does not exist in pure form, and has been abstracted from the healthy aspects of many different individual lives. So what happens to disrupt this developmental pattern? What acts to damage the I-Self connection across life's ages? And what are the effects of these disruptions in our lives? This takes us further into the study of the primal wound of nonbeing, and the primal splitting of the human spirit.

5

The Primal Wound

On the earth the broken arcs; in the heaven, a perfect round.
—Robert Browning

Having explored the genesis, nature, and development of human being, we may now discuss further the primal wound to that being— nonbeing. Most simply, the wound of nonbeing occurs as there is an experienced disruption in the empathic mirroring relationship between the personal self or "I" and Self. Since the I-Self connection provides a sense of personal being, any apparent disruption in that connection automatically brings with it the threat of nonbeing.

Such disruptions occur within the specific relationships in our lives. It is as if the connection to Self is distorted or wounded by the inability of particular life relationships—particular unifying centers— to actualize this connection:

> My father suddenly shouted at me in a blind rage. I was shocked. I felt crushed, stupid, betrayed, completely alone. I wanted to disappear, to die. It was like falling through empty space, nothing to hold onto. I felt like an astronaut cut loose from his space ship, falling into infinite black nothingness. All I could do was stand there. I was frozen.

The failure of a unifying center undercuts our sense of personal self, threatening that self with fragmentation, abandonment, and annihilation. As we shall see later in this chapter, a person will go to great lengths to avoid such encounters with nonbeing, including splitting oneself into parts.

Much study has been devoted to disruptions of being and the consequent threat of nonbeing. Let us first look at what some noted psychological thinkers from different schools have said about the threat of nonbeing.

PSYCHOLOGY AND NONBEING

As we have seen, nonbeing is akin to what Winnicott (1987) calls the annihilation of personal being or, simply, annihilation. Winnicott maintains that this annihilation is caused in infancy by a failure of the caregiver-infant connection that disrupts the infant's continuity of being. Thus, such caregiver failure creates what he termed the unthinkable or archaic anxiety derived from this threat of nonbeing. He further points out that continuity of being and annihilation are dynamics that operate well before concepts of life and death are developed.

Similarly, Kohut (1977) speaks of *unnameable dread* and *disintegration anxiety* arising from the danger of the dissolution of the self. This threat is caused by a lack of empathic response from, a disturbed connection with, the significant other or selfobject. Here, too, we can recognize the core wound of nonbeing and the anxiety related to this. Kohut also places issues of being and nonbeing at a deeper level than life and death—witness his study of those willing to face death rather than betray self.

In a like way, the psychoanalyst Michael Balint (1968) describes what he calls the *basic fault*. This basic fault is characterized by feelings of "emptiness, being lost, deadness, futility" (p. 19) that are caused by a "lack of 'fit' between the child and the people who represent his environment" (p. 22). Again, we can see the concept that broken relationship leads to experiences associated with nonbeing.

We can recognize nonbeing, too, in the thought of Erich Neumann. Neumann talks about a break in the child's "primal relationship" with the mother/Self which then causes the anxious experience of "hunger, pain, emptiness, cold, helplessness, utter loneliness, loss of all security and shelteredness . . . a headlong fall into the forsakenness and fear of the bottomless void" (Neumann 1973, 75).

Turning from these schools of depth psychology, we can of course find much about being and nonbeing in the school of existential psychology. Following the likes of philosophers Søren Kierkegaard and Martin Heidegger, existential psychology has from the beginning maintained a focus on nonbeing and its accompanying existential anxiety. For example, Rollo May describes anxiety as "the realization that one may cease to exist as a self," and, after theologian Paul Tillich, called this the "threat of nonbeing" (May 1977, 183).

The existentialist May is in agreement with psychoanalysts Kohut and Winnicott (1987, 47) that the dynamic of being-nonbeing exists at a more fundamental level than life and death. May suggests further that nonbeing anxiety can actually cause physical death. He cites the mysterious phenomenon of voodoo death, which can occur when a member of a tribe has broken a communal taboo. These deaths seem the direct result of the nonbeing anxiety caused by a break between the person and the community, and modern medicine has proven impotent in healing the tribal member so doomed. As May says, here one is literally "cut dead" or "scared to death." Such deaths illustrate that a connection to the unifying center—the communal holding environment or selfobject matrix—is more fundamental than life or death, truly Kohut's "oxygen line."

By the way, the dynamics of voodoo death are akin to those operating when an unhealthy family system bends a child to its oppressive rule, because such domination wields the potent threat of disconnection and nonbeing—"Be who we need you to be, or you won't exist at all." And the adult seeking later to heal these childhood wounds will, like the threatened tribal member, face the profound nonbeing anxiety of transgressing a tribal taboo.

Another existential psychotherapist, Ludwig Binswanger, states that anxiety is caused by a broken continuity between self and world, leading to "the delivery of the existence to nothingness—the intolerable, dreadful, 'naked horror'" (Binswanger 1958, 205)—a vivid description of nonbeing arising from a break in relationship. Existentialist concepts such as anxiety, nothingness, anguish, angst, and dread all point to a perception of the nonbeing underlying human life caused by "the gap . . . between the individual and his world" (May 1977, 48).

We can find a somewhat analogous point of view in the attachment theory of John Bowlby, which is focused on the dynamics of parent-child bonding. Bowlby states that anxiety may not be always the complex secondary phenomenon often held forth by psychoanalytic thought, but may be a primary response to the disrupted bond between the child and the caregiver (Bowlby 1973, 31, 376–7).

Finally, we can turn to humanistic psychology, the movement that seeks models of humanness based on psychological health and positive self-actualization. Even within such an optimistic orientation, Abraham Maslow (1962) points to broken relationship as the cause of an anxiety that cripples human growth. He sees this wound in terms of the primal, terrifying danger created by the parents not meeting the child's fundamental needs for safety and belongingness. Without this basic secure connection, the child's "inner Being" or "Self" will be lost, yielding to a "pseudo-self" and "pseudo-growth." Maslow's thinking seems quite the same as Winnicott's notion that the threatened annihilation of the true self causes the formation of a defensive false self.

> *"There's nothing to be afraid of." The ultimate reassurance, and the ultimate terror.*
>
> —R.D. Laing

It appears then that psychoanalysis, analytical psychology, attachment theory, and existential-humanistic psychology all recognize the crippling wound to being caused by the threat of broken significant relationships. This wounding caused by the threat of nonbeing can be called the primal wound.

The Primal Wound

It is clear why a disruption in an empathic connection to a unifying center gives rise to the threat of nonbeing—this is a disruption in the continuity of being that flows from this connection. These moments of primal wounding are what self psychology calls *empathic failures* or *selfobject failures*—those events in which we were not treated as living, conscious human beings, but as objects, as things. In Kohut's words, "What leads to the human self's destruction, however, is its exposure to the coldness, the indifference of the nonhuman, the nonempathically responding world" (Kohut, 1984, 18). In Buber's (1958) terms again, here are not empathic "I-Thou" experiences, but cold, impersonal "I-It" experiences. In these experiences we are torn away from human being and thrust toward human nonbeing, and our sense of self is profoundly wounded.

Such wounding may be overt or covert. The overt type includes obvious violence, sexual abuse, or physical abandonment, but the covert category is surely more pervasive. The covert types include such things as emotional battering, emotional incest, and enmeshment; unresponsiveness, depression, or self-involvement on the part of the caregiver; caregiver compulsions and addictions that remain unrecognized and untreated; a constant unresolved tension between caregivers, manifested in outward conflict or invisibly pervading the family atmosphere; the leaving of a child alone to face an overwhelming situation; and forcing the child into a limiting role (especially that of partner or even parent to the adult):

> I was always my mother's "special man." I basically took the place of my father. They never really got along, so I was elected to fill in for dad. I don't mean sexually or anything, but I was always the one she confided in, always the one she came to when she wanted to share about things. What I didn't realize until my mid-forties was that I never got to be a kid, and that there was a lot of abandonment and rage deep inside me.

Even the apparently healthy family can covertly inflict debilitating wounds in the children via the unconscious wounding in the caregivers. Such caregiver wounds constitute blind spots in the caregiver mirroring function that cannot but create areas of nonbeing in the child—"When I look I am not seen, so I do not exist." Here caregiver psychological blindness to certain sectors of human experience leaves vacancies in the child—holes of nonbeing, so to speak—in the unfolding personality. In this way wounds can be inflicted by the very process of bonding to the wounded personality of the caregiver:

> For a long time I never knew what I was feeling. Or even what a feeling was. I was confused when someone said I looked sad or asked me why I was angry. I thought they were crazy. In therapy I learned to feel my feelings, though. My family just never talked about feelings. It was as if feelings didn't exist.

The effects of covert wounding may not therefore be ultimately traceable to particular disruptive events (although there will certainly be these), but will be embedded in the overall caregiver-child relationship, forming an atmosphere of wounding in which the child grows up. According to Kohut, the gross traumatic events of childhood may be only "crystallization points" for the trauma inflicted by ongoing contact with the wounded personalities of the caregivers and with the disturbed early environment in general: "But clinical experience tells us that in the great majority of cases it is the specific pathogenic personality of the parent(s) and specific pathogenic features of the atmosphere in which the child grows up that account for the maldevelopments, fixations, and unsolvable inner conflicts characterizing the adult personality" (Kohut 1977, 187). For example, bonding to the high-functioning persona (Jung) or false self (Winnicott) of the caregiver can only give the child, too, a false self. Such a child may look as self-actualizing and gifted as the parent, but this merely hides the fact that the unconscious inner emptiness of the parent has been passed on to the child.

As Alice Miller points out, the caregiver may wound the child even while expressing genuine affection and love. In Miller's words, the love is not expressed "in the way he [the child] needs to be loved" (Miller 1981, 34). Love and affection do not necessarily mean there is an empathic connection. Empathy is transcendent-immanent—it can exist whether one is feeling loving or angry, happy or sad. What makes a relationship empathic is not necessarily what one is doing, sensing, feeling, or thinking; what makes a relationship empathic is

recognizing and respecting the actual, unique, individuality of the particular human being.

An example of the difference between love and empathy occurred
when a husband looked at his wife quietly reading across the room,
felt overwhelmed with love for her, and rushed over to hug her. This
triggered a loud and irate response in the woman, because her experience in that moment was not of being loved by him, but of having
him suddenly and violently break into her peaceful contemplation—
leading to an argument with hurt feelings on both sides. Here the man
was not acting empathically towards her, but responding only to the
excitement of his own loving feelings. The unique experience of the
woman in that moment was unseen, and so transgressed.

Much the same can happen when caregivers express their love
and care for the child, or their excitement over the achievements of
the child—the emphasis may be upon their love and care, upon their
excitement, rather than on the unique experience of the child.
Without empathy, love and affection will not be directed at the person, but at some aspect of the person or, worse, at one's own fantasy
of the person.

So in a very real way there is here a level of respect and responsiveness deeper than normal conscious behavior, resting finally in the
fundamental empathic ability of one's own core identity. Here is
Kohut pointing to this most essential level of connection and wounding beyond conscious behavior and good intentions: "The *nuclear* self,
in particular, is not formed via conscious encouragement and praise
and via conscious discouragement and rebuke, but by the deeply
anchored responsiveness of the self-objects, which, in the last analysis, is a function of the self-objects' own nuclear selves" (Kohut 1977,
100). This level of caregiving is beyond "conscious encouragement"
or "rebuke," beyond good values, beyond parenting manuals, beyond
childrearing techniques. This is a level of being, of core selfhood, at
which the health or wounding of the child derives not so much from
what the caregiver does or does not do, as from who the caregiver *is*.

Winnicott, too, recognizes this essential core-self level of caregiving: "Mothers who do not have it in them to provide good-enough

care cannot be made good enough by mere instruction" (Winnicott 1987, 49). He points out that good enough care is not a matter of knowledge or technique, but derives from the psychological ability of the caregiver to deeply empathize with the infant. Here again, the wounded ability of the "I" of the caregiver to reflect the "I" of the child translates directly to a wounding of the child.

Therapists like Kohut, Miller, and Winnicott seem to be saying that if the caregiver is wounded at this fundamental level, the caregiver's empathic mirroring function will be distorted or limited, and thus the child's self will reflect this wounding. Covert trauma is not simply a function of outward behavior, but is more a result of faulty mirroring causing faulty reflections. It thus seems that the wounded spirit of the caregiver cannot help but create a wounded spirit for the child, no matter how seemingly knowledgeable and attentive the parenting appears. The very best caregiver effectiveness training may therefore involve facilitating self-knowledge, self-empathy, healing, and self-transformation for the caregivers themselves.

The Ubiquity of Primal Wounding

Stepping back a moment, one can dimly perceive here a powerful, broad, invisible river of wounding flowing down through the generations via empathic failures, completely hidden by supposedly normal parenting practices and cultural beliefs.

As mentioned in the introduction, it seems the further one goes back in the history of Western civilization, the more nonempathic response, neglect, and abuse characterize our treatment of children. Historians Philippe Ariès (1962) and Barbara Tuchman (1978) both write about this nonrecognition of childhood in the Middle Ages. Here is Tuchman:

> Of all the characteristics in which the medieval age differs from the modern, none is so striking as the comparative absence of interest in children. (P. 59)

and:

> On the whole, babies and young children appear to have been left
> to survive or die without great concern in the first five or six years.
> (P. 52)

It seems reasonable then, that there is a tidal wave of wounding coming to us from past ages, which we recognize by our new sensitivity to
trauma both in children and in the childhood levels within adults (the
inner child movement). We believe that this blossoming sensitivity
to child mistreatment marks a collective participation in an evolution
of empathy with others, ourselves, and the world.[1]

So this historical flow of wounding is a social, political, and cultural phenomenon. We do not believe there truly can be good enough
caregiving without a good enough society. For example, if infant girls
are seen as less valuable than infant boys by the culture, this attitude
will be transmitted by the caregivers at some level, whether conscious
or unconscious. We are talking here about wounding from the whole
interpersonal matrix of the growing child—any and all of the unifying centers that make up the broadest of holding environments. We
are not talking only about those of us who have been obviously abused
and neglected, but about the human condition itself. In Lenore Terr's
words, "Childhood 'psychic trauma' is not so 'abnormal.' It, or lesser
shades of it, plays a part in the ordinary development of any young-
ster" (Terr 1990, 24). The primal wound is a level of human suffering
that none of us escapes.

Moreover, it may well be that primal wounding is so pervasive that
it can begin as early as intrauterine life. Rowan posits that even in the
womb the person may experience being "invaded by some aggressive
force" (Rowan 1990, 122). Rowan states that in response to this confrontation with extinction and annihilation (nonbeing) there is a
traumatic splitting of the person which he calls the *primal split*. Here
is clearly intrauterine trauma and splitting.[2]

In their book, *The Secret Life of the Unborn Child* (1981), Thomas
Verny and John Kelly discuss intrauterine bonding, describe sympathetic communication between fetus and mother, and outline research
that shows the importance of the empathic connection between

mother and fetus. They report that the fetus is highly attuned to the mother and will react negatively to a rejecting attitude in the mother even when the mother herself is unconscious of this attitude. Again, mirroring and empathic responsiveness are not necessarily conscious matters, but they are a function of a deeper, relational core of the personality.

Finally, a focus on the trauma of conception itself is provided by Christina Grof in her practice of Holotropic Breathwork. Grof, in working with people who uncover memories of their own conception, reports these individuals often describe a deep and pervasive grief that comes with taking a human form: "They say they feel cut off from their true nature, that somehow conception has wrenched them away from an expansive sense of freedom and unity and ensnared them in an individual, material body" (Grof 1993, 41). In our terms, this would be an instance of primal wounding, a break in the I-Self connection suffered at the time of conception.

Transpersonal theorist Thomas Armstrong (1985) suggests that this type of intrauterine separation from Spirit is the source of the *infant exile motif*, a theme found in religions and mythologies throughout the world.[3] Here the child feels the loss of a golden age, exiled in a foreign land, and must undertake the hero/heroine's path of return. As we shall see shortly, this theme was recognized by Freud and Rank as the *family romance*.

It seems clear that what we are calling primal wounding is so ubiquitous, so embedded in the fabric of human existence, that it may seem almost natural. But this normal, pervasive wounding profoundly disrupts natural human development at the deepest levels. Normal does not necessarily mean natural.

A Trauma of Incarnation?

Although Grof and Armstrong see this fundamental trauma of alienation and grief as inherent in incarnation, we would speculate rather that this is a function of engaging a world in which one is not empathically mirrored. As Stolorow and Atwood point out, painful events per se do not cause trauma; it is a break in the empathic connection which causes trauma:

> It cannot be overemphasized that injurious childhood experiences—losses, for example, in and of themselves need not be traumatic (or at least not lastingly so) or pathogenic, provided that they occur within a responsive milieu (Shane and Shane 1990). *Pain is not pathology.* It is the absence of adequate attunement and responsiveness to the child's painful emotional reactions that renders them unendurable and thus a source of traumatic states and psychopathology. (Stolorow and Atwood 1992, 54, emphasis added)

Pain is not pathology. That is, we can hypothesize that painful events, whether prenatal or afterwards, do not necessarily cause primal wounding. The cause of primal wounding is not the suffering itself but the absence of some empathic other and, thus, the threat of nonbeing. The protection provided by the empathic bond even within the womb is recognized by Verny and Kelly:

> Her [the mother's] love is what matters most; and when her child senses that love, it forms a kind of protective shield around him that may decrease or in some cases neutralize, the impact of outside tension. . . . (Verny and Kelly 1981, 46)
> Occasional negative emotions or stressful events are not going to affect intrauterine bonding adversely . . . The danger [to the child] arises when he feels shut off from his mother or when his physical and psychological needs are consistently ignored. (Pp. 94–5, emphasis in original)

We would say that Verny's and Kelly's "protective shield" is a function of the transcendent-immanent bond between child and mother, a bond that need not be broken by anything at all since it is distinct from all content and process (their use of the word "love" implies something beyond loving feelings). The natural processes of life, whether painful or pleasant, do not in themselves inflict nonbeing wounding—only empathic failures do this. There is no inherent reason why the spiritual, transcendent-immanent I-Self connection need be broken by the natural processes of conception, gestation, or birth.

In fact, an increasing number of psychologists, physicians, and parents today do not accept that gestation and birth need be traumatic; they are doing everything they can to provide a more responsive milieu for the human journey from conception through birth.

One may speculate, therefore, with many nature-centered spiritualities both old and new, that we are naturally at home in the universe. We are not in truth strangers here, but feel isolated and alone only because of our primal wounding. We are not wounded by a "fall into matter," but by a break in our connection to Self caused by nonempathic unifying centers.

Matter or nature is not the culprit here, and to believe so can support a devaluation of the physical body, mothers, women in general, and the natural world. It may even be that this dualistic belief of a "fall into matter" actually produces empathic failure at conception—if we do not think that conception is completely natural, healthy, and spiritual, then we will not be able to mirror this for our newly conceived children.

More research is needed in this area, but this research must be open to discovering the sources of wounding and not assume that trauma is inherent in the natural order. We must differentiate between pain and primal wounding; the former implies stress to the organism, perhaps threatening death, while the latter implies actual annihilation and nonbeing. Furthermore, since the I-Self connection can remain intact even in the face of death (cf. Kohut), it takes a special kind of threat to disturb this connection—something beyond soma and psyche alone. The ubiquity of primal wounding, its normality, must not be taken as a sign that this is necessary, innate, or natural. Again, normal does not necessarily imply natural.

In any case, we can see that debilitating wounding is caused by failures in the unifying center, creating a disturbance in the I-Self relationship and so the threat of nonbeing. Since the threat of nonbeing is perhaps the most profound threat a human being can face, moments of primal wounding constitute extremely powerful assaults on the person. Such events are fraught with potent negative energies such as anxiety, dread, disintegration, and despair, which were recognized by the various psychological thinkers above.

The impact of these wounding events must be handled in some way by the human organism. Some method must be devised by which to maintain a relationship with external unifying centers even when these centers fail to see us as we truly are. Only in this way can we avoid the unimaginable fall into the bottomless void of nonbeing. The way we manage this monumental task is by splitting ourselves into parts.

SPLITTING THE PERSONALITY

When a unifying center fails as an empathic other, the connection between "I" and Self is disturbed. The very oxygen line to the source of one's being is threatened, and one faces a headlong fall out of the universe, a plunge into nothingness, a seeming rejection by the Source of Being itself. So how is one to survive this unthinkable contradiction apparently at the foundation of existence: that the Source of Being is now a source of annihilation?

In order to preserve the connection to Self, we split our experience of the failing unifying center into two separate parts, one positive and one negative. The positive side of the unifying center, based on the empathic I-Self relationship, is preserved as a pure, good unifying center from whom we feel love and acceptance—the *positive unifying center*. Conversely, the negative side of the unifying center, based on wounding nonempathic responses, forms a *negative unifying center* from whom we feel hate and rejection:

> I've had two images of my dad in me. For most of my life all I could see was how good he was, how lucky I was to have him for my dad. I felt great about myself and about life. But then I began to remember my abuse, entered therapy, and I began to see another side of him. I even began to see him as totally bad, that his goodness was fake. That was hard, seeing him like that, because it felt like a terrible betrayal and that I would be cast out or something. He was bad. I was bad. The world was a bad place. Now I am starting to see both the good and bad parts of him. Seeing him more as he was.

By separating our interactions with a failing unifying center into positive and negative images, we can then keep the positive safe from the negative. We hereby begin to live in two different worlds, one of trauma and one of security, and never allow one to get near the other. "My dad loves me" and "my dad abuses me" are kept separate, protecting the positive world from the negative. Splitting our experience in this way, we seek to preserve the sense of a positive I-Self relationship, but the price we pay is to split our sense of being, our most basic experience of ourselves and the world.

The recognition of this good-bad splitting stands at the very beginnings of Western psychotherapy. Freud described it as occurring when an instinctual drive within the person met with disapproval from the environment. This conflict was resolved by a psychical dissociation in which the unacceptable and bad was made unconscious, while the acceptable and good remained conscious. This splitting of the personality formed what Freud called "the nuclear complex of a neurosis," which subsequently became more specific in his theory of the Oedipus complex (Freud 1981b, 214). He also referred to the general splitting dynamic as a splitting of the ego in which "two contrary and independent attitudes" are formed within the person (Freud 1981c, 204).

After Freud's insights, the notion of good-bad splitting became a centerpiece in the thinking of Melanie Klein, who even referred to this at times as *primal splitting*. She maintained that splitting of internalized good and bad objects (internal unifying centers) is a natural process in which the child preserves the good object, and so attains a secure sense of self: "To return to the splitting process, which I take to be a precondition for the young infant's relative stability; during the first few months he predominantly keeps the good object apart from the bad one and thus, in a fundamental way, preserves it—which also means the security of the ego is enhanced" (Klein 1946, 191).

Following Klein, Fairbairn describes splitting in terms of the internalization and repression of inner representations of the traumatizing parents or *bad objects*. He asserts that it is intolerable for the child to have a parent who is at times supportive, nurturing, and good, and then at other times frustrating, neglecting, and bad. The child therefore splits the inner figure of the mother into a bad mother and good mother, or into a bad object and good object. The bad object then is repressed, banished to the unconscious: "I find it useful [with patients] to speak of the bad objects as being, as it were, buried in the cellar of the mind behind a locked door which the patient is afraid to open for fear either of revealing the skeletons in the cupboard, or of seeing the ghosts by which the cellar is haunted" (Fairbairn 1986, 65n). This splitting and repression allows the child to maintain a relationship with the outer parents by relegating all wounds to the "cellar." In other words, the negative internal unifying center that inflicts nonbeing wounding is hidden from consciousness. The child can thereby consciously feel safe in what now appears to be a benign holding environment, enjoying a positive sense of self. In Fairbairn's words, "the internalization of bad objects represents an attempt on the part of the child to make the objects in his environment 'good' by taking upon himself the burden of their apparent 'badness,' and thus to make his environment more tolerable" (p. 164).

However, it is not only the unifying center that is split, but one's sense of self as well. That is, when I feel attacked by the negative unifying center, I feel I am bad, unworthy, and hated—I form a negative identity. But when I feel connected to the positive unifying center, I feel good, worthwhile, and loved—I form a positive identity. These two very different experiences of myself go with the two different unifying centers, leaving me with two different experiences of who I am.

Freud, Klein, and Fairbairn all recognize this splitting of identity when they speak of the splitting of the ego, e.g., Freud's two different and independent attitudes. In psychosynthesis terms, these positive and negative identities can be called the *positive personality* and the *negative personality*. Positive personality is connected to the positive unifying center, and the negative personality is connected to the negative unifying center. Figure 5.1 shows how the split into these two major sectors might be diagramed.

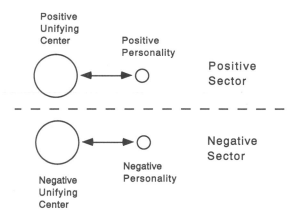

Fig. 5.1

This diagram illustrates a split that creates two types of relationship, one positive and one negative. The positive personality (I am good) relates to the positive unifying center (you are good), while the negative personality (I am bad) relates to the negative unifying center (you are bad). In the positive sector one might feel the peace, joy, and beauty inherent in a perfect connection to the purely positive unifying center (a good or idealized object), while in the negative sector one might be made to feel anxious, shamed, and traumatized by the negative unifying center (the bad or traumatizing object). These two sectors represent a kind of holographic break in the I-Self relationship—the unifying center positions are the split representations of Self, while the personality positions are the split representations of "I."[4]

Splitting: Some Current Views

It seems clear that much current developmental research and psychological theory recognizes the phenomenon of positive-negative splitting, although there are many individual variations among theories (see for example, Grotstein 1986). We shall now briefly touch upon some of these theories.

Developmental researchers such as Mahler, Pine, and Bergman (1975) believe the infant's early ability to differentiate pleasurable/good experiences from painful/bad experiences is the basis for possible later pathological splitting. Stern (1985) also sees the infant categorizing various experiences into pleasurable and unpleasurable clusters, but he believes that what many see as later splitting may be the synthesizing of these earlier experiences into more highly articulated models of good and bad.

In the field of psychoanalysis, Otto Kernberg (1992) and James Masterson (1981), among others, recognize such extreme positive-negative splitting as occurring in the borderline and narcissistic disorders. Both authors describe good self and good object images, which are in opposition to bad self and bad object images.

According to Masterson, for example, the narcissistic personality consists of an "omnipotent fused object representation that contains all power, perfection, direction, supplies, etc.," which is fused with a "grandiose self-representation . . . of being superior, elite, exhibitionistic, with an affect of feeling perfect, special, unique" (p. 15). Here is quite clearly a strongly positive sector of the psyche—an example of what we are calling the positive personality and unifying center. Masterson further says that this good ego-object dyad in narcissism defends against the underlying negative dyad consisting of an "object representation that is harsh, punitive and attacking and a self-representation of being humiliated, attacked, empty, lined by the affect of the abandonment depression" (p. 15). This seems a quite precise description of the "cellar," of an extremely negative personality and unifying center.

We can clearly see the two worlds caused by splitting. One is a world comprising positive personality and positive unifying center (good ego-object dyad), reflecting an ideal I-Self relationship. The other is the world of negative personality and negative unifying center (negative ego-object dyad), reflecting a negative I-Self relationship.

As discussed below, however, we believe the splitting of the personality into positive and negative sectors is a normal—although not natural—aspect of human development. It is to be found not only in the extremes of narcissistic and borderline conditions, as recognized by Masterson and others, but in all of us. As Fairbairn writes, "For that matter, it also applies to the 'normal' person. It is impossible for anyone to pass through childhood without having bad objects which are internalized and repressed. Hence internalized bad objects are present in the minds of all of us at the deeper levels" (Fairbairn 1986, 64–5).

We would add only that the positive personality and positive unifying center are also hidden, not in the "cellar" perhaps, but in the "attic" of the human psyche. By such a "repression of the sublime" (Haronian 1974), the positive is further protected from the trauma and so is preserved. Again, the wounding we all have suffered in childhood has created a fundamental split in our psyches between positive and negative sectors.

Lastly, the work of Michael Washburn (1994) is highly significant in that he elaborates positive-negative splitting within the context of transpersonal psychology and analytical psychology. Washburn describes splitting not only in terms of a split between good and bad representations of self and object, but as a splitting of the archetypal, numinous, and magical Great Mother into representations of Good Mother and Terrible Mother. He thereby shows splitting to be a transpersonal dynamic, one that separates us from our deepest spiritual potentials.

Washburn's description of the split between the Good Mother and Terrible Mother is quite analogous to our view that splitting forms positive and negative sectors of the unconscious. He too maintains that the magnitude of this splitting is such that the positive and negative sectors do not come together in early development, as some object-relations theorists maintain, but are instead repressed, forming a dichotomy within the unconscious that will be encountered in later years. He also laments this splitting as causing a repression of deeper psycho-spiritual potential as well as an alienation from others and the world.

Washburn even states that this splitting is ultimately the result of "fear of object loss, anxiety of losing the primary caregiver" (p. 56)— what we would call the threat of nonbeing caused by primal wounding. He also understands later transpersonal development as involving an encounter with a wound or "black hole" at the seat of the soul, which we would describe as an encounter with this primal wound of nonbeing—the result of primal wounding suffered over the course of a lifetime.

Washburn appreciates the magnitude and profound effects of the splitting phenomenon. It is not at bottom simply a splitting of the representations of caregivers, but a splitting of our relationship to Ultimate Reality. Unifying centers channel our connection to Self, to the Ground of Being of all things, so splitting here is not simply to have positive or negative images, but to perceive reality in positive or negative terms. These "objects" are not contents of our consciousness, but form the very context of our consciousness. They are the broken lenses through which we perceive life as a whole.

Note well, however, that we are not using the term *splitting* to describe a necessary developmental event, a natural differentiation within the personality, or a simple discrimination of painful and pleasurable experiences. While these all may underlie the splitting process, it is only a wounding to being itself that can cause a basic structural separation between major sectors of the person.

Splitting in our view is caused essentially by a failure in the environment to mirror the wholeness of the person; it is a desperate dividing of oneself in order to preserve a relationship to nonempathic unifying centers and so avoid nonbeing. As outlined earlier in the description of authentic personality, without the primal wound the personality would exhibit a natural, fluid multiplicity with no need to isolate major sectors of experience. Primal splitting, like primal wounding, is indeed ubiquitous and normal, but again, this is not to say it is natural and necessary.

We therefore do not believe that splitting is solely an attempt by the child to manage instinctual drives. For example, we strongly disagree with Klein's (1946) view that splitting is caused ultimately by the child's primordial anxiety regarding her or his own innate "death instinct" (e.g., the child's supposed oral-sadistic and cannibalistic desires). In our experience, the violent aggression underlying splitting, when surfaced in adult psychotherapy, invariably turns out to be a rage reaction to an empathic failure on the part of an external unifying center.

Similarly, the most basic primordial anxiety does not seem to concern one's own inner drives, but again, the threat of nonbeing arising from a failed empathic relationship. Such fragmenting rage and anxiety are not naturally occurring aspects of the unmolested human personality; they are valid and proportionate responses to nonempathic agents within the interpersonal milieu. What is primary here is not the rage and anxiety, but the wound that causes these.

Blaming the Victim

In our view then, aspects of the personality are split off not because of basic conflicts among them or because of a necessary conflict between them and society, but because the environment is unwilling or unable to respond empathically to full human being. Good enough empathic response from the environment will allow a sense of I-amness that can engage and manage the widest range of psychological experience, including the many natural polarities of the human personality: affection and anger, pain and pleasure, dependence and independence, or contact and withdrawal, for example. Within an empathic holding environment, such dynamic polarities can be held as part of a larger whole, with no need to split them dualistically into completely separate sectors. While splitting is a defense, it does not defend primarily against inherently conflictual aspects of the inner world. Rather, it defends primarily against the nonempathic response of the environment.

And as self psychology points out, working with splits in the personality demands that the therapist search for empathic failures, both in the client's past and within the therapeutic relationship itself. To assume splitting is a natural phenomenon and not simply the norm is to be blind to the underlying primal wounding that caused it. If we study the splitting process by focusing upon the inner world of the client alone, it is as if we study an assault victim while ignoring the fact of the assault. We then can misinterpret the person's rage as innate sadism and the person's fear as a persecutory anxiety triggered by the sadism. In other words, such a theory prevents an empathic connection to the experience of the one who is wounded. Higgins captures this point: "Since so many forms of distress originate in assault, we need to refocus on what is disrup*tive* to people rather than obsessively categorizing those who are disrup*ted*" (Higgins 1994, 13, emphases in original). This is also the meaning of Terr's term "the psychology of the external" (Terr 1990, 10).

Recognizing the primal wounding beneath our psychological disturbances does not of course absolve us from taking responsibility for our reactions to this wounding. While we are not responsible for having received the wounding itself—an insight crucial to healing—we are responsible for how we handle the wounding, and therefore for any damage to self and others caused by acting out our anxiety, pain, and rage. Understanding that we are all victims at a fundamental level is different from blaming others for the state of our lives and thereby justifying behaviors ranging from aggressive dependence to physical violence. Acceptance of this wounding is not to fall into a victim role, but to touch a basic truth from which to begin the healing process.

So note that we are not talking "mere theory" here. A theoretical system within the field of psychotherapy is much more than mere theory—it is a mirror, a unifying center, which may or may not be able to reflect the plight of those it seeks to serve. And psychological theory that ignores the wounding agent, that blames the victim by locating psychological disturbances solely within the client, amounts to an egregious empathic failure—and cannot help but re-traumatize those seeking psychological help.

In sum, what is primary to our view of splitting is not a life instinct and a death instinct, not a need for union and a need for autonomy, not a libidinal drive and an aggressive drive, but something far more simple and far more destructive—radical wounding to the human spirit, inflicted by an other.

Even though many psychological thinkers do not recognize the centrality of empathic failure to the splitting phenomenon, the recognition of this positive-negative splitting in the personality seems widespread in contemporary psychological thought. In the remainder of this chapter we shall examine more closely the results of primal splitting—the negative and positive sectors of the personality.

PAIN AND PERFECTION

Note once more that the essential pattern of the I-Self relationship is reflected in both the positive and negative sectors created by the primal wound: the personality positions dimly reflect "I" or personal self and the unifying center positions dimly reflect Self. It is as if our essential I-Self connection, our basic experience of being, is reflected in two parts of a distorted, broken mirror.

The trauma of nonbeing disrupts our continuity of being, not by actually breaking the connection between "I" and Self—for that would mean absolute nonrelationship and nonbeing—but by causing the individual to create split-off experiences of pain and perfection, of trauma and idealization. In this way, relationship and being is maintained in the face of trauma. As Freud said of splitting, this is a "very ingenious solution" and "almost deserves to be described as artful" (Freud 1981d, 275, 277).

Furthermore, the more there grows a negative sector caused by empathic failures, the more there is a need for a compensating positive sector. In the words of Klein, "The infant's relative security is based on turning the good object into an ideal one as a protection against the dangerous and persecuting object" (Klein 1946, 49). This balancing of positive and negative can also be seen in psychoanalyst Harry Guntrip's words: "The real parent is 'idealized' in equal proportion to the badness of the parent figures who have been repressed" (Guntrip 1961, 328). It seems the positive and negative realms must be balanced, one against the other, for the split to be maintained, and so for the wounding to remain hidden.

However, we posit that normally the extremes of *both* positive and negative sectors are eventually repressed. The wounding is simply too profound, and the positive and negative too polarized, for these extremes to remain conscious. In forming a stable sense of identity, both the depths of wounding and the heights of perfection are to some extent eliminated from consciousness over the course of normal development.[5]

What the psyche needs in order to counterbalance primal wounding is not most centrally a particular conscious attitude, persona, or identification (although these are important), but an equal amount of positive material within the unconscious. Personal consciousness can be viewed as a fulcrum between the painful and perfect realms of the unconscious, a fulcrum which seeks to balance not only the conscious and unconscious, but more basically, the negative and positive unconscious.

In other words, there is always a negative *and* positive shadow. Jung (1968) does admit the possibility of a positive shadow and not simply a negative one, but he does not seem to allow for the existence of both types of shadow in one personality. We, with Assagioli, are saying that this duality of the shadow is the norm.

We would maintain, for example, that if there is an unconscious wound from childhood incest, there may perhaps be an unconscious image of a valiant savior. Or if there is an unconscious trauma of neglect, there may perhaps be an unconscious ideal of being seen as the most special. Or if there is an unconscious memory of abandonment, there may be an unconscious hope for a perfect union. There is not only a repression of the negative, but a proportional repression of the positive:

> I hid my goodness so my mother wouldn't consume it like she consumed everything else of me. She hurt me so much that I wasn't going to let her have the pleasure of seeing me. The only power I had was not to express myself. Now it's a struggle to get back what I hid from my mother.

This sense of goodness, potential, and perfection is not an illusion, but is formed by our connection to Self via positive unifying centers— good experiences with caregivers, peers, nature, spirituality, etc. The positive that is split off here is not simply the goodness of the caregiver, as stated by object relations theory. The positive that is split off is our sense of a good connection to Self, from which unfolds authentic personality. Here our relationship with the Divine, with Ultimate Reality, with the deeper meaning of life is broken off and repressed. The positive unconscious may hold our deepest sense of beauty, joy, and creativity; our ability to appreciate art, nature, and other people; our sense of a transpersonal connection to all of life.

And to the extent we have been wounded, this type of profoundly positive experience is split off and hidden, often not only from the environment, but from ourselves as well. We may remain somewhat aware of this positive dimension in childhood hero worship, salvation fantasies, and daydreams, or we may later in life project this positive realm outward and seek it there.

This search for lost perfection can be seen in some childhood abuse survivors who become caught up in a desperate quest for final salvation from the effects of childhood trauma. There is frequently an obsessive search for the right technique, therapist, or group by which to realize a state of being that is untouched by the trauma—a state of perfection. Here the positive shadow or positive unconscious is projected onto external objects, and then sought in those objects—just as the negative shadow or unconscious can be projected onto external objects and in those objects be feared and hated.

This driven search and idealized hope has been called the Flying Dutchman Syndrome by Jungian Anthony Stevens (1982) and the Heaven Is Just Around The Corner Syndrome by Ann Gila (Russell, 1990), which has been described in this way: "Here there is the hope and quest for some magical situation—the right house, life-style, therapy, relationship, religious practice, etc.—that will trigger the idealized spiritual state, or 'true self.' The often-unconscious assumption is that the treasure at the end of the quest will erase the wounds of life, and eliminate the need for creating a realistic lifestyle which accepts these wounds" (Firman 1991, 27).

This same type of compulsion can be seen in the person seeking an "enlightenment" that is understood as a unitive state untouched by the fragmentation and suffering in the world and, as we shall see later, it is a drive that underpins the addictive process as a whole. Psychoanalyst Christopher Bollas describes much the same motivational drive as the quest for what he terms the transformational object: "We see how hope invested in various objects (a new job, a move to another country, a vacation, a change of relationship) may both represent a request for a transformational experience and, at the same time, continue the 'relationship' to an object that signifies the experience of transformation" (Bollas 1987, 16). Bollas sees this quest behind the criminal's search for the perfect crime, the lover's search for the perfect partner, and the compulsivity of the gambler's game.

Even the addict who prowls the streets for his angry "fix" and the assassin who stalks his fated prey are reaching out for being.

—Huston Smith

Working with this sense of perfection and its related compulsivity is often a central part of psychotherapy, recovery groups, and spiritual practice. The painful realization that such perfection can be glimpsed but not finally attained is called the *crisis of duality* in psychosynthesis theory (see chapter 8).

Although the experiences comprising the positive and negative sectors of the unconscious may or may not have been conscious at different times in life, over the course of development the person generally seeks to avoid both extremes in favor of a more balanced, if less energetic, personality configuration—one cannot live in either agony or ecstasy for very long. In the service of a stable sense of self and world, both the extremes of pain and perfection are repressed, creating two separate sectors of the unconscious.

These positive and negative worlds then normally lie dormant in our lives as adults, allowing a stable, adjusted existence. The conscious identity maintains itself as a fulcrum, balancing these two sectors of the psyche (akin to the function of Fairbairn's *central ego*). However, either sector may later break into consciousness, as when shocking and painful abuse memories suddenly emerge into awareness or when peak moments of beauty and joy burst into our mundane lives.

We shall return to the emergence of the two sectors shortly, but let us first examine the work of a man who not only recognized this type of positive unconscious, but also traced the effects of this in worldwide mythology, the early psychoanalytic thinker Otto Rank.

THE POSITIVE UNCONSCIOUS: OTTO RANK

Indications of this compensating, positive unconscious can be found in Otto Rank's (1990) study of what he, after Freud (1981a), calls the *family romance*. According to Freud and Rank, the family romance is a common childhood fantasy uncovered in adult psychoanalysis. Rank maintains that the child, under the impact of parental neglect and hostility, inwardly splits off the positive side of the parental figure and develops this into a private idealized story, the family romance.

According to this inner story the child believes that she or he does not in reality belong to the family at all, but is the son or daughter of noble parents from whom he or she has fallen into the current, lowly, adoptive family. Here is much the same dynamic as described in the splitting of internal unifying centers. One can also clearly see in the family romance the universal infant exile motif researched by Armstrong (1985).

This myth-making by the child is fueled by pain and aggression in relationship to the real parents, who are hereby disowned in favor of a higher birthright. But, as Rank says, by splitting off the goodness of the parents and locating this in the idealized noble parents, the child preserves the parents' goodness in the face of their negative side: "The entire endeavor to replace the real father by a more distinguished one is merely the expression of the child's longing for the vanished happy time, when his father still appeared to be the strongest and greatest man, and the mother seemed the dearest and most beautiful woman" (p. 62).

As discussed in chapter 2, infancy is grounded originally in reality and not fantasy, so this vanished happy time is not an illusion based on some sort of early innocence but an ideal of perfection caused by the wounding itself. The sense of this lost Golden Age is the result of splitting the empathic factors within the early environment from the nonempathic factors. In developing the romantic fantasy, the child enshrines the positive qualities of empathic relationship—in our terms, the qualities of the ideal I-Self relationship—and so preserves them as ideal seeds of redemption and vindication hidden from the traumatic environment. By this means, the child forges hope within an otherwise hopeless situation.

Pia Mellody, a strong voice in the recovery movement, offers an accurate contemporary description of the family romance, pointing to its possible physiological underpinnings as well:

> One way such children may escape the pain of severe abandonment by the parents is to fantasize about being rescued by a hero of some kind. Little girls may imagine a knight in shining armor who has loving feelings for her and who does things that demonstrate this love by connecting with her, finally giving her life meaning and vitality. The fantasy is often very much like the fairy tale Sleeping Beauty, in which Sleeping Beauty lies asleep, out of touch with herself and her surroundings, until the life-giving kiss of Prince Charming awakens her. Children spend so much time in this fantasy world because it creates a state of euphoria. I spent hours as a child daydreaming about my knight in shining armor. If I felt bad I could play out this fantasy in my mind, get high in about ten minutes, and stay there for at least two or three hours. I think that when we put a pleasurable picture in our minds and think about it, we can stimulate an emotional response to it that may lead to the release of endorphins into our system. Endorphins literally relieve emotional pain and create varying degrees of euphoria. (Mellody 1992, 16–17)

Mellody is here clearly describing the formation of an ideal realm that is kept separate from the wounding environment, and so preserves the hope of salvation from that environment. Such childhood idealization often then becomes unconscious over time, although the psychic energy it represents will become a strong force in addictions and compulsions as it is projected outward and sought in people, places, and things.

Rank points out, too, that the family romance is ultimately a vehicle for the idealization of oneself as well. In other words, there is not only a positive unifying center position, but also a positive personality position. He says the culmination of the family romance is found in the statement, "I am the emperor (or god)" (p. 77). Here a person can feel special, seen, and adored—precisely the opposite of the traumatic feelings of being despised, ignored, and abandoned.

This inflation of self indicates an ideal state of being that has been established to counteract trauma. Here the individual ultimately feels not only in communion with the Divine, but Divinity itself. And while this experience is in a way quite valid, as seen in the profound union of "I" and Self (see chapter 2), it is here distorted by being split off from other aspects of life experience. That is, it is not a true unitive experience because it is based on a separation from major dimensions of reality. But these heights of perfection serve well to counterbalance the depths of the negative sector.

As mentioned earlier, both Kernberg and Masterson recognize this positive sector in the narcissistic and borderline disorders. In their insight into the narcissistic fusion of ideal self and ideal object, we can see the inflated self—"I am god"—to which Rank points as the ultimate state of idealization in the family romance. The oscillation between these two sectors, the bipolar swings between highs and lows, between pride and inadequacy, between good and bad, can be seen throughout the entire range of human personality, although perhaps most markedly in the borderline and bipolar disorders.

Rank takes his work further by claiming that this family romance is reflected in the hero stories found in world mythology (cf. Armstrong's infant exile motif). Such myths describe a fall of the hero from his original high state into a realm of humble circumstances, oppression, and persecution, over which the hero triumphs against all odds. These myths glorify the struggle and victory of the nobly born hero in a way which closely resembles, according to Rank, these childhood family romances.

We might add that this type of story is often found at the core of dualistic metaphysics as well (e.g., many Gnostic myths), in which human beings are seen as essentially good sparks of pure spirit that have fallen into an evil world to be oppressed by the rule of a malevolent demiurge (see, for example, Jonas 1963, Couliano 1992).

Classically, the dualist believes that good and evil are separated into a spiritual world of a Good Divinity (positive unifying center) and material world of an Evil Divinity (negative unifying center), and that salvation lies in a return to the spiritual realm beyond the material.

✓ In dualistic systems, as in the family romance, one can sense a masked rage and aggression toward the parents (and world) for empathic failure. This rage seems evident, for example, in the historical dualist negativity towards marriage—marriage is to be blamed for the trapping of pure spiritual beings in the prison of the body (see Nigg 1962). Aggression towards parents is, according to Rank, the energy that fuels the formation of the family romance, and it is revealed in some hero myths as well: "The youthful hero, foreseeing his destiny to taste more than his share of the bitterness of life, deplores in a pessimistic mood the inimical act which has called him to earth. He accuses the parents, as it were, for having exposed him to the struggle of life, for having allowed him to be born" (p. 65). This passage describes well the dualistic sensibility: one has been thrown down from the spiritual heights into an evil, abusive world, and must climb back up the scale of being to attain the original lost spiritual glory. Here is the source of a divine homesickness; a feeling of alienation from normal daily life; a sense one is special, elite, or chosen; a sense one needs to learn to incarnate; a felt secret knowledge or "gnosis" of a higher reality; and an abiding hope in the myth of return.

The Gnostics themselves knew what real suffering was, and consequently the spirit of any man who has languished in similar darkness will respond to the Gnostic creed.

—Walter Nigg

This type of dualism entails a profound perception of suffering and evil, coupled with a vivid vision of perfection, which together comprise a cosmic splitting and polarization of creation and the Divine alike into good and evil. It just may be that dualistic metaphysical systems derive in part from the deeply felt experience of wounding in life, and from a resultant keen insight into the evil of the world.

In any case, it seems that the psychological truth of all such mythology lies in the myth's embodiment of the hope of the wounded human spirit. Here is a hope that finally one day the hidden truth—the evil oppression of one's noble birthright—will be revealed, and salvation will be attained from imprisonment in a false self and false society.

As we close this discussion of the family romance, note that Rank does not consider the family romance as merely an unrealistic idealization formed by impossible wishes and desires; rather, he considers the idealization to be formed from the *actual* goodness experienced in lived relationships. We would say that the treasure hidden away in the realm of perfection is treasure gained from whatever empathically attuned relationships one may have had—and in psychosynthesis terms, these positives derive ultimately from the I-Self relationship as facilitated by empathic unifying centers.

But in order to protect this goodness from destruction, it has been split off from the rest of existence, and thus idealized. In object relations terms, the good parent has been preserved as an inner ideal. In philosophical terms, qualities such as love, joy, and beauty have been preserved by seeing them as ideal forms separate from matter. In religious terms, God is seen as separate from creation, as solely transcendent rather than as transcendent-immanent.

So again, what is illusory in this positive sector is not the goodness itself, nor even perhaps the ultimate redemption of this goodness, but rather the splitting that separates this goodness from the world, that locates it in a glorious, heavenly realm having nothing fundamental to do with this terrestrial "vale of tears."

THE TWO SECTORS OF THE UNCONSCIOUS

Allow us at this point to summarize our position regarding the negative and positive sectors of the personality.

Under the impact of the primal wound of nonbeing, the personality undergoes what can be called the primal split: the personality splits into negative and positive sectors which normally over time become more or less unconscious, leaving the conscious personality to function relatively protected from the extremes of pain and perfection, of trauma and idealization. On one hand we have the sector representing a negative, wounding experience of the I-Self relationship, and on the other hand we have a sector appearing as a positive ideal I-Self relationship unsullied by wounding.

Thus, although the negative sector seems more related to the primal wound, and the positive more related to the true I-Self relationship, in fact both positive and negative sectors are conditioned by the underlying trauma. Both sectors are distortions of the I-Self relationship, and neither would exist in their isolation were it not for primal wounding. It is as if one buries the wounding not in one or the other side of the split, but deep at the bottom of the chasm *between* them.

On one hand one can avoid the threat of nonbeing by identifying with personality structures conditioned by the positive sector, for example: "I am perfectly loved" (positive personality) or "I am all-loving" (positive unifying center). But in this business of avoiding nonbeing, it works equally well to identify with structures conditioned by the negative sector: "I am worthless, hopeless" (negative personality) or "You are worthless, hopeless" (negative unifying center). Both positive and negative sectors operate to give some sense of identity and thus protect against nonbeing.

The strong bonding, and even fusion, between each personality and unifying center in each sector allows the pairs to operate somewhat in isolation from each other, thus constituting the primal split. In psychoanalytic terms, this is object cathexis operating as a repression barrier. As long as these sectors operate independently, even though drawing us under their sway at different times, the underlying wounding will not emerge in its fullness.

Clearly then, it is only as these two sectors begin to come into relationship, as one begins to bridge both of them, that the threat of nonbeing and the hidden primal wounding will emerge. Only then can a person begin to heal the split in the whole personality.

And please note again here that *both* of these sectors are valid and real. The positive unconscious is not simply "infantile hallucinatory gratification" (Klein) nor merely a defense against a supposed basic existential isolation; indeed, this realm represents much of our capacity for spiritual insight, inspired creativity, unitive experiences, and altruistic ideals. However, the positive sector is not the true world of union and perfection, while the world of trauma and pain is an illusion. Rather, both sectors are components of our authentic experience. The inauthenticity of these sectors, if we can call it that, derives simply from the separation between these two aspects of experience.

The only illusion operating in all of this is the mistaken perception that transcendent-immanent being does not include both these sectors of human life. The lives of many involved in psychological and spiritual healing show us beyond a doubt that this major split in the psyche can in fact be bridged, leading to a more profound ability to engage both the heights and depths, the joys and pains, the unions and separations, of living. As someone said, healing involves "feeling better"—feeling better the joy, feeling better the pain, feeling better all that life may bring.

These concepts of negative and positive sectors of the unconscious can, in our view, be equated with Assagioli's concepts of a lower unconscious and a higher unconscious, respectively. Although Assagioli did not precisely elaborate his understanding of these sectors, we believe he himself would have been in accord with this further expansion of his theory.[6] We shall now look more carefully at these higher and lower sectors of the unconscious, and later we shall examine how the primal split between them can be healed.

6

The Higher and Lower Unconscious

Looking at my life from one vantage point,
I see nothing but devastation. Yet, like the moon,
my life has another side, one with some luminosity.
—Sylvia Fraser

The primal wound arises from failures in the empathic functions of significant others—of external unifying centers. These are moments when one is faced with the unimaginable prospect of personal nonexistence, of individual annihilation, of nonbeing. In response to this threat of nonbeing, the personality splits into positive and negative sectors.

The negative sector resonates most obviously with the primal wounding. It comprises our ability to see the wounding in ourselves and others, and is organized as a relationship between the negative personality and the negative unifying center. The positive sector comprises much of our ability to perceive unitive and spiritual aspects of reality and is organized as a relationship between the positive personality and the positive unifying center. These two sectors are largely repressed, leaving the conscious personality in a more stable configuration, relatively oblivious of the heights above and depths below. In this way the positive is conserved, the negative hidden, and a secure normality is attained. Although there may be many variations of this, the positive-negative split seems a basic pattern of the human personality. Even though many psychologists understand this splitting as a splitting of inner representations of parental figures, it is far more profound than this might seem. We here split up our most basic experience of ourselves, of others, of the cosmos, and of Divinity. It is as if our ability to see red were broken away from our ability to see blue, and both were broken away from our ability to see yellow. We then live our lives looking through only the yellow lens, oblivious of the reds and blues that surround us. It is only later, when we begin to integrate the red and blue sectors, that we begin to see reality in all the richness of its true colors.

Remember that the primal wound splits our experience of being itself. The being flowing to us from Self is in effect separated into negative and positive streams. Here is not a split in something we can reflect and act upon, but a split in the place from which we reflect and act. Deeper than consciousness. Deeper than will.

These positive and negative sectors of the personality can be called, respectively, the higher unconscious and lower unconscious. Adapting Assagioli's (1965) model, these two sectors are represented in figure 6.1.

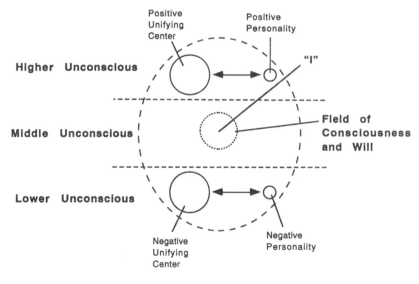

Fig. 6.1

"I" or personal self is represented in the center of the diagram with the field of consciousness and will that was discussed in chapter 3. The middle unconscious is that area of the personality that is unconscious but not repressed, comprising unconscious aspects of ourselves that are accessible in our normal functioning in the world. The higher unconscious and lower unconscious, however, represent sectors of our experience that are split off by primal wounding and forcefully kept from our awareness by repression. The dotted lines indicate that this repression is not complete and that these areas of ourselves nevertheless influence our conscious lives. Let us examine these lower and higher sectors in turn.

The Lower Unconscious

If the threat of nonbeing derives from an empathic failure on the part of an external unifying center, we might assume that every personality is riddled with greater or lesser amounts of primal wounding. Human life is rife with moments and periods of nonempathic response from significant others, either covert or overt, intentional or unintentional. Even if these periods of primal wounding took place in the distant past, they exist now in the present.

Recalling the ring model of the personality (figure 4.3), we might envision each psychological age, each inner ring of the personality, marred by the threat of nonbeing. All of these moments together constitute a network or matrix that is the structure of the lower unconscious. The material of the lower unconscious comprises experiences associated with the threat of personal annihilation, of destruction of self. This is the threat that creates Kohut's disintegration anxiety, "a deeper unnamable dread experienced when a person feels that his self is becoming seriously enfeebled or is disintegrating" (Kohut 1977, 105).

Of course, phenomenologically there is not in truth an absolute nonbeing state that can be experienced. The reason for this is simply that, in a true nonbeing state, there would be no experiencing subject present at all—no one is there to have the experience. By definition then, such a state in pure form lies forever beyond experience. Tillich says that anxiety is facing the "unknown which by its very nature cannot be known, because it is nonbeing" (Tillich 1952, 37). Kohut affirms this insight: "Clearly, the attempt to describe disintegration anxiety is the attempt to describe the indescribable" (Kohut 1984, 6). And Winnicott dubbed this *unthinkable anxiety*, placing it beyond the purview of psychological analysis (Winnicott 1987, 61).

Personal annihilation is unimaginable, unthinkable, and terrifying at a level far beyond the reach of consciousness. From this threat of unimaginable nothingness issues a profound and deadly power, the energy that makes up the lower unconscious. Among these negative energies, qualities, or experiences are those listed below:

Anxiety and disintegration

A lack of meaning in self or world

Feeling lost, trapped, or buried

Isolation, abandonment, banishment

Feeling overwhelmed, helpless, or hopeless

Emptiness or hollowness

Endless despair; Wanting to die; Shame and guilt

Overwhelming terror at the possible loss of other

A sense of inauthenticity or falseness

Low self-esteem or worthlessness

Primal, terrifying danger (Maslow)

Angst, anguish, dread (cf. May)

The Dreadful (Binswanger)

Falling forever (Winnicott)

Loss of direction, lack of intentionality (Tillich)

Having no relationship to the body (Winnicott)

Hunger, pain, emptiness, cold, helplessness (Neumann)

Falling, darkness, oppression, dejection, contraction (Laski)

Utter loneliness, loss of all security and shelteredness (Neumann)

Falling into the forsakenness and fear of the bottomless void
(Neumann)

All of these qualities of experience are symptomatic of a break in an empathic connection, causing the threat of nonbeing. These experiences are the direct opposite of feeling held securely in being, and imply instead a falling towards nonbeing. (Compare these negative qualities to the lists of the workshop participants in chapter 1.)

These types of experience also tend to link with similar experiences over time, creating continuous chains of like memories throughout the personality. Such a personality structure organized around a common element is what Jung (1969b) calls a *complex*, what Stan Grof (1975) terms a *system of condensed experience* or COEX, and what Kohut (1971) calls "the telescoping of genetically analogous experiences."

For instance, moments of shame as a toddler will be aligned with later moments of shame in grade school, then with similar moments of shame in adolescence, and so on, until finally the experience of shame in adulthood involves a complex organization of memories, physical sensations, feelings, and thoughts. Such stratification within the lower unconscious can be seen, too, when one has bonded to a wounded parent or has been brought up in an abusive environment; here the ongoing threat of nonbeing infuses each layer of the personality as the layer develops. However they are acquired, these traumatic experiences will constitute branches throughout the inner layers or ages within the personality. Depth psychotherapists are well aware of the process by which clients often sort through these experiences layer by layer in their healing process.

Although conditioned by nameless and unimaginable nonbeing wounding, the lower unconscious is nevertheless an organization or structure of experience. As such, it provides an identity, a mode of being, but this is a *negative* identity or mode of being. This is the realm of negative personality and negative unifying center, a broken image of the deeper I-Self connection. At this level, the traumatized child learns, for example, that life is an abusive experience, and comes to accept abuse as simply the way things are. Later in life, such a person may fall into abusive relationships—as perpetrator or victim—and these relationships, although painful at one level, may in some way feel familiar and comfortable, offering a negative mode of being.

Fairbairn (1986) also recognizes this preference for negative relationship over the actual loss of relationship. He describes Freud's discussion of a case of demonic possession suffered by a seventeenth-century artist who, depressed after the death of his abusive father, sought relief by signing a pact with the devil. This pact was made not to gain any sort of hedonistic pleasure, but solely so the devil would agree to be his father. In Fairbairn's view, the pact was made in order to maintain the relationship with his abusive father in the form of the devil: "What he sold his eternal spirit to obtain, accordingly, was not gratification, but a father, albeit one who had been a bad object to him in his childhood" (p. 71). That is, according to Fairbairn, the devil symbolized the artist's "internalized bad father, whom he had either to embrace *or else remain objectless and deserted*" (pp. 71–2, emphasis added). In other words, the man would rather face damnation itself than confront nonbeing. The human being opts for a negative relationship rather than face the unimaginable terror of pure nonbeing, absolute nonrelationship.[1]

It is again the relationship itself that is so important in creating a sense of being and providing a defense against nonbeing. It is through our significant relationships that we are connected to Self and receive a sense of personal selfhood; thus the threatened loss of such a relationship—whether it is positive or negative—will raise the specter of nonbeing. Even the painful and oppressive relationship between negative personality and negative unifying center gives a sense of being—the negative mode of being characteristic of the lower unconscious.[2]

In sum, the lower unconscious arises from primal wounding, from the threat of nonbeing arising from a disturbance in the I-Self connection. The more such wounding there has been in our lives, the more we will split this off from, and so protect, the empathic experiences we have in life. Thus, the more developed the lower unconscious, the more developed is its opposite—the higher unconscious.

THE CONNECTION TO SELF

Before discussing the higher unconscious, it is important to emphasize that it is formed by splitting off aspects of our innate natural ability to experience our connection to Self. This connection is glimpsed in moments such as this:

> I suddenly felt I was united to all things, to the whole universe. Something or someone was holding the universe and me in an unbreakable unity. Everything was absolutely safe. I could not fall out of the universe. There were no cracks. I could still feel my grief, but now it and I were held by something greater.

The universe is here felt to be a cosmic unifying center infused by a connection to an empathic Other beyond "I." As we have seen, this transcendent-immanent connection to Self produces an enduring sense of transcendent-immanent "I" that can engage love and grief, union and fragmentation, fullness and emptiness, and all the other experiences encountered over the course of a human life.

And since the I-Self connection is transcendent-immanent, abiding through all stages of life, each stage of life has a stage-specific ability to appreciate a connection to this deeper holding presence. Of course, the adult's connection would be moderated by adult external unifying centers (e.g., the night sky, a religious community, a spiritual teacher) and adult internal unifying centers (e.g., mature cognitive and moral functioning), while an infant's connection, for example, would be facilitated by different external unifying centers (e.g., the mother, the secure setting) and internal unifying centers (e.g., early developmental structures). Nevertheless, each age has its own potential for experiencing a connection to the universality of Self. Aldous Huxley's *The Perennial Philosophy* affirms the ability to experience this reality at any stage of development: "But direct awareness of the 'eternally complete consciousness,' which is the ground of the material world, is a possibility occasionally actualized by some human beings at almost any stage of their own personal development, from childhood to old age, and at any period of the race's history" (Huxley 1945, 20-1).

In Judy's (1991) terms, this unitive awareness would be a conscious contact with the Divine Ground of Being that infuses all our
relationships from infancy onward, at all levels, both interior and
exterior. Such a unitive holding experience would be possible at any
of Judy's four levels of community: phyletic, nature, mystical, or polit-
ical/geographic (see chapter 4). In Wilber's
terms this would seem to be a stage-appropriate
consciousness of the ultimate Unity that inter-
penetrates "all levels, realms, and planes, high
or low, sacred or profane" (Wilber 1980, 74).
And for Washburn (1988), this would seem to
be contact with the Dynamic Ground.

We know that children
are capable of peak
experiences and that
they happen frequently
during childhood.

—Abraham Maslow

In a nontraumatizing world, this awareness of
a connection to Self would abide through all
the unfolding stages of human development.
There is no inherent reason why consciousness of this connection
need be broken in natural development—this connection is the
source of personal freedom and responsibility, and the axis of development throughout the life span.

But in primal wounding, specific unifying centers fail to reflect
this connection to Self, and consciousness of this connection is split
off and repressed. As this wounding occurs at the various stages of
development, more aspects of this consciousness are increasingly dissociated, forming the higher unconscious.

In this process the connection to Self is experienced as existing
in a higher or "more sublime" sphere separated from the conscious
identity and daily life. Consciousness of the I-Self connection begins
to exist in a perfect realm of being which seems to have very little to
do with the mundane or painful aspects of life. Here is created a higher
platonic realm, filled with ideal contents and energies separated from
everyday reality—the higher unconscious.

But of course, it is only splitting that creates the impression of a
higher realm. In actuality these ideal contents and energies are very
much a part of everyday reality, embedded in every aspect of our here
and now existence. It is simply that we have been made blind to them.

Our ability to see them—our "lens" for viewing this aspect of reality— has been broken off and forgotten.

Accordingly, using the ring model of the personality, the formation of the higher unconscious and lower unconscious over time might be diagrammed in the manner depicted in figure 6.2.

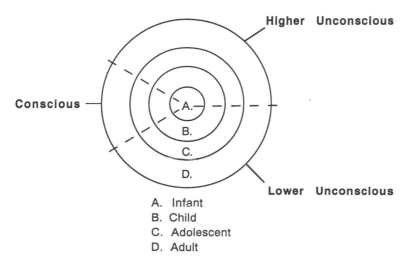

A. Infant
B. Child
C. Adolescent
D. Adult

Fig. 6.2

In this figure, the sector to the left represents what is included in one's usual mode of consciousness: one is here aware of the adult mode of being (D) and can draw upon certain memories and developmental capacities from earlier ages (A, B, C). In this sector would be also the unrepressed unconscious—the middle unconscious—those contents that are not defensively kept out of awareness, but that are unconscious by virtue of natural development (e.g., deep physiological processes, integrated transpersonal qualities, developmental achievements).

The upper sector of the diagram represents the higher unconscious. Here are unintegrated higher states of consciousness that have been present as potential throughout the life span (A through C) and continue to be split off in the present. A repression barrier operates to keep these states out of awareness, whether these are memories of past experiences or potential new experiences in the present (as usual, dotted lines indicate the interpenetration of these various sectors).

The lower sector is the lower unconscious, again separated from the whole by a repression barrier. Here psychological wounds remain safely outside of everyday awareness, whether these are memories of past traumatic experiences or wounding events taking place in the present. So this sector too includes elements from all developmental levels (A through C).

The raptures of wonder and beauty, the terror of violation and abandonment, all may exist at any age of life whatsoever. The primal split between higher unconscious and lower unconscious moves forward in time as one, reflecting in every stage, every formation, of the developing personality.

So as we now explore the higher unconscious, keep in mind that it is formed from authentic consciousness of the Deeper Source from which we come. It is inaccurate to consider this higher dimension of human being fantasy, delusion, or pathological. The use of such terms in this regard illustrates a naivete often exhibited by Western psychology vis-à-vis transpersonal experience.

THE HIGHER UNCONSCIOUS

As previously discussed, the experience of "being" splits into positive and negative modes—into positive and negative experiences of the I-Self relationship—as a way of surviving nonbeing wounding. Through splitting and then repression, the experiences most closely associated with the threat of nonbeing are organized into the lower unconscious, which appears as a negative I-Self relationship (negative personality and unifying center). This leaves a compensatory and protected realm of idealized I-Self relationship (positive personality and unifying center), or what can be called the higher unconscious.

The higher unconscious then comprises potential states of unitive consciousness, creative abilities, transpersonal energies, and numinous forms that embody a purely positive I-Self relationship insulated from the lower unconscious. In principle, this perfect union can function much like Robert Firestone's (1987) *fantasy bond*, or Helmuth Kaiser's (1965) *fusion-delusion*, whereby some form of ideal connection and being is achieved while the underlying dissociation from painful experiences is preserved. This also seems akin to the mechanism recognized by Kernberg and Masterson in the fusion between the idealized ego and idealized object, and by Freud and Rank in the family romance.

While the lower unconscious is infused by the type of negative experiences listed above, the higher unconscious includes quite opposite experiences that can be called *transpersonal qualities*. Maslow (1962, 1971) called such qualities *being values* and *being cognitions*, and they can been seen in Richard Bucke's (1967) cosmic consciousness, in those moments William James (1961) studied as varieties of religious experience, in what Marghanita Laski (1968) explored as *ecstasy*, and in the *peak experiences* researched by Maslow (1962, 1971).

Transpersonal qualities are probably infinite in variety, but at one point Maslow (1971, 106) distills this list from his study of peak experiences:

Truth, Beauty, Wholeness

Dichotomy-transcendence, Aliveness-process

Uniqueness, Perfection, Necessity

Completion, Justice, Order

Simplicity, Richness, Effortlessness

Playfulness, Self-sufficiency

Another list of transpersonal qualities was published circa 1970 by the Psychosynthesis Institute in Redwood City, California:

Beauty, Compassion, Comprehension

Courage, Creativity, Energy, Power

Enthusiasm, Eternity, Infinity, Universality

Freedom, Liberation, Detachment

Cooperation, Friendship

Generosity, Goodness, Goodwill

Gratitude, Appreciation, Admiration, Wonder

Harmony, Humor, Inclusiveness

Joy, Bliss, Light, Love

Order, Patience, Positiveness

Reality, Truth, Service

Renewal, Trust, Faith

Serenity, Peace, Silence, Quiet, Calm

Simplicity, Synthesis, Wholeness

Understanding, Vitality, Will, Wisdom

As Maslow points out, these characteristics describe how the world appears to a person during and after peak experiences. In other words, they are descriptions of a particular relationship to the world, a relationship involving an ideal sense of connection and unity (dichotomy-transcendence, universality) and a sense of being fully oneself (self-sufficiency, uniqueness, will).

The I-Self relationship can be seen underpinning these qualities—the universality and unity of Self juxtaposed with the uniqueness and individuality of "I." Taken together, transpersonal qualities are like an energy field set up between the pole of "I" and the pole of Self. They are essential properties of this primal relationship which, once split off, characterize the higher unconscious. (Of course, many aspects of these qualities are not split off and have been integrated into ongoing functioning.)

The Opposition of Higher and Lower

It is interesting to compare these lists of transpersonal qualities with the list of lower unconscious experiences. The contrast is striking, and one can see the vast chasm separating these two realms of human experiencing. This opposition of higher and lower is pointed out by Marghanita Laski in her classic empirical study of higher unconscious experiences described in her book *Ecstasy* (1968). In addition to ecstasies, Laski described what she called *desolation experiences* and noted a symmetrical opposition between these and the higher experiences. Here are a few examples from her research in which she describes first a quality of a particular ecstasy and then the opposed qualities of desolation, reported in the actual words of her subjects:

> For feelings of unity, we find feelings of uncoordinated diversity: e.g., "an inextricable jumble."
> For feelings of a new world, another life, we find feelings of the horrors of this world and of hell: e.g., "the pains and torments of hell," "this wretched life."
> For feelings of contact we find feelings of loneliness and isolation: e.g., "abandoned," "cast out," "an object of contempt to all, especially to its friends," "appalling self-centredness," "exiled and cast out."
> For feelings of "up" we find feelings of "down": e.g., "cast away," "the uttermost depths," "fell," "cast down."
> For feelings of light we find feelings of darkness: e.g., "darkness," "the shadow of death," "perpetual fog and darkness," "grievous darkness."
> For feelings of enlargement, improvement, we find feelings of emptiness and loss: e.g., "a profound emptiness," "lost this spiritual light." (Laski 1968, 162–3)

So here are the transpersonal qualities of the higher unconscious—unity, light, enlargement—juxtaposed to the isolation, darkness, and constriction of the lower unconscious. This lends credence to the idea that there is a mutually compensating relationship between these two sectors, a balanced opposition ideally suited to maintain the

primal split and hide the primal wound. The higher and lower unconscious contain and separate the sublime and traumatic experiences
that the person has deemed too overstimulating for a stable, consistent mode of being in the world.

Since the connection to Self exists throughout the stages of life,
empathic failures may split off aspects of this experience throughout
these stages. The higher unconscious, like the lower unconscious, can
thus be found to be layered; it too pervades the many "rings" of the
personality (see figure 6.2). In addition, as transpersonal aspects of
particular ages are split off and repressed over time, these aspects may
form the same type of linking found in the lower unconscious—but
now the chain is forged from similar positive experiences linked
together over time. This type of chained structure is what Grof (1975)
calls a positive COEX—a positive complex that is organized around
positive rather than negative experiences.

Because of this "geological" stratification and complexes of the
higher unconscious, a long-standing method within psychosynthesis
has been to facilitate contact with higher unconscious states by recalling transpersonal experiences from the past, reliving them in the
imagination, and integrating their energy into the present. An excellent example of this technique is Ann Gila's exercise, "Integrating
Transpersonal Experiences" (Russell 1977). A similar method for contacting the higher unconscious is to explore an entire higher unconscious complex or positive COEX: follow one's experience of, for
example, peace or joy, back through one's life, discovering the many
instances of this experience in the past. The energies thus contacted
can then become available in the present.

Such approaches to the higher unconscious are extremely useful
in psychotherapy and can become a standard part of taking a client
history. In this way, even the committed atheist often finds that he or
she has had spiritual and mystical experiences, although long forgotten, minimized, or misinterpreted. These moments then can be made
available to the therapeutic process, and other avenues to the higher
unconscious may become possible as well.

Through such methods one is able to access higher states of consciousness in vivid, authentic, and energetic ways, even though they were thought to be experiences forever in the past. These higher levels are thereby made available in the here and now and, once integrated, serve to enrich the present. Approaching the higher unconscious in these ways is clearly aimed at healing the split that separates us from the direct experience of this rich realm of human being.

Transpersonal Defenses

In order to guard the nonbeing wounding, we hide the abiding presence of the lower and higher unconscious from ourselves by using a number of defenses besides the basic splitting. Since the operation of defenses vis-à-vis the lower unconscious is well known, let us look at some defenses operating in relationship to the higher unconscious— what might be called transpersonal defenses.

For example, the repression of the higher unconscious insulates us from the joyous heights of human life, causing us to live with little or no passion or idealism, viewing the world as a humdrum place in which to live out a humdrum existence. This is what psychosynthesis psychotherapist Frank Haronian (1974), after Robert Desoille (1945), elucidated as the repression of the sublime. The repression of the sublime is akin to the defense mechanism of mistrust and cynicism that Maslow (1971) termed *desacralizing*—the distrust of the possibility of values and virtues.

Another important transpersonal defense is that of projecting the ideal higher unconscious energies onto other things. This is the mechanism by which we idealize the past and the future; idealize a person, group, or idea; and idealize just about anything one can name, from Cosmic Unity to the Eternal Void.

From Wilber's work, the following can be added to our list of transpersonal defenses:

Rationalization: "Transcendence is impossible or pathological."
Isolation: "My consciousness is supposed to be skin-bounded!"

Death-terror: "I'm afraid to die to my ego, what would be left?"
Substitution: A lower structure is substituted for the intuited higher
   structure.
Contraction: Contraction of the higher into forms of lower knowledge or experience. (Wilber 1980, 91)

And finally, from psychosynthesist Piero Ferrucci we can add the following:

Compensation: Developing a new trait opposed to the superconscious quality.
Defensive pessimism: "I am too old," "I am not bright enough," "I
   am too hung up."
Routinization: Turning the superconscious into some form of
   organization, bureaucracy, or routine, from which the original
   creative element is gone.
Dogmatization: Superconscious becomes superego, e.g., "I have
   to be joyous" or "loving" or "enlightened." (Ferrucci 1982, 157)

Note that all such mechanisms defend not against the higher unconscious per se, but against the hidden primal wounding. That is, the
resistance here is not to peace, love, and unity, but to the experiencing of some earlier wounding event—e.g., loss of control, being overwhelmed, or loss of identity—which will come to light if the higher
unconscious is contacted. Why do I feel anxious in contacting universal love? Because my mother controlled me with her supposed love.
Why do I feel isolated and unworthy in the face of a Cosmic Thou?
Because my father was controlling and abusive. Why do I fear surren-
dering my ego to experience my insubstantiality? Because moments of
surrender and vulnerability in my life have been traumatic. Here is
psychosynthesist Diana Whitmore: "Finally, for many, a fear of letting
go and trusting (surrender) is evoked by transpersonal experience.
There was a time in early childhood when we *ran to life with open arms*,
and for most of us this trust was betrayed. The promise of the transpersonal reminds us of this deep trauma and can evoke terror" (Whitmore
1991, 133, emphasis in original).

We defend against any experience—whether lower or higher

unconscious—that threatens nonbeing, that disrupts our continuity of being, our stable sense of self. Relational wounds are the core here, not the higher unconscious qua higher unconscious or the lower unconscious qua lower unconscious. Both higher unconscious defenses and lower unconscious defenses serve to maintain the primal split, thus burying the primal nonbeing wounding.

THE HIGHER AND LOWER DYNAMICS IN ADDICTION

The lower unconscious and higher unconscious, although repressed, do of course profoundly affect our lives. In the following chapter we shall see how these affect the formation of other psychological structures. However, one of the most common ways these two sectors impact us is in our addictions, compulsions, and attachments. (For the purposes of the current discussion, these three terms are considered equivalent.)

You will recall from the workshop described in chapter 1 that addictions embody the primal wound—every addiction seems based upon the strongly destructive dynamic between the higher and lower unconscious. It is as if an addiction comprises a painful synthesis of positive and negative, each force continuously at odds with the other. This interplay of positive and negative qualities can be represented by simple questions and answers such as these: Why must I rage all the time? Not only to avoid feeling small and powerless (lower unconscious), but to feel strong in myself (higher unconscious). What is the experience I seek in my alcohol? Not only to overcome my feelings of emptiness (lower unconscious), but in order to connect to other people (higher unconscious). Why do I compulsively seek so many sexual partners? To escape my inner sense of worthlessness (lower unconscious), but also because sex is the only time I feel loved (higher unconscious).

Each of the above questions and answers symbolize an addiction: an addiction to rage, to alcohol, and to sex. And there is not only an avoidance of lower unconscious qualities (e.g., powerlessness, emptiness, worthlessness), but also a positive quest here, too, a search for

personal strength, connection, self-worth, love—a search for the positive kernels of transpersonal qualities. Each addictive structure contains a drive away from negative qualities and a thrust toward positive
qualities. We can visualize this dynamic in figure 6.3.

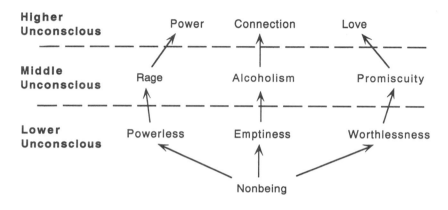

Fig. 6.3

The middle unconscious, that sector closest to our awareness, contains the observable addictive structures and processes that reflect the
larger primal split: (1) rage is underpinned in this example by powerlessness but includes a feeling of power, (2) beneath alcoholism is the
experience of emptiness but a need for connection, and (3) the compulsive promiscuity is driven by an experience of worthlessness, but
also by a search for love. Each addictive process is a holographic representation of the larger primal split, each containing a positive and
negative image of the I-Self relationship.

This dual dynamism between higher and lower unconscious qualities can be seen in all addictions, compulsions, and attachments,
including such things as:

> Attachment to power
> Alcohol and drug abuse
> Envy, jealousy, and greed

Compulsive exercise and dieting
Anti-social and isolating tendencies
Sex, relationship, and romance addiction
The people-who-love-too-much syndromes
Defenses such as displacement, projection, denial, etc.
Obsession with stimulation, avoidance of solitude and silence
A driven search for spiritual experience or enlightenment
Cold detachment or possessive clinging in relationships
Implosive withdrawal and passive aggression
Compulsive overeating, compulsive gambling
Co-dependence, extreme need for approval
Preoccupation with fantasy and mythology
Bigotry, chauvinism, xenophobia
Needing always to be right
Workaholic, Rageaholic
Religious addiction
Seeking revenge
Perfectionism
Fanaticism

In such addictive processes, there is often a continuous cycling between positive and negative experiences: the initial feeling of comfort from acting out the addiction; then guilt, shame, remorse; then more acting out to gain comfort; and so on. This cycling, however destructive, yet serves to hide the primal wound of nonbeing (see figure 1.4).

In fact, upon closer examination we can see that it is not so much the lower unconscious that is avoided in addictions as it is nonbeing. Even this painful cycling between positive and negative is preferable to nonbeing. As we saw in our discussion of the lower unconscious, even when it appears that negative qualities alone are all that are offered by a relationship, this is yet preferable to nonbeing. Given a choice between an abusive relationship or absolutely no relationship at all, we will choose the abuse. This of course only applies to areas of primal wounding; it is the pressure of the underlying nonbeing wound that forces such tragic attachments. The primary factor in the addictive process is the primal wound, and the lower and higher unconscious are secondary to this.

These deeper experiences of wounding will fully reveal themselves only as the person is able to enter recovery and begin to "feel and heal" the primal split. One cannot simply delve into the lower unconscious, but must engage both sectors of the personality. Only in this way can the split be mirrored within healing relationships, and so gradually be mended.

Attachment/Detachment and Addiction/Recovery

This dual dynamic of addictions is recognized in the recovery movement, for example, in Pia Mellody's work with love addiction. Love addicts are people who become destructively overly involved in their romantic relationships based on an idealization of their partners. Such people often have been the victims of an abusive or neglectful childhood, engendering deep feelings of abandonment, fear, shame, guilt, and emptiness—lower unconscious qualities. In order to manage these feelings, love addicts project their childhood idealizations onto their partners. Here is Mellody:

> Love Addicts do not see who the other partner really is, but instead see the image they created in childhood. They focus on this fantasy image, which they placed like a beautiful mask over the head of the real human being. Love Addicts assign to their partners all the qualities of their childhood fantasy rescuers. Ignoring their partner's reality, good qualities and bad, Love Addicts truly believe that their partners have the fantasy rescuer's attributes and will soon create a wonderful life of wall-to-wall loving and caring. (Mellody 1992, 22)

In the psychoanalytic world, Bollas shows clearly this twin negative-positive motivation underlying compulsions, addictions, and destructive attachments. He recognizes not only the driven quest for perfection, but also the hidden wounding of self that instigates this quest:

> The search for the perfect crime or the perfect woman is not only a quest for an idealized object. It also constitutes some recognition in the subject of a deficiency in ego experience. The search, even though it serves to split the bad self experience from the subject's cognitive knowledge, is nonetheless a semiological act that signifies the person's search for a particular object relation that is associated with ego transformation and repair of the "basic fault." (Bollas 1987, 8)

Here is the quest for that perfect something that will deliver us from the wounding of self—the Flying Dutchman Syndrome (Stevens) and the Heaven Is Just Around The Corner Syndrome (Gila), driven by the basic fault (Balint) of broken I-Self relationship. Perhaps another term for this syndrome might be *personal millenarianism*, the sense that something will happen soon to make everything all right.

In transpersonal psychology, this addictive process has been recognized by Roger Walsh and Frances Vaughan in their discussion of attachment. They state that attachment plays a central role in the cause of suffering in the world and imply that the threat of nonbeing underlies this: "Insofar as we believe that our identity is derived from our roles, our problems, our relationships, or the contents of consciousness, attachment is reinforced by fear for personal survival. 'If I give up my attachments, who and what will I be?'" (Walsh and Vaughan 1980a, 56). Here one is enmeshed, identified, attached to things, and the possibility of losing these things brings with it the threat of nonbeing, the fear for personal survival. Religions both East and West speak therefore of non-attachment or detachment, and psychosynthesis speaks of disidentification, as the way of liberation from these attachments.

We would add that, without nonbeing wounding, there would be no drive for such destructive attachment at all. Attachment does not indicate here the natural connection of "I" and Self via a unifying center, but what Bowlby (1973) termed *anxious attachment*—a clinging overdependency caused by a disruption in the natural connection with others. Attachment is a result of the primal wound.

This powerful addictive push-pull that dominates human life derives neither from overpowering natural desires of lust, greed, and revenge nor from some intrinsic illusion of the natural world that enthralls and ensnares us, but from a wounded sense of self. The primal wound sweeps us into a desperate struggle for being, bringing us all under the thrall of addiction. Ironically, of course, true being is freely flowing to us from Self, and any struggle for being belies this freely given foundation of our existence.

As we shall see, letting go of attachment is indeed the path to freedom, but this will very often necessitate a journey through the black hole of nonbeing. The principle expounded in different ways by many religions—one must die to self—seems to indicate this engagement with nonbeing. Here are to be found the spiritual experiences of purgation and the "dark night of the soul."

It is important to emphasize that because this addictive being-nonbeing dynamic is a function of a disturbed I-Self connection, it shares in the transcendence-immanence of that connection. That is, since the I-Self relationship is distinct from any content, energy, process, or forms of consciousness, and therefore can be present within any of these, *anything at all may become the object of addiction.* One may become addicted or attached not only to the more usual gamut of addictive substances and processes, but to particular feelings, thoughts, or states of consciousness as well.

> *For facing the God who is really God means facing also the absolute threat of nonbeing.*
>
> —Paul Tillich

One can therefore find such addictions/attachments in extremely elusive and hidden forms, e.g., Wilber's (Wilber, Engler, and Brown 1986) subtle and causal disorders, or Chögyam Trungpa's (1973) concept of *spiritual materialism.* In these types of attachments one may, for example, become addicted to spiritual love while dissociated from personal power and responsibility. Or one may become attached to peace, avoiding healthy boundaries and creative conflict; or rush up a supposed ladder of enlightenment, ignoring the abiding presence of Self exactly where one is.

We can become addicted to anything, from the comfort of morphine to the thrill of romance, to the creative process, to the intuition and higher states of consciousness. One might say that any level of consciousness, on any spectrum of consciousness, can become grist for the addictive process. Again we can see vividly here the profound pervasiveness of the primal wound, as it transects all types of experience and all stages of development.

The addictive process can even touch the seemingly untouchable—the void sometimes encountered in deep meditation. Here we attach to contentlessness or transcendence and consider all experience—and the world itself—as illusory. This identification can be called *morphophobia*, meaning "fear of form, of manifestation." (The complementary term is *morphophilia*, meaning "attachment to form, to manifestation.") Wilber called this attachment the ultimate pathology—"a failure to integrate the manifest and unmanifest realms" (Wilber, Engler, and Brown 1986, 144). And Hui-neng, the sixth patriarch of Zen, warns us about just such an addiction to the void: "In conversation with others, externally be detached from phenomena in the midst of phenomena; internally be detached from the void in the midst of the void. If you are entirely attached to the phenomenal, you would fall into perverted views. On the other hand, if you are entirely attached to the void, you would only sink deeper into your ignorance" (in Wu 1975, 89).

So, having had a profound experience in which I saw through the illusion of my separate self and realized my union with Ultimate Reality, I may become addicted/attached to this particular state of consciousness. I may seek this state just as fervently as the addict seeks the needle or the alcoholic seeks the bottle. All addictions are similar at their core. The skid row alcoholic and the obsessed spiritual athlete may be much closer than they appear, brothers or sisters in the grips of the being-nonbeing dynamic. The primal wound clearly has a quality of transcendence-immanence—it can be found in any and all states of consciousness, types of personality, and stages of development.

The Lower Unconscious and
Higher Unconscious in Daily Life

The split between the higher and lower unconscious allows the person to remain oblivious to these two realms of experience in an ongoing way. It is not that these realms exist simply in the past or only as sectors of our hidden inner world, but that they fundamentally condition our here and now experience at all levels. As a disturbance in the I-Self relationship, this split is a basic characteristic of our total, daily being in the world. In Freud's (1981d) terms, splitting is founded upon a disavowal of reality. So insofar as we avoid both the higher and lower dimensions of ourselves, we also are blind to these dimensions in the world around us. The "doors of perception" are not only clouded and in need of cleansing as William Blake understood. They are broken and in need of healing as well.

If, then, our transpersonal defenses are breached for a moment, we may in the words of C. S. Lewis (1955) be "surprised by joy." Here we may even be overwhelmed and disoriented by a sudden inflow of higher unconscious energy and contents. Our normal state of awareness may suddenly be uplifted by a profound aesthetic experience, by a felt connection to the universe, or by falling deeply in love with someone. We here feel ourselves in the presence of a higher realm, formerly hidden, compared to which our normal state of consciousness now seems dry and lifeless. In other words, we realize we have been split off from this dimension of living, perhaps for most of our lives.

Here is that earliest Western transpersonal psychiatrist, Richard M. Bucke, writing (in third person) about a transpersonal experience he had in 1879:

> For an instant he thought of fire, some sudden conflagration in the great city; the next, he knew that the light was within himself. Directly afterwards came upon him a sense of exultation, of immense joyousness accompanied or immediately followed by an intellectual illumination quite impossible to describe. Into his brain streamed one momentary lightning-flash of the Brahmic Splendor

which has ever since lightened his life; upon his heart fell one drop of Brahmic Bliss, leaving thenceforward for always an aftertaste of heaven. (Bucke 1967, 10)

The study of such experiences has been central to humanistic and transpersonal psychology, forming an important touchstone around which these approaches have evolved. Over the course of many years, these psychologies have laid down a body of work that validates the reality and health of the higher unconscious, defending this dimension of human being against those who would dismiss it as irrelevant or reduce it to psychopathology.

And as this dissociation from the higher unconscious is healed, as these peak experiences become integrated, our doors of perception are healed. We might, for example, become more aware of the beauty, joy, and love surrounding us or begin to feel less alienated and more cognizant of our belongingness in the universe. It is not that we leave the world to enter a higher realm; it is that we realize that the world itself *is* that higher realm—the world has only *appeared* to be devoid of this transpersonal richness because we had split off our ability to perceive this richness.

Researchers at Yale University in 1979 concluded that the violent family is not an aberrant subtype but is really a typical American family.

—Victoria Tackett

By the same token, the repression of the lower unconscious is not something in the distant past either, but it constitutes a basic truncation of present experience. Here we are oblivious to the tremendous level of abuse and neglect that pervades modern life, and we may be unaware of this even when we are direct victims or perpetrators ourselves. This repression of the traumatic supports naive optimism, otherworldly spirituality, and unrealistic idealism.

If this negative dimension of reality suddenly reveals itself, we may be "surprised by pain." We will perhaps be shocked, surprised, and at first disbelieving when stumbling upon:

- Inner forms of self-abuse, ill-will, and addiction
- Insidious ways we hurt those close to us
- Hidden abuse among one's own family and closest friends
- Subtle forms of sexual harassment in the workplace
- Covert institutionalized racial prejudice
- The epidemic of domestic violence
- Collective atrocities throughout the ages
- Injustice embedded in fundamental social institutions
- Overwhelming ecological disasters

This often dramatic and literally disillusioning discovery of the destructive side of life, both inner and outer, is a very common experience for the abuse survivor who has done some amount of healing work. The scales fall from the eyes of such a person, and he or she becomes acutely aware of neglect and abuse in personal relationships, on the job, and in the world at large. We can see a collective expanded awareness of this realm when many formerly trusting American citizens were shocked to discover their government lying to them about the Vietnam War and engaging in the misdeeds of the Watergate scandal. Here the ideal, "perfect family" of American democracy was shattered, revealing a hidden, darker side. More recently, the same type of disillusionment can be seen in the English, as their adoration of the royal family has yielded to a realization of the dysfunction, wounding, and pain within that family.

It just may be, too, that at least some of what we consider paranoid delusion may have its roots in an expansion of consciousness into the lower unconscious, especially as the latter interfaces with the lower collective unconscious. Here one may become terrified and overwhelmed, or obsessed and violent, in perceiving the immensity of evil in the world. One may not understand that what he or she is now seeing is something that has been there always; that is, it is not (perhaps) some new conspiracy, not some new network of evil that threatens but, rather, one is simply experiencing a heightened awareness of the lower unconscious as it operates throughout the world—

the *collective* lower unconscious, akin to what Vaughan (1985) calls the *transpersonal shadow*.

The Politics of Agony and Ecstasy

The splitting and repression of these profound levels of agony and ecstasy in human life is not only an issue of the past—these condition every moment of every day. And the repression of these two realms can be recognized in the common surprise and shock that frequently occur as awareness of either breaks into our daily "normal" lives. We then discover that our usual state of consciousness is largely split off from immense sectors of reality.

As we have seen, both these repressions serve to maintain the primal split, hiding the deeper threat of nonbeing. Even the cynic, firmly entrenched in a negative stance towards life, is still protected from the true tragedy of the world—the gaping pit of nonbeing. This chasm will yawn as the cynic dares to allow some hope and joy into his or her world. Here the negative system will be destabilized, triggering an identity crisis with feelings perhaps of being lost and confused ("Who am I now?"). She or he will feel the grip of nonbeing from which the cynic identification had offered some protection. Like fish who do not recognize the ocean around them, we breathe an invisible atmosphere of empathic failure that maintains the split between the higher and lower realms of human existence.

One of the advantages of psychosynthesis is that it can recognize and validate both these dimensions of human life and thereby address the traumatic split between them. Therapists do not need to discount feelings of union with nature or the Divine as instances of regression to an archaic state or as mere defensive delusions and wish-fulfillment, nor do they need to ignore the violence, trauma, and wounding that also are a part of human life, placing these latter on a lower rung of the scale of being. Rather, both sectors of human experience can be understood and respected, and thus the I-Self relationship can begin to be healed. Psychosynthesis encourages a mirroring of the whole person, affirming the sense of "I" that can engage both the heights and depths of human experience.

Why is it that transpersonal experiences alone cannot provide a stable sense of being, as we so often seem to hope? The answer is, of course, that the energies and states of the higher unconscious have been split off from the lower unconscious. They represent only a limited part of our whole life experience, leaving out the painful world of human limitation and brokenness. Therefore, in order to heal our true sense of being, we must bridge these two sectors of life, engaging both the heights of the higher unconscious and the depths of the lower unconscious—and thus brave the primal wound hidden beneath the split.

The difficulty is that these heights and depths tend to overpower us—that is why they are normally repressed. It is as if our sense of "I" is not strong enough to engage these sectors on their own terms. So it would seem we are trapped in a seamless prison bounded on one side by the lower unconscious and on the other by the higher unconscious.

However, we are not alone. Self is present throughout both the higher and lower unconscious, transcendent-immanent within them both. Therefore, through an increasingly intimate relationship with Self, we can begin to partake of Self's ability to experience both positive and negative dimensions. As this relationship develops, the image or reflection ("I") becomes an increasingly accurate representation of that which it reflects (Self), gaining an ability to engage a wider range of experience. One becomes more able to experience the joy and wonder, as well as the pain and terrors, of existence. One is less engulfed, stuck, or identified with any point on the wide spectrum of experience and so finds an openness to the entire spectrum.

Of course, this increasingly empathic connection between "I" and Self also leads to the surfacing and healing of primal wounding, both past and present, beneath the primal split. This conscious relationship with Self—and this alone, it seems—can finally release us from the powerfully addictive dynamics that are created by the interplay of the higher and lower unconscious. It is the building of this conscious I-Self connection, what will be explored later as Self-realization, which is the fundamental axis of all work in psychosynthesis therapy.

Before looking at the path of Self-realization, let us look at two more major effects of the primal split caused by the primal wound: the multiple splitting of subpersonalities and the splitting between authentic personality and survival personality.

7
Personalities and Subpersonalities

The human spirit will endure sickness;
but a broken spirit—who can bear?
—Proverbs 18:14

Since the primal split is created by a wound in the I-Self relationship, it constitutes a split at the most fundamental level of personality organization. Here one's deepest sense of self-in-relationship—one's sense of being—is fragmented. We have looked at this fragmentation as a split between the higher and lower unconscious, but there are two other significant splittings to consider. The first of these is the splitting into subpersonalities, the second is the split between authentic personality and survival personality. Let us look at each of these in turn.

SUBPERSONALITIES

A major ramification of the primal split is the formation of what Assagioli (1965) called subpersonalities. Subpersonalities are those semiautonomous aspects of the personality that, in Rowan's (1990) words, act like "people inside us" and are caused by trauma. As we have seen, Rowan describes a primal split between a non-OK self and an OK-self. He sees this split continuing to spread throughout the personality, creating OK subpersonalities and non-OK subpersonalities.

Within psychosynthesis, therapist and theorist Chris Meriam (1994) has developed an understanding of subpersonality formation that is based upon object relations theory and psychosynthesis. Meriam agrees that wounding from the environment causes a major splitting in the personality, forming the higher unconscious and lower unconscious. He also recognizes the higher unconscious as comprising the positive personality and positive unifying center (what he calls the positive ego and positive object), while the lower unconscious comprises the negative personality and negative unifying center (what he calls the negative ego and negative object).

But Meriam takes this positive-negative splitting one step further and builds a bridge to subpersonality theory. He maintains that these two higher and lower dyads, comprising these four components, in turn condition the formation of subpersonalities. For example, the positive personality might generate a Perfect Pleaser or Idealistic Savior type of subpersonality, and the positive unifying center might produce a Guru, Wise Father/Mother, or Great Leader subpersonality. Similarly, the negative personality might condition a Wounded Child or Helpless One, while the negative unifying center produces a Harsh Critic or Perfectionist subpersonality. Following the diagram in the last chapter, Meriam's thinking might be schematized as shown in figure 7.1.

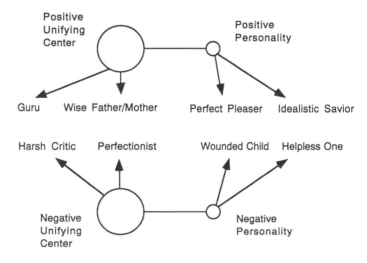

Fig. 7.1

With Meriam, we can readily see the negative unifying center in critical and shaming subpersonalities who aim their criticism inwardly and outwardly, the negative personality in the various types of wounded child subpersonalities most directly related to the impact of early wounding, the positive personality in the confident and heroic self-actualizing subpersonalities, and the positive unifying center in the acceptance, nurture, and love of higher subpersonalities. A subpersonality is like the visible tip of an object-relations "iceberg" whose main mass lies beyond the reach of normal awareness.

In his object-relations exploration of subpersonality formation, Meriam also recognizes the underlying dynamics of the higher unconscious, the lower unconscious, and nonbeing. He implies that both the negative and positive personality/unifying-center systems are responses to a deeper threat of nonbeing: "Any perceived impingement upon the basic structure of a positive or negative object relationship is viewed by each component within the relationship as a threat. The object resists change for fear of *loss of identity;* the ego will not abort or leave the relationship for *fear of abandonment*" (p. 25, emphases added). Both positions of the lower unconscious—and both positions of the higher unconscious—resist change, because change triggers the more profound threat of nonbeing, in this case abandonment and loss of identity. Their relational bonds, whether positive or negative, support a sense of being and defend against a confrontation with nonbeing. This implies that there is a nonbeing wound somewhere behind the more obvious relational patterns. As Rowan's work indicates also, subpersonalities seem ever shadowed by wounding.

This underlying nonbeing dynamic of subpersonalities also appears in the early work of psychosynthesis therapist Betsie Carter-Haar. In discussing a clinical case, she describes a subpersonality named the Loser who is strongly conditioned by the lower unconscious:

A positive experience is simply not acceptable to the "Loser" because its quality is different from, and inconsistent with, that of his self-image. But it goes even further: a positive experience is actually threatening. What if he were not really a Loser? Who would he be then? As we saw earlier, this fear of loss of identity, of a deep void or inner emptiness, if not correctly understood is often too overwhelming to be faced. In such a situation it frequently seems less painful to have a negative sense of self than no sense of self at all. (Carter-Haar 1975, 70)

Carter-Haar's phrase "negative sense of self" indicates a negative mode of being that is derived from the negative personality and unifying center. And the underlying threat of nonbeing is clear in her account: a deep void or inner emptiness, and no sense of self at all. From this perspective it becomes understandable why a person might defend a low self-image and chronic self-criticism against all onslaughts of positive feedback, because to accept the positive energy would be to destabilize the negative system, threaten a loss of identity, and so induce the deeper threat of nonbeing. On the other hand, we also can understand the person who has an extreme sensitivity to even the most gentle criticism—this negative energy would destabilize the positive identification and trigger the threat of nonbeing.

So when dealing, for example, with an anxious and shame-based underdog subpersonality (conditioned by the negative personality), in conflict with a perfectionistic and critical top-dog subpersonality (conditioned by the negative unifying center), we can see that at a deeper level both subpersonalities are connected. Their relationship allows a continuity of being and a defense against the greater threat of nonbeing. The Loser's negative sense of self, which is derived from such negative relationships, is infinitely preferable to no sense of self at all—actual nonrelationship and nonbeing.

By the way, Carter-Haar also describes a dual subpersonality formation that precisely reflects the original higher-lower split. She describes a strong, self-sufficient Striver subpersonality that developed out of an earlier Rejected Child subpersonality. The Rejected Child, thwarted early in its need for acceptance by the family—what we would say is the need for an empathic, mirroring connection—was repressed, and this need then was channeled into the extroverted and driven Striver subpersonality. Thus we have the positive mode of the Striver driven both by a negative mode of being and by the deeper nonbeing wounding of the Rejected Child. Carter-Haar's work clearly shows the primal wound, as recognized in some of the earliest development of subpersonality theory.

Transpersonal Subpersonalities

Some clarification of the higher unconscious or transpersonal subpersonalities—those conditioned by the positive personality and positive unifying center—is in order. Such subpersonalities often are so loving and wise that they are not recognized as subpersonalities at all.

As mentioned in chapter 5, the higher unconscious carries an impression of perfection that is sufficient to compensate for the wounding nonbeing experiences of the lower unconscious. There is a balance between the higher and lower sectors that allows for stability within the personality. The higher unconscious subpersonalities will thus, as Meriam indicates, often be highly transpersonal, creating positive personality subpersonalities such as the Warrior, Aspirant, or Server and positive unifying center subpersonalities such as the Guru, Wise Person, or Sage.

An excellent case example of work with these transpersonal subpersonalities, as well as with lower unconscious subpersonalities, appears in the therapy work done by "Sharon," as reported by psychosynthesis therapist James Vargiu (1974). Sharon, working in a guided imagery session, first recognized her critical Hag subpersonality (reflecting the negative unifying center), then the fearful Doubter subpersonality (reflecting the negative personality), and then experienced a striking disidentification from the Idealist subpersonality (reflecting the positive personality) with whom she was normally identified. Here is the section of the session transcript in which Sharon experiences this disidentification, and in so doing recognizes the Idealist for the first time (G is the therapist):

G: Okay. Now things are going to change slightly. Step back and observe Sharon . . . (pause) . . . now be aware of the Doubter as well . . . and of the Hag . . . .

S: Yes, they are all there . . . and Sharon is just one of them . . . . I can really see her clearly now. She's not Sharon, she's . . . the Idealist! I'm not her! I *have been her*, but I'm not her, am I? She's the Idealist! Oh, wow! (P. 68)

This is a clear disidentification from a major subpersonality—the Idealist—who had involved Sharon in an unrealistic and unbalanced pursuit of spiritual development. The Idealist is a subpersonality conditioned by the positive personality, a major identification split off from the lower unconscious. As the Hag said later, "The Idealist wanted you to be so pure that you'd never have bad feelings, and you pretended you didn't have them" (p. 71).

Disidentification from the Idealist subpersonality allowed Sharon to then contact a fourth subpersonality, representing the positive unifying center, whom she calls the High Me. The session continues:

G: Good . . . . This is an important insight . . . take some time to experience it.

S: (long pause) yes . . . now there's someone else . . . there's someone else here too . . . kind of the greater me, the high me.

G: And what is the "high you" like?

S: She's what I want to be. She's looking at the Hag, and the Doubter, and the Idealist. And what's so special is that she accepts them. All of them. And she feels compassion towards them. She knows the Hag is critical and twisted, and the Doubter afraid, and mistrusting, yet she accepts them. And she sees through the Idealist too, the unrealistic ideals and the refusing to accept her limitations, the pretension and the desperate spirituality. She accepts them all, and loves them in spite of their faults. (Pp. 68–69)

Figure 7.2 shows how Sharon's disidentification from the Idealist and her recognition of the High Me might be diagrammed:

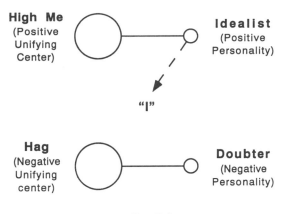

Fig. 7.2

The realization that Sharon is distinct from the Hag and Doubter, and then distinct from the major Idealist identification as well, produces an expanded awareness that allows her to recognize the new High Me subpersonality conditioned by the positive unifying center. In other words, her experience of being transcendent of these subpersonalities translated immediately into an increased experience of immanence, a greater ability to engage all the parts—a vivid instance of the transcendent-immanent function, a blossoming of I-amness (cf. chapter 3).

This contact with the High Me put Sharon in touch with an aspect of her personality that offered unconditional love and wise guidance. Discussing this moment in the session, Vargiu writes, "Next came a spontaneous influx from the superconscious, in the form of a subpersonality-like formation of a transpersonal nature . . . " (p. 75). This is clearly a subpersonality conditioned by the positive unifying center, a palpable ideal of goodness, love, and wisdom with whom Sharon began to relate.

Subpersonalities as Unique and Archetypal

None of these many subpersonalities, nor their four conditioning personality positions and unifying center positions, constitute the personality as a whole; they are fragments of the wholeness that was potential before the primal split. However, we can at times see these four basic positions reflected in different types of people: the person with a chronic sense of low self-esteem (negative personality), the cynic constantly critical of the world (negative unifying center), the idealistic believer (positive personality), and the charismatic leader (positive unifying center). Each of these types of person would presumably have the other three positions as well, but the other positions would be obscured by the major identification.

A power of psychosynthesis theory can be seen here, because it understands that "I" can identify with all the many different subpersonalities conditioned by these four positions. It is not a mystery that we may be arrogantly critical (negative unifying center) and then feel depressed and worthless (negative personality); or that we may at another time feel passionately obsessed with something (positive personality) and then later gloriously grandiose and self-congratulatory (positive unifying center).

Also, as Meriam explains, it may not be one, or even two, but many different subpersonalities that are generated by each one of these four major positions. One might, for example, have a Wounded Child, a Victim, and a Helpless One all organized by the negative personality position. Meriam further points out that specific subpersonalities may draw from several different personality and unifying center positions, both negative and positive. As an example of this, he describes an Achieving, Anxious Pleaser subpersonality that is formed from the relationships among all the different positions. Given such interrelationships among the different positions, we have a theoretical understanding that allows us to describe the rich variety of unique subpersonalities so familiar to those who work in this way.

Thus, even given such a coherent underlying pattern of subpersonality formation, both Meriam and Rowan agree that, in Rowan's words, "We have now left the age when everyone had to have the same subpersonalities completely" (Rowan 1990, 196). That is, the diversity of subpersonalities within the individual seems destined to remain a reflection of the uniqueness of the particular person-in-relationship, ultimately defeating all attempts at neat classification. This view is important therapeutically because it encourages us to maintain the empathic attitude so crucial in working with subpersonalities—they are not "It's" to be catalogued or synthesized, but unique "Thou's" with whom to relate.

Whether we see one major split into positive and negative sectors, or more than one basic split, it appears that the vast range of different subpersonalities are conditioned by primal wounding in the early facilitating environment. It does seem true however, as Rowan points out, that collective patterns—social, ethnic, cultural, and universal—do condition subpersonality formation as well. In Jungian terms, one might say that the individual complexes are conditioned by the collective archetypes as expressed within early relationships.

But these general patterns or universal archetypes cannot be separated from one's own unique relational matrix. Such patterns are abstractions of specific lived human relationships with self, other, and environment. In short, archetypal patterns are generalized forms of human relationship, naturally distinct but never separate from the specific relationships of individual human beings: "The paradoxical truth about the evocation of human archetypes consists in the fact that their activation is dependent from the outset on the dimension of social relationship between human beings" (Neumann 1989, 85).

Furthermore, if archetypes are, as Jung said, "the deposits of all our ancestral experiences" (Jung 1966, 190), then one could make the case that many archetypes are created by these major divisions in human beings in the first place. It is not that all archetypes flow from the Divine Ground to condition us, not that they are chosen by God, but that many are the collective imprint of countless fragmented psyches belonging to countless human beings. Thus, the Great Mother/Father may have been formed by the positive unifying center position, the Warrior or Hero by the positive personality position, the Terrible Mother/Father by the negative unifying center position, and the Victim or Abused Child by the negative personality position. Although now these archetypes operate like collective habits in our collective personality, conditioning individual development, they nevertheless stem from mortal, flawed human beings. The human relationship to nature, the social environment, and to the Divine may constitute the fount of many archetypes.

It is of crucial importance to psychotherapy that this relational context of symbols and archetypes is understood. The reason for this is that therapists and clients alike can operate at the level of these abstract patterns and never touch the concrete specifics of wounded relationships. Here is author and former psychoanalyst Alice Miller powerfully voicing this concern:

> The patient of a Jungian analyst, for instance, can allow himself to confront the "savage goddess Kali"—that is socially acceptable, because Kali is abstract and not the concrete mother. Then painful memories, such as being dragged across the floor as a child by his drunken mother, unfortunately will not have to come to the surface, and he will consequently be unable to free himself from the repetition compulsion. When he later reenacts his repressed experiences with his own child, other archetypal explanations can be offered. (Miller 1984b, 202)

We would not lay this mistake at the door of the Jungians, but at the door of any therapist who focuses more upon the archetypal than upon the unique situation of the client. In these cases, the world of imagery, symbol, and myth operates not as a way of adding meaning and richness to the person's life (as it can and should do), but instead becomes a defense, offering a positive or negative mode of being that is dissociated from the underlying wounds caused by actual life relationships. The therapist hereby deals only with the symbolic and universal, while the actual existential situation of the unique person—the I-amness transcendent-immanent in spacetime—is unseen.

In other words, remaining at this abstract, symbolic level alone constitutes a retraumatization of the client, creating yet another non-mirroring relationship in the person's life. This same type of nonempathic attitude can be supported by subpersonality work that relies exclusively upon personal imagery and symbolic resolution (Vargiu) while ignoring the specific human relationships underlying subpersonality formation and healing.

Psychotherapy and Subpersonalities

Since the higher unconscious and lower unconscious comprise the major mass of an iceberg of which the subpersonality relationships are the visible tips, an understanding of this substratum is central to psychosynthesis therapy. While dealing with the subpersonality level, the therapist remains aware of these more basic dynamics and is ready to address them as they surface. Therapist and client alike then are prepared to engage such things as the gradual surfacing of traumatic memories, the positive and negative aspects of potent transference-countertransference dynamics, and the patient, intimate, long-term empathic mirroring needed for deep healing work (in or out of therapy).

Knowledge of these deeper structures does not imply that the elegant simplicity and directness of subpersonality work is lost. Such work will ever remain an important asset to psychosynthesis. Indeed, whenever possible, the ideal is to begin at the subpersonality level and attempt to resolve the presenting problem there.

However, if the relational foundation of subpersonalities is not recognized in therapy, a variety of difficulties can arise in working with them. One of these is the same danger we saw in working with archetypes and imagery—the therapy may actually serve to hide the early relational dynamics. That is, although addressing subpersonalities can be quite powerful and liberating, creating an immediate sense of disidentification and a new experience of oneself, it may omit deeper unconscious dynamics. One can disidentify from subpersonalities, uncover and abreact many of the early experiences that form them, and even transform them into more positive attitudes and behaviors, all without engaging the deeper childhood relational matrix in a serious and ongoing way.

Such limitations in the theory and practice of the subpersonality method have not gone unnoticed in psychosynthesis. Psychosynthesists

Meriam (1994), Yeomans (1992), and Tackett (1988) all have warned of subpersonality work that does not fully recognize and engage the foundation of childhood experience. Here is Yeomans' suc-cinct statement of these concerns: "The disadvantage of subpersonali-ties is that they don't take you into the more unconscious patterns of the personality and to those complexes which are, in fact, shaping their reactions—the deep structure. Subpersonality work alone, therefore, conducted without regard for this deeper dimension, is palliative, but incomplete in affecting real personality change" (p. 2).

Of course, this lack of engagement with deeper structures of expe-rience is not the sole property of uninformed work with subpersonali-ties, but can be found in any therapy that does not recognize the primal wounding underlying psychological symptoms. For example, psychoanalysis also often misses these core wounds of the spirit, as the writings of Jeffrey Masson (1984, 1990) and Alice Miller (1981, 1984a, 1984b) have so well illuminated.

Having said all this about subpersonality work, however, we must emphasize again that this approach to the multiplicity of the person-ality has a tremendous amount to offer. The immediate clarification of inner conflict, the insight into the nature of "I" and disidentifica-tion, the instant relief it often affords, and the empowerment of the client are just some of the beneficial aspects of such work. Combined with an understanding of the relational matrix which conditions subpersonalities, such work can include a deeper level of healing as well, making an important contribution to the development of psychotherapy.

As one examines the many varied subpersonalities within the human personality the question arises, "How does anyone manage to function in any stable and consistent way given this splitting?" The answer seems to be that "I" becomes identified with a relatively stable system or structure comprising those subpersonalities and other per-sonality functions that are not too highly charged with energy from the higher or lower unconscious. This deeper structure allows the indi-vidual to cohere the multiplicity and maintain the primal split while at the same time adapting to the nonempathic environment. Since its function is to survive in a nonempathic environment, this structure can be called the *survival personality*. It is depicted in figure 7.3.

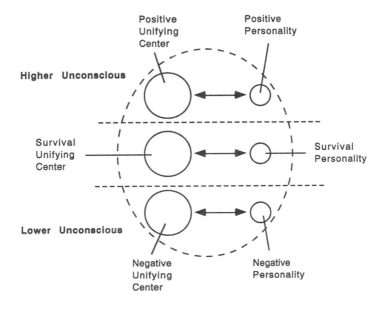

Fig. 7.3

This diagram illustrates the situation of the normal person caused by primal splitting. To borrow a phrase from Fairbairn, this is the basic endopsychic situation of most of us. The higher and lower unconscious are separated from each other and from consciousness, and there is a central defensive or compensating system comprising those subpersonalities and personality contents with which we tend to identify on a daily basis—survival personality along with its attendant *survival unifying center*. Let us examine each of these important structures in turn.

SURVIVAL PERSONALITY

Primal wounding is a break in the I-Self connection via a nonempathic unifying center. The unifying center does not respond to the essential I-amness of the person, but instead views the person as an

"It" to be used for the unifying center's own ends. Here there is a powerful message to our very core that, if we want to avoid annihilation and nonbeing, we had better become what is demanded of us. Instead of being "me," I must become the one who, for example, is destined to save my caregivers from a meaningless life or difficult marriage, or who must fulfill my caregivers' desire to have a child of a particular gender, or who will be someone's object of perverted sexuality, or who must do all the things my caregivers failed to do in their lives. Feel free to add to the list. It is probably infinite.

This lack of empathic connection is a severe disruption of the blossoming of I-amness through space-time, a truncation of authentic personality—the natural unfoldment of the personality that gives one a sense of authenticity, freedom, and continuity of being. Instead of expressing who we are in the environment, we hide our true natures and become what the environment needs us to be. This derailment of authentic personality is what Winnicott and others recognize as the false self: "The False Self has one positive and very important function: to hide the True Self, which it does by compliance with environmental demands. . . . In this way it is possible to trace the point of origin of the False Self, which can now be seen to be a defence, a defence against that which is unthinkable, the exploitation of the True Self, which would result in its annihilation" (Winnicott 1987, 146–7).

It is clear that Winnicott is describing a mode of being that is created by the primal wound—the threat of annihilation. Survival personality or false self is developed in order to survive within a nonempathic environment; one exists, as Winnicott states, "by compliance with environmental demands." Here, instead of enjoying the blossoming of my unique self, I am forced by the demands and expectations of the environment to become someone I am not.

By developing survival personality, the individual seeks to sustain a connection to a nonempathic external unifying center—and so continue to maintain a sense of self—in the only way offered by the situation. Survival personality is an attempt to form some sense of selfhood in the face of a potential fall into the pit of nonexistence.

As Winnicott's psychoanalytic theory recognizes true self and false self, so psychosynthesis recognizes survival personality and authentic personality. You will remember that the authentic personality is "the true expression of I-amness, in union with Self, conditioned by the person's unique genetic endowment and facilitating environment." This expression of I-amness takes place over time, actualizing and including the unfolding potential of each phase of development. Thus, we have the image of concentric rings, each ring representing a developmental stage and the whole of the rings representing the continuous, cumulative, coherent expression of all stages. This ability to have all the riches of ongoing development available is self-empathy—an empathic connection to all the psychological ages, creating Assagioli's psychosynthesis of the ages.

But the primal wound disrupts this ongoing wholeness and self-empathy, causing the development of personality patterns that are not the natural expression of "I," and that are geared instead to survive in a nonempathic environment. This is survival personality, based on a truncation of natural self-empathy through a dissociation from core aspects of one's experience.

It must be emphasized that, since primal wounding and splitting are so commonplace, the survival mode is the starting place for all of us. Survival personality is not merely a one-dimensional facade, an empty shell devoid of depth and richness. Quite the contrary, this mode can often allow a functioning well above the average level, commanding truly impressive talents and abilities.

One can engage tremendous depths of lower unconscious wounding, abreacting memories of childhood abuse, or disidentify from many different subpersonalities, or move into the heights of the higher unconscious, enjoying the complete transcendence of ego in a union with the Divine—*and do all of this while leaving survival personality intact.* The most powerful experiences may never ultimately touch the place from which we are operating, our survival ground of being. This is why, as Winnicott and others have seen, therapy can go on forever, never reaching the core personhood. This also is why, as spiritual communities have seen, truly advanced spiritual leaders may yet be controlled by their psychological wounding.

So here we might find the person who can be sensitive, creative, humorous, and spiritual, yet who is unconsciously controlled by the survival orientation. As Winnicott (1987) points out, the false self can sometimes perfectly mimic the true self. And according to Kohut, "Every self, not only in the narcissistic personality disorders but also in the structural neurosis and in health, consists to a greater or lesser extent of compensatory structures" (Kohut 1977, 44).[1]

Up to this point we have been describing survival personality that is, for the most part, conditioned by the higher unconscious. The high-functioning survival personality enjoys a comfortable level of self-esteem, feels held by the environment, and does not for the most part identify with feelings of anxiety, worthlessness, and isolation (although these lurk in the background).

However, survival personality also may be conditioned by the realm of the lower unconscious. Dominated by the negative personality, for example, one may ever feel the helpless victim, ever oppressed by the powers that be, ever isolated from any hopeful expectations for life (except perhaps salvation in the next). This type of survival personality expresses itself in philosophies of despair and in an affect of depression. Here, an identification conditioned by the negative sector allows the avoidance of an even deeper abyss—nonbeing. Such painful personality formations are as violently defended against self-esteem and hope as the positive survival personality defends against worthlessness and despair.

Survival personality can also be conditioned by the negative unifying center. For example, this formation seems quite evident in the violent macho personalities of some urban gang members or the violent fanaticism of militant cults. The antisocial rage and rebellion of such a personality is a way of basing a sense of self upon the inner perpetrator rather than the inner victim. This sense of potency provides protection from the helplessness, futility, and victimization beneath the surface.[2] Of course this dynamic is in no way limited to these extremes of antisocial behavior, and can be recognized in many law-abiding citizens, from the person who verbally abuses his/her spouse to the office despot to the raging automobile driver.

In sum, survival personality is a reaction to primal wounding in which we split our true expression of I-amness—disrupting the unfoldment of authentic personality—and so avoid the threat of nonbeing. But let us look more closely at the unifying center that supports and controls the survival personality: the survival unifying center and the powerful trance in which it places us.

The Survival Unifying Center

For survival personality to exist, it must of course be relating to some sort of unifying center; it must have its own object relation from which it draws its being. The center that provides the holding environment or context for the survival personality can be called simply the *survival unifying center*. Here again we see a familiar pattern: the survival personality reflects the "I" position, while the survival unifying center reflects the Self position, allowing some shred of personal being. The survival unifying center has two aspects, one having to do with a consciousness of personal identity ("who I feel myself to be") and one having to do with will or action ("what I do, how I act")—reflecting the consciousness and will functions of "I."

The consciousness aspect comprises an image of a relationship to Self, to the Ultimate, which is contaminated by the image of the relationship with nonempathic caregivers (structurally analogous to the Freudian ego-ideal). This image therefore dictates the mode of consciousness or sense of identity one is to assume within the constricted world of the family. This type of identity is illustrated by the common problematic roles of The Hero, The Scapegoat, The Lost One, The Clown, or The Placater (Kritsberg 1985). Not fulfilling this role, one becomes a target of outrage, disgust, and contempt from the unifying center and experiences feelings such as low self-esteem, worthlessness, and personal defectiveness, that can be called collectively *survival shame*—a tension between one's current mode of consciousness and that held forth by the survival unifying center.

The will aspect of the survival unifying center relates more to behavior, to what one does, and comprises the core family moral principles (akin to the Freudian superego). The survival unifying center is the repository of constricting family rules such as "Do not speak of feelings," "One does not grieve," or "Never speak to outsiders about the family." Disobeying these dictates, one's behavior will become the target of outrage, disgust, and contempt. Disobedience may feel like committing an unforgivable sin, giving rise to despair, a sense of incompetence, and a terror of punishment, all of which can be termed *survival guilt*—a tension between one's actions and those decreed by the survival unifying center.[3] Survival guilt, as survival shame, is underpinned by the threat of nonbeing: one feels the anxiety of potential personal annihilation. (Authentic guilt and shame will be discussed in a subsequent chapter.)

The bond with this survival unifying center, first the external unifying center and later the internal unifying center, is often felt as an actual agreement or contract one has made, a *survival contract*. It is as if one's very existence depends on fulfilling the terms of this commitment to be a particular way and to do particular things. We have here, in effect, contracted to sell our souls (or at least split our souls) in order to survive. Accordingly, any movement away from these habitual modes of will and consciousness will be felt as breaking this contract and opening oneself to dire consequences:

> Talking about my father in therapy felt like I was betraying him. He was abusive as hell to me, but I felt this strange loyalty. It scared me to talk about him, like *I* was a bad son, a bad person—like I was the one being mean and not him!

> Every time I stand up for myself I feel guilty. I can hear my mother saying, "You're so selfish. You're always thinking about ol' number one." I have to be this all-giving person with no needs, or I feel selfish and uncaring.

If we begin to transgress the survival contract, tension is increased with the survival unifying center and we begin to feel guilt and shame.

Attempting to break the contract, we will disturb our oxygen line and will face the deeper threat of nonbeing. Violating the terms of the contract—e.g, speaking to outsiders, daring to speak of feelings, refusing to act the role, or entering therapy—we may feel as though we are doing something terribly wrong. We may feel anxious and ashamed, and that we risk abandonment, isolation, and even damnation itself. Such movements toward recovery, toward becoming more authentic, may feel like a betrayal of some ancient sacred vow—a breaking of a tribal taboo, a violation of the survival contract.

THE SURVIVAL TRANCE

This powerful bond to the survival unifying center—both internal and external—significantly limits self-empathy; that is, it significantly limits our ability to be open to the wide range of our authentic experience. The unfoldment of authentic personality is derailed, and we instead struggle to survive in an oppressive environment. Whenever we are bonded to such a constricting unifying center and identified with the constricted role dictated by that center, a very curious thing happens: we enter a trance.

The phenomenon of trance is dramatically demonstrated by the stage hypnotist working with a subject to entertain an audience. Here the hypnotist becomes a unifying center, and the subject's experience is controlled by the hypnotist. The subject bonds to the hypnotist, accepts a truncated experience, and assumes an identification within the confines of this truncated experience. While there may be the experience of free will on the part of the subject, the exercise of both consciousness and will is in fact highly conditioned by the hypnotist.[4]

However, unlike stage hypnosis or even therapeutic hypnosis, the survival unifying center does not hypnotize us for a limited time. We can be conceived, born, and mature, all within this fundamental and pervasive trance. As Charles Tart (1987) points out, this childhood entrancement is involuntary and time-unlimited, can use physical and emotional force, draws upon positive reinforcement and trust of the parents, and is expected to last a lifetime. The trance therefore does not become a matter for reflection and choice, but simply "the way things are." Furthermore, since in this case the hypnotist also is within us—i.e., the internal survival unifying center—the trance can last throughout our entire lives.

The Family Trance

The survival trance found within the family system can be called, using John Bradshaw's (1988a) term, the *family trance*. The family trance is a hypnotic state, an addictive thrall, that has its roots in the family of origin and early environment. In the family trance— the fount of all other trances—the family is the unifying center that forces a constricted identification or role upon the family member. To be in the trance is to be so completely identified with one's role in the family, so identified with the values and world view of the family, that important aspects of one's own personal experience remain unconscious. The trance is ultimately the family demanding compliance rather than authenticity, demanding conformity rather than free will, and no small vulnerable child has the ability to say "No" to this.

The family trance defends against the possibility of being abandoned by the family system and thereby confronting nonbeing. Here the survival personality and survival unifying center form a tight-knit, closed system that is defensively cut off from other areas of experience. The child scrambles for scraps of safety and belongingness in the only way offered, and pays for it by relinquishing authenticity.

For example, the trance may completely prevent traumatic events from becoming conscious, as in the case when one has blank spots in memory of significant years or events in life (cf. Kohut's *horizontal split*). Or one may be able to remember the concrete details of childhood while remaining dissociated from the raw emotional experience, e.g., the pain, shame, and rage. In the latter case, for example, trauma may be masked by interpretation and reframing within the rules of the trance, as when physical abuse is remembered as "rightful punishment which I deserved" (cf. Kohut's *vertical split*).

The family trance often presents itself vividly in psychotherapy. Many clients, obviously in great pain from emerging feelings, thoughts, and memories of childhood wounding, nevertheless can say: "I had a normal, happy childhood," or, "But it wasn't really that bad." Here is psychoanalyst Harry Guntrip: "One patient started analysis by saying 'I have the most wonderful mother on earth,' which immediately made me realize that her mother was her real problem, as turned out to be the case" (Guntrip 1971, 97). Such statements from clients at times have a flavor of a programmed response or memorized axiom, lacking the vitality of other statements that are connected to the person's spontaneous experience. Listening to such statements, one feels very much in the presence of a posthypnotic suggestion. This trance is extremely powerful, and any competent clinician knows well that these waters run deep and must be entered with the utmost care and respect.

One woman, recognizing the criticism and shaming she received from her parents even as an adult, determined not to go to her parents' house for Thanksgiving one year. Even with this strong resolve, however, she found herself—"as if in a trance"—telephoning them to ask what she should bring for Thanksgiving dinner. This condition is indeed a hypnotic state, because the person appears to be functioning normally in all respects, yet is dissociated from vast realms of his or her experience.

Again, the trance is so pervasive and powerful because it derives from a unifying center that allows some sense of safety and connection. Locked in one's family role and world view, the individual feels secure, protected, and held in being (even when one is in fact not safe at all). Accordingly, the dispelling of the trance means a discontinuity in the ongoingness of being—the threat of nonbeing. Entertaining the possibility that perhaps one does not have the most wonderful mother on earth, for example, means experiencing oneself outside the motherly unifying center, cut off from the holding environment and from the source of one's existence—alone, abandoned, and facing potential nothingness. The person in effect faces the voodoo death inherent in the breaking of a tribal taboo. This is why, even when clients begin to realize painful depths of childhood abuse, they can still maintain a belief in a normal, happy childhood.[5]

The Trance of Everyday Life

The tremendous pervasiveness of the survival trance has been recognized in the work of Arthur Deikman (1982) and Charles Tart (1987). Both believe that we are all unknowingly enthralled in a deep collective trance, living our lives in a state of normal unconsciousness. Deikman calls this the *trance of ordinary life*: "Most persons who stop to observe their thoughts, concerns, and desires become aware that they pass most of their time in a sleep of fantasy—a trance—even if, at the same time, they are consciously pursuing practical goals" (p. 126).

Tart, who calls this the *consensus trance: the sleep of everyday life*, claims that this trance completely pervades our waking lives. He writes this striking phrase: "About one-third of our lives is spent at the level of nocturnal sleeping and dreaming, the remaining two-thirds in consensus trance" (p. 213)!

At this cultural level of the survival trance, the accepted norms of society, our shared scientific and philosophical paradigms, and the very cultural atmosphere we breathe all place us in a thrall in which our perception of reality is broken and our true selves are hidden. Again, here is the function of a relationship with a unifying center—the cultural milieu is the survival unifying center, our collective hypnotist. As Deikman points out, traditional psychotherapy cannot see beyond this trance because traditional psychotherapy itself operates within the trance. Both Deikman and Tart diagnose the same trance and prescribe the same remedy: waking up through the practice of self-observation, or in our terms, the awakening of "I."

It is important to point out, however, that awakening from the survival trance does not mean eliminating our dependence on unifying centers in order to gain some sort of free-standing individuality. Remember, we are *always* dependent; our being flows to us from Self via unifying centers.

As discussed in the following chapter, the path to awakening involves consciously choosing increasingly *authentic unifying centers* that can support our healing and growth and that do not constrict our I-amness. We find practices, ideas, values, people, and milieus that more accurately reflect the I-Self relationship and so can facilitate authentic personality—the business of all mystical science (Deikman) through the ages. Although we are ever dependent, we can seek increasingly accurate, expanded, and universal unifying centers in which to be dependent. Paradoxically, it is only by acknowledging our dependence upon these centers, and so upon Self, that our independent essential selves will blossom—the dependent-independent paradox.

In an ultimate way, it can even be said that we will always be in trance. Even if we awakened to the widest range of experience, the broadest awareness of reality possible to a human being, we would still have a limited view of the entirety of the cosmos. From this point of view we perhaps have the choice between a survival trance and an authentic trance, between a trance that reflects the demands of others and a trance that reflects the necessities of our own being in relationship to Self and world.

RAGE

Finally, in addition to the survival unifying center and survival trance, rage seems to play a central role in sustaining the survival personality. This rage was dubbed *narcissistic rage* by Kohut (1978) because it is a direct result of an assault to the self (a narcissistic injury).

Rage is not anger, although the two are related. Anger is an affect that can accompany natural self-assertion, while rage results from a violation of self. Rage is a powerful and violent energy flowing directly from the primal wound. It allows the person both to dissociate from the wound, as well as gain a power with which to deal with the violating agent. It is a primal energetic response to the threat of nonbeing, and it can be difficult to get beneath it to the more primary wounding of nonbeing.

We believe this rage is what many psychoanalytic thinkers point to as the "aggression" behind splitting. Unfortunately however, these ideas are imprisoned in Freudian drive theory and lend themselves to the notion that splitting is the result merely of an overactive aggressive drive—tending to minimize the fact that there is an actual wounding to which the aggression is a response. We believe that any such difficulties with one's supposed aggressive drive are quite secondary to trauma. Rage is not some natural drive, but the fury of a wounded spirit. Kohut does not make this mistake of falling back on drive theory alone, and traces this central rage to a wound to the self—thus the term "narcissistic rage."

Rage is not a feeling or emotion in the usual sense, and often can be expressed as a logical, willful, philosophical stance toward the world. It can condition one's entire life, as seen in what has been called the rageaholic personality, or in the more coolly intellectual obsession with revenge. On a small scale, one can recognize rage in the automobile driver who becomes furious, irrational, and dangerous in response to the minor misdeeds of another driver ("road rage"), or the impotent rage at not being able to find a mislaid personal possession, or one's obsessive enjoyment in hating a particular person and the glee felt when that person meets ill. Such events and people are experienced as acute threats to the self and indicate an underlying vulnerability; they point to unhealed wounds from past wounding experiences.

The depth and power of rage, reflecting its source in a wound to transcendent-immanent being, can be seen in its total disregard for the welfare of oneself or other people. This is an energy far beyond any caring about life and death. It is in this sense free from all constraints of the world, transcending physical needs, emotional gratification, or intellectual belief. One of Kohut's examples of this rage is Ahab, the obsessed ship captain in Herman Melville's *Moby Dick*, who destroyed himself and his crew in his quest to kill the elusive white whale. Nothing could stop Ahab's determined, destructive pursuit of this whale who had been the cause of injury to his sense of self.

One can even recognize an "Ahab complex." Caught in the grips of this complex, one will stop at nothing, even evil itself, in order to root out and destroy the evil in oneself and the world—thus succumbing to the very evil one seeks to obliterate. Rage here creates an inversion or distortion of the purposeful life direction characteristic of an unwounded I-Self relationship.

Rage fuels the lust for revenge, the wish to get even, and it has tremendously destructive consequences for individual lives as well as society at large. Alice Miller (1991) traces the evil of such men as Hitler, Stalin, and Ceausescu to the rage and revenge created by an abusive upbringing. It just may be that the violence, hatred, and wars rampant in human history flow not from a supposed primitive aggressive drive, but from the rage caused by wounds to the self, both personal and collective.

From one point of view, the purpose of rage is the destruction of something that has violated one's deepest values, one's most fundamental sense of self and world. But from another point of view, following Bollas's (1987) notion of *loving hate,* the rage may be seen as a way of actually maintaining a connection—though a negative connection—to the offending other. Think of the couples who continuously bicker and fight, finding a sense of comfort and identity in their constant conflict. Changing such a negative pattern invariably will involve a confrontation with nonbeing—a stepping into the unknown, a grappling with the question "Who are we?" and a transformation of the old way of being.

However we conceptualize its precise mechanism, rage gives one a sense of apparent transcendent power over traumatic events, a sense of personal potency against the wounds to our spirit, a sense of being in the face of nonbeing. In short, rage is an ideal energy to fuel any and all methods—from addictions to the survival personality—that serve to protect us from our wounding. Challenge anyone's addiction or compulsion, or anyone's survival personality, and you will feel the heat of rage, covertly or overtly expressed. Even the most benign and pleasant personality, when suddenly threatened by the loss of a favorite defensive substance or activity, can suddenly flare with the rage of a wounded spirit.

The Primal Split in Daily Life

The primal split represents a traumatic impact to the I-Self relationship—the primal wound—and an attempt to manage this impact. The tremendously powerful interplay of the lower and higher unconscious across the split forms a dialectic that pervades not only the personality, but the human condition as a whole.

Thus perhaps, the violence, abuse, and injustice so endemic in human life may not be caused by instinctual drives of sex, power, and aggression that we are unable to tame. Human suffering may instead be largely the result of primal wounding to our natural human relatedness, causing the primal split. We may have difficulty with our natural drives only because of nonbeing trauma, by which the drives are used in compulsive, defensive, and destructive ways. Our natural sexuality, personal power, and transpersonal awareness, for example, here function in the service of survival rather than self-expression.

If this is so, we agree with Guntrip that the "security for babies and mother outweighs every other issue" and should be "the overriding fact that should determine our social goals" (Guntrip 1971, 114–15). Furthermore, this social justice agenda should include all of childhood, including not only prenatal care, family life, and schooling, but social, political, and environmental conditions as well.

But such an agenda seems a dream when we realize the seamless nature of the being-nonbeing trap. The being-nonbeing dynamism is the very warp and woof of our lives. We are caught in a desperate search for the right person, career, community, or ideology that will finally give us a firm sense of being from which to act with integrity and meaning. And the universe itself may seem far from a holding environment, looming instead as an infinite nonempathic emptiness in which we must struggle for a brief time before lapsing into nothingness. No wonder we grab for any shreds of being we can find. This state of human existence is what Assagioli called the fundamental infirmity of man:

> In our ordinary life we are limited and bound in a thousand ways— the prey of illusions and phantasms, the slaves of unrecognized complexes, tossed hither and thither by external influences, blinded and hypnotized by deceiving appearances. No wonder then that man, in such a state, is often discontented, insecure and changeable in his moods, thoughts and actions. Feeling intuitively that he is "one," and yet finding that he is "divided unto himself," he is bewildered and fails to understand either himself or others. No wonder that he, not knowing or understanding himself, has no self-control and is continually involved in his own mistakes and weaknesses; that so many lives are failures, or are at least limited and saddened by diseases of mind and body, or tormented by doubt, discouragement and despair. No wonder that man, in his blind passionate search for liberty and satisfaction, rebels violently at times, and at times tries to still his inner torment by throwing himself headlong into a life of feverish activity, constant excitement, tempestuous emotion, and reckless adventure. (Assagioli 1965, 20–21)

This is an excellent description of a human being who has suffered primal wounding and primal splitting, and so is "divided unto himself." Here we are cut off from the extremes of agony and ecstasy of life, caught in survival personality, and enthralled by the family and cultural trance (hypnotized). Our empathic connection to ourselves and others is broken (i.e., in failing to understand either himself or others), leaving us isolated and alienated, feeling outside of life and looking in upon it. No wonder we attempt to "still our inner torment" by destructive attachments to violence, sex, and power, and by addictions to people, places, and things.

In the end, the question finally becomes not *whether* primal wounding is operating in our lives, but *how* it is operating. There seems to be no sphere of human existence that is not covertly or overtly influenced by this wounding. So what is the way out?

The door out of the being-nonbeing prison opens only with the recognition that we are indeed in a prison. We realize that we are in important ways powerless, addicted, and inauthentic, and that significant aspects of our lives are at the very least empty and unfulfilling. We begin to see that our comfortable conscious view of ourselves— whether positive or negative—is hiding deep streams of unconscious pain, fear, depression, and rage. We discover that these deep streams of experience are not "back there" in childhood past, but are fundamental aspects of our daily life. We begin to awaken from the survival trance. In short, we begin to realize we are living from survival personality.

However, survival personality can be so resilient and so hidden that often it will remain completely invisible until a personal crisis dramatically disrupts it. Perhaps a brush with death, a struggle with an addiction, or the loss of a loved one will finally bring us to our knees and reveal this deeper conditioning of our lives. In some way it may be that the struggle with survival personality begins only with an act of grace. We are so identified with this orientation that even our best efforts to escape from it are themselves conditioned by it.

Once survival personality is revealed we can begin to be aware of how this orientation pervades our daily living, from disguised relationship and sexual addiction to habitual alcohol and drug use, from hidden spiritual pride to subtle revenge motives, from spiritual materialism (Trungpa) to compulsive service to others. As we address these tendrils of survival, we can uncover the primal wounding at their core and gradually begin to move towards authenticity.

Although we can begin this process in therapy, this is not a single insight or breakthrough experience but a lifelong journey—such is the depth and pervasiveness of primal wounding. As with primal wounding, the question is never *whether* survival personality is operating, but *how* it is operating. We can always expect our experience to comprise fluctuating percentages of survival and authenticity.

As elaborated in the next chapter, success in addressing survival personality entails transforming the survival unifying center into a more authentic unifying center. We here reach empathically to our core trauma, our wounded "inner children," and provide them with a new holding environment, one that can let them grow according to their own natures. We find a matrix of relationships that can hold us as we develop self-empathy and a conscious relationship to Self, a stable authentic unifying center (internal and external) that can support the unfoldment of authentic personality. In this manner we heal the broken connection to Self, and open to a lifelong relationship to Self, or Self-realization.

It is this radical and faithful openness to Self, and so to the vicissitudes of human experience, that marks the path out of the addictive bipolar prison, out of the craving and aversion of the primal split. In order to guide this awakening, healing, and growth, it then can be helpful to have an understanding of the overall process of Self-realization. As we shall see, Self-realization is not an orderly progression up through developmental levels, but an often dizzying roller coaster ride, one moment plunging us to the depths, the next moment rocketing us to the heights, and the next moment presenting us with the mundane duties of everyday living. We shall now examine this unpredictable journey founded on a relationship to Self.

8

Self-Realization

*That is to say, even the enlightened person remains what he is,
and is never more than his own limited ego before the One who
dwells within him, whose form has no knowable boundaries,
who encompasses him on all sides, fathomless as the abysms
of the earth and vast as the sky.*
—C. G. Jung

Self-realization is an assent to the intimacy of the I-Self relationship. We are all most likely doing this right now, to a greater or lesser extent, via the significant relationships in our lives, both inner and outer. In Self-realization, a conscious ongoing relationship to Self develops that will—as with all relationships—entail an openness not only to the joys of life, but to the pain, uncertainty, and limitations of life as well. Here enlightenment does not mean attaining a particular type of higher experience or developmental stage, but developing a committed relationship to the source of our being, a willingness to follow the call or vocation of our deepest truth no matter the experiences in which we find ourselves.

The enduring presence of the I-Self relationship in all stages of life and all types of experience indicates the transcendence-immanence of "I" and Self. That is, "I" endures through all changes in our bodies, all changes of feeling and belief, and all the changing roles that make up our personal lives. And Self abides through all changes in unifying centers, from family, friends, and communities to ideals, goals, and values. Ergo, the I-Self relationship continues through all this change as well, distinct but not separate from all the many transformations encountered over the course of a human life span. No matter where you go, there you are. No matter where you go, there is Self.

Therefore, the conscious development of a relationship to Self may lead us virtually anywhere. We may find ourselves at various times engaging in a wide range of experiences:

- The depths of traumatic pain
- The heights of spiritual insight
- Unresolved childhood issues
- The denial around our addictions and compulsions
- Archetypal images or paranormal experiences
- The dynamics of our family systems
- A struggle with life values and choices
- Decisive social and political action
- The healing of our relationships with others and world

The type of experience we face in Self-realization at any one time depends on whither our relationship to Self leads us.

The idea that Self-realization may lead us almost anywhere has many ramifications for the human journey. For one thing, it means that we cannot assume that our path leads inexorably upward from the lower unconscious to the higher. Nor is this an ascent through increasingly more harmonious planes of existence. Neither can we be assured that our highest experiences of spiritual unity, noself, or cosmic consciousness are necessarily Self-realization.

Obviously then, describing Self-realization presents something of a challenge. It cannot be equated with any particular content or form of experience, no experience of contentlessness or formlessness, no particular state of consciousness, and can occur—or not—at any stage of life or moment of the day.

This chapter will employ several approaches to the elusive phenomenon of Self-realization. The first will be to outline the two dimensions of Self-realization: personal development and transpersonal development. Then we shall discuss the psychological transformation related to Self-realization: the development of an authentic unifying center and the expansion of the middle unconscious.

Throughout, we will discern the brokenness from the primal wound and gain some hints about how this is healed.

THE TWO DIMENSIONS OF SELF-REALIZATION

In presenting a broad view of Self-realization, we can draw upon the psychosynthesis conception of human development as comprising two dimensions: (1) personal development, what Assagioli called *personal psychosynthesis*, which involves the increasing ability to express a sense of unique, well-articulated individuality and (2) transpersonal psychosynthesis, which Assagioli called *transpersonal psychosynthesis* or *spiritual psychosynthesis*, which includes a growing contact with unitive states of consciousness, mystical sensibilities, and a sense of universality.[1] Using the chart created by James Vargiu (Firman and Vargiu 1977, Firman and Vargiu 1980), these two dimensions of human development can be diagrammed as shown in figure 8.1.

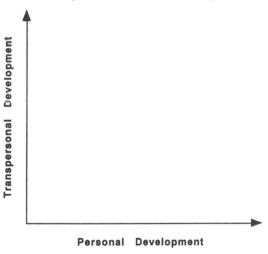

Fig. 8.1

Personal and transpersonal development together outline the broad psychospiritual terrain in which Self-realization takes place, and can thereby serve to illuminate the nature of Self-realization itself. We posit that an unwounded I-Self relationship, facilitated by empathic unifying centers, would allow both these lines of development to unfold in the growing individual, from the earliest moments of life through old age. This unfoldment would naturally embody the "synthesis of individuality and universality" that is a characteristic of the communion between "I" and Self (Assagioli 1973, 113). However, given the ubiquity of primal wounding, progress along either of these axes and the integration of the two will invariably involve some amount of healing work.

In figure 8.1, movement along the horizontal axis represents an ability to function as a volitional and well-individuated personality with a good measure of personal power. The personality that is well developed along this dimension is what Maslow called the *nontranscending self-actualizer*. He describes such people as "more essentially practical, realistic, mundane, capable, and secular people, living more in the here and now world . . . 'doers' rather than meditators or contemplators, effective and pragmatic rather than aesthetic, reality-testing and cognitive rather than emotional and experiencing" (Maslow 1971, 281).

Because of the personality integration and personal power occurring along the personal dimension, many developing here would find themselves successful in the world, able to achieve society's goals of education, family, and career. Due to primal wounding, this development involves a healing at the levels of the middle and lower unconscious: "This [personal psychosynthesis] includes the development and harmonizing of all human functions and potentialities at all levels of the lower and middle area in the diagram of the constitution of man [and woman]" (Assagioli 1973a, 121).

Of course, there is seldom an aspect of the human journey that does not include material from all levels of the unconscious. Personal development, while more obviously engaging lower and middle unconscious contents, will involve the higher unconscious as well—for example, one very often encounters transpersonal qualities when working through early trauma. In a way, one can think of personal development as referring to where one is currently focused in the overall healing of the split between the lower and higher unconscious.

Personal development does not necessarily involve the application of formal methods of education, counseling, or therapy—surely it most often occurs simply in the living of our lives. In the process of rising to meet the challenges of our personal and professional lives we develop our unique gifts and abilities, attain more harmony within our personalities, overcome feelings of survival guilt and shame, and transform fears and anxieties. In an effort to live authentically, we will often find personal wholeness blossoming and old wounds healing. But in many cases too, much time and struggle can be saved by consciously working at personal development with a trained professional.

On the other hand, vertical movement on the diagram, or transpersonal development, represents an increasing communion with higher, unitive, or mystical states of consciousness, e.g., the *cosmic consciousness* of Bucke, Maslow, and others—"The . . . holistic perceiving of the cosmos as a unity" (Maslow 1971, 274). Given primal wounding, this development includes integrating material from the higher unconscious and so healing our separation from this ability to experience our union with something greater than ourselves. In Assagioli's words: "The specific therapeutic task . . . is that of arriving at a harmonious adjustment by means of the proper assimilation of the inflowing superconscious energies and of their integration with the pre-existing aspects of the personality; that is, of accomplishing not only a personal but also a *spiritual psychosynthesis*" (p. 55, emphasis in the original).

A movement up the vertical represents becoming less aware of uniqueness and individuality and more aware of unity and universality. For example, attaining the uppermost area of the vertical with no proportional movement along the personal, one would experience no differentiated individuality at all, but only universality. This level of experience may be akin to what Wilber called the *causal level*, in which "the centralizing ego-sense is entirely subordinated, lost in largeness of being and finally abolished" (Wilber, Engler, and Brown 1986, 73). Here is the realization that although "I" appears to be self-existent, "it has, in reality, no autonomous substantiality," to use Assagioli's words (Assagioli 1965, 20). (This experience of personal no-thingness is quite different from the frozen terror in facing the non-being wound, although the former may trigger the latter.)

As with personal development, transpersonal development may often occur naturally, with no need for any psychological work at all. Whether via striking peak experiences or gradual shifts in consciousness, the transpersonal dimension reveals itself and becomes a center of meaning in our lives. Through meditation, prayer, ritual, music, art, service, and community, we seek to commune with this higher, more unitive dimension of existence.

However, transpersonal experiences can be difficult to integrate at times. For example, if one has an intense experience of solidarity and compassion for all humankind, this may lead afterwards to a heightened sensitivity to one's own feelings of hatred or revenge—here feelings are surfacing that obstruct the expression of compassion. Or perhaps a strong experience of unity with nature may reveal the personal attitudes and beliefs which have caused us to violate this union in the past—attitudes and beliefs that are obstacles to right relationship with nature. And of course, transpersonal development may easily find us struggling with any of the transpersonal defenses outlined in chapter 6. It is as if the older habits, attitudes, and feelings that would obstruct the concrete expression of the transpersonal experience are thrown into stark relief by the light of the experience itself (this dynamic has been discussed as *induction* in Firman 1991).

In such cases active and intentional psychological work on the problematic reactions can help a great deal, and this will invariably entail work with the lower unconscious. Here again is the reciprocal interplay of the higher and lower unconscious, revealing a larger process in which the healing of the higher-lower split—the primal wound—is the agenda.

Understanding these two dimensions of human growth as distinct, we can account for the observation that a person can be highly developed along one dimension and underdeveloped along another. Far along the horizontal, the strong nontranscending self-actualizer might be powerful and creative, operating successfully in the world, but have little or no sense of transpersonal realities. Along the vertical dimension, the transcender might have an ongoing knowing of Ultimate Unity and the insubstantiality of personal identity, but may be hard put to operate creatively within intimate interpersonal relationships and the practical tasks of the mundane world. As is now well recognized, even those who are highly experienced in the transpersonal realm can be firmly in the clutches of major addictions, debilitating compulsions, and abusive patterns of behavior (e.g., see Zweig and Abrams 1990).[2]

The two-dimensional model also accounts for transpersonal experiencing in childhood and throughout the life span. A sense of a transpersonal reality is not the summit of personal development, but is possible at every point of development. The infant or child, as well as the adult, may experience both individuality and union with the Ground of Being, both personal and transpersonal growth. Childhood spirituality has been documented and discussed at length (Armstrong 1985, Laski 1968, Robinson 1983).

As we shall discuss shortly, there is no correct path of human development implied in this model. An individual life journey may range widely throughout the area of this diagram, leading now toward one dimension and now toward the other, or perhaps even tending to emphasize one dimension to the relative exclusion of the other.

However, there are two crises that indicate that there is a general human tendency to include some amount of both of these developmental directions over time. These crises occur when there is an imbalance toward either of these two dimensions, thereby indicating the need to include the other dimension as well. The crisis found along the vertical axis is the *crisis of duality*, while the crisis along the horizontal is the *existential crisis* (see Firman and Vargiu 1977, 1980).

The Crisis of Duality

Development along the transpersonal dimension with the relative exclusion of the personal may at some point land one in a crisis of duality, an experience in which one realizes that no matter how high one goes, the unitive state is not permanent. One's desire for a stable, conscious union with the Ground of Being seems forever thwarted:

> I'd do intensive periods of meditation practice and feel wonderful. Even when they were hard, there would always come a time when I'd feel beyond duality, knowing All was One. But coming home, I would lose it all. I was back into the same old stuff—the fear, the feeling bad about myself, the anger. And I still couldn't do relationships. I was in a lot of pain. I couldn't see why my practice wasn't changing my life.[3]

This type of crisis can be coupled with a painful sense of the dissonance and unbridgeable chasm between the unity and beauty of the heights and the brokenness and suffering of the world, between the mundane and sublime realities, between the manifest and unmanifest. Here one faces—perhaps in grief and despair—a seemingly final, inescapable duality between the human and the Divine.

The crisis of duality usually involves morphophobia: there is a fear of form, a turning away from the world of individuality and boundaries in an attempt to maintain an exclusively unitive consciousness. This seems related to what Wilber calls the *ultimate pathology*—"a failure to integrate the manifest and unmanifest realms" (Wilber, Engler, and Brown 1986, 44). But how do such profound transpersonal states of consciousness become problematical? They do so by becoming split off from other dimensions of experience. These unitive experiences do not in fact embrace the widest unity because they leave out the personal, the individual, and the unique. The transpersonal realm, while certainly extremely meaningful and transformative, is nevertheless only one dimension of an even more fundamental reality that includes differentiation and individuality.

The crisis of duality seems to indicate that the experience of the transpersonal is split off from the whole by primal wounding, because reorientation away from the transpersonal most often does surface this underlying wounding. A letting-go of the transpersonal and a movement towards the personal dimension involves facing the results of early trauma: perhaps a fear of being entangled in the illusion of matter, an inflated rage at the stupidity of the human race, an attachment to dualistic metaphysics, a debilitating anxiety about losing one's spirituality in the mundane world, a desperate need to withdraw from the conflict and turmoil of life, or a fear of being overwhelmed by interpersonal relationships and everyday duties—all issues with early traumatic roots that will need to be addressed in some way.

Ultimately, the crisis of duality is an opportunity to reorient oneself along the personal dimension. This may involve a difficult disidentification from the transpersonal, perhaps giving up a quest for enlightenment or detaching from unitive states of consciousness. But in this "parting with god for God's sake" (Eckhart in Blakney 1941, 204), one can begin to include the personal dimension and discover that this, too, can be an integral part of one's Self-realization. Here one is invited to work through some amount of psychological wounding, to attain a new level of personal integration and, in the end, perhaps to express transpersonal awareness more fully in the everyday world.

The Existential Crisis

The second crisis of reorientation derived from this model is the existential crisis arising from an imbalance toward the personal and away from the transpersonal. In this case we might find a person who is highly individuated, operating well in the world, and powerfully decisive—well developed along the personal dimension—but for whom life becomes less and less meaningful:

> The person now begins to wonder if he is ever going to find fulfillment. An increasing sense of meaninglessness pervades all of his

normal activities. Pastimes and interests which he formerly found rewarding do not bring the same pleasure they did before. His family, friends, and career simply do not interest him as they had. As this progresses, the person may experience at various times apathy, fear, and even despair. What is missing in his life? He has a strong identity, a well-integrated personality, and can function very well in the world. He is not neurotic; he has more than successfully attained the level of functioning termed "normal" by modern mental health standards. Logically he should be happy. (Firman and Vargiu 1977, pp. 69–70)

The person "has it all," but none of it satisfies a need for deeper meaning and purpose in life. This has also been called the *existential vacuum* by Viktor Frankl (1967) and the *existential neurosis* by S. R. Maddi (1967), and amounts to an invitation to reorient oneself toward the transpersonal dimension.

As in the crisis of duality, this reorientation toward the transpersonal can also reveal indications of the earlier wounding underlying the split between the two dimensions: the fear of letting go of one's worldly identity; anxiety about losing control; a defensive, cynical attitude toward higher human potential; pain from abusive experiences with church, theology, or clergy; or a strong attachment to the concrete, tangible, and material—morphophilia.

This earlier wounding can be addressed in counseling and psychotherapy, while a relationship with the transpersonal might be developed via spiritual practices such as prayer and meditation, and by engaging new external unifying centers that can reflect and support this growing connection to the transpersonal (spiritual communities, religious reading, retreats, etc.). Thus the existential crisis invites one beyond individuality and toward a growing communion with more unitive spheres of value and meaning.

The crisis of duality and existential crisis together indicate that full human growth very often tends toward a bringing together of the higher and lower; we seem to be called from the extremes toward a more integrated experience of ourselves and the world.

The 2-D Model and Self-Realization

Two important things need to be kept in mind about this two-dimensional model and, we think, any model that seeks to outline personal and transpersonal development. Allow us to make each point, and then speak of their importance taken together.

The first point is that, throughout the personal and transpersonal spectra, we are talking about the experience of an individual human being—"I." Remember, in order for anything to be experienced directly, and then reported, means ipso facto that there was someone present having the experience. This includes even those experiences of noself or ego transcendence. In the succinct words of Deikman:

Emptiness does not mean that things don't exist, nor does "no self" mean that we don't exist.

—Jack Kornfield

"He knows 'I am' to be a misconception. Who knows that?" (Deikman 1982, 41).

In psychosynthesis terms "I" is the "who" who knows "I am" to be a misconception. "I" is the essential "you" who sees through the illusion of isolated selfhood to realize the insubstantiality of personal identity. "I" is the experiencer of whatever is arising. This abiding presence of "I" also holds for reports of psychotic experience: who is the one who can later describe ego disintegration or loss of boundaries? Not ego—it was in a state of disintegration—but "I."

The experience of ego or "separate sense of self" does of course evaporate along the transpersonal dimension. However, "I" is ever-present, whether experiencing pure no-thingness or pure fullness—or you never would have known anything took place at all. One can transcend the ego, but one can never transcend "I," because "I" is the one who does the transcending.

The second point about the two-dimensional diagram and other spectrum models is this: Self transcends, and so is immanent within, all points throughout the spectra. In Wilber's words, Self is "the *ground* of every stage of development" (Wilber 1980, 25). Self is not then to be equated with any point on the graph, nor with either axis, nor with the entire field delimited by the axes, nor with a supposed third dimension on a par with the other two.

Taking these two points together—that both "I" and Self are ever-present throughout the human journey—we can arrive at the conclusion: the I-Self relationship is potentially present throughout the entire field outlined by the two dimensions. One may therefore have a direct, conscious connection to the Ground of Being from anywhere on the diagram at all. One's relationship to Self is independent of any stage of growth, life experience, or state of consciousness, whether personal or transpersonal.

Quite practically then, this means that Self-realization can take place at *any point* charted by these two dimensions. That is, one might be called by Self to function as a strongly individuated personality deeply immersed in the world, with little time for transpersonal development, or be called to take up a contemplative lifestyle, devoting oneself to prayer and meditation with little focus on the personal dimension. By the same token, one may develop a survival personality (and subpersonalities as well) along either of these dimensions that can limit Self-realization; either a spiritual, transpersonal survival personality or a pragmatic, worldly survival personality may work against hearing the call of Self. Indeed, the two crises described earlier would indicate the disruption of some such developing survival orientation.

Clearly, it is difficult to judge Self-realization from the outside according to a set of standard criteria. This discernment is not so much a matter of theoretical models as an intimate affair between the person and deeper Self at every stage of the human journey, facilitated by important relationships to other people and the world.

So while the two-dimensional diagram charts a broad area on the spectrum of human consciousness, it charts only the terrain of Self-realization, not the journey itself. The journey will be a unique path unfolding from one's own relationship to Self, and may take one anywhere in the terrain at different times—from powerful personal expression to humble personal nothingness to a paradoxical synthesis of the two.

In other words this model, as other models of personal and

transpersonal development, is useful in understanding where you are on your journey, but does not indicate where to go on your journey. Such models cannot tell you whether you need psychotherapy or spiritual direction, whether to join a self-help group or take up meditation, or whether or not to pursue a particular life goal. Such answers can only evolve from an open and responsive relationship to Self, as manifested in the internal and external unifying centers of our lives.

So the fundamental characteristic of Self-realization is not a specific higher experience or state of consciousness, but a commitment to one's truth, a dedication to one's deepest sense of values, life direction, and dharma. We might say that having a transpersonal experience or spiritual awakening is like falling in love with Self, while Self-realization is like getting married to Self. Some religious traditions even speak of a spiritual marriage between the human and Divine.

Self-realization, as any committed life-long relationship, is not conditional; it is not dependent upon states of happiness, union, or bliss, but is "for better or worse." The key element is less a state of consciousness than a state of will—a commitment to be true, come what may. But this is not a static, stagnant state; it is a dynamic, living orientation expressed anew each minute of every day. One may be continually challenged and transformed, as well as held and nurtured, by this unpredictable marriage to Self.

Assagioli describes Self-realization most clearly as a dialogue, governed by mutual influence, between personal will and transpersonal will. He says the transpersonal will can be experienced as "a 'call' from God, or a 'pull' from some Higher Power" that "sometimes starts a 'dialogue' between the man and his 'Higher Source,' in which each alternately invokes and evokes the other" (Assagioli 1973a, 114). Such a dialogue is transcendent-immanent within both the transpersonal and personal dimensions of experience; it does not depend upon transpersonal unitive experiences but can be facilitated by a wide variety of unifying centers, e.g., deeply held values, an inner voice of wisdom, important nocturnal dreams, friends and family, an empathic community, or synchronistic events in one's life.

This emphasis on a personal response to call is very like Jung's concept of fidelity to the law of one's own being, of the individual's obedience to the law of his life inborn in him (Jung, 1954), and is also like Kohut's "the realization, through his actions, of the blueprint for his life that had been laid down in his nuclear self" (Kohut 1977, 133n). Assagioli's examples of people who have trod well the way of Self-realization include Mahatma Gandhi, Florence Nightingale, Martin Luther King, and Albert Schweitzer. Assagioli would say, however, that Self-realization is the prerogative of all people, and not only that of the famous heroes and heroines among us.[4]

Note again that the I-Self connection is not a despotic one-way relationship between "I" and Self, but operates under the principle of mutual influence, I-Thou relationship, and dialogue. The essence of the I-Self relationship is an empathic resonance, an intimate communion in which individuality and free will are respected and supported. Indeed, individuality and free will *arise* from this relationship.

This openness to an intimate relationship with Self, together with an openness to one's authentic experience, comprises authentic personality. Authentic personality is not dependent on any stage of development or particular content of consciousness, nor upon a relatively nontraumatic childhood, but simply upon a responsiveness to the call of Self and an openness to the experiences encountered in following this call.

Just as survival personality is connected to the survival unifying center, so authentic personality draws its being from the *authentic unifying center*. The authentic unifying center is a good enough "true link, a point of connection between the personal man and his higher Self" (Assagioli 1965, 25) capable of facilitating Self-realization throughout the life span. Thus, working with the authentic unifying center is another way to approach the business of Self-realization.

THE AUTHENTIC UNIFYING CENTER

The authentic unifying center is the unifying center that reflects Self accurately enough so that authentic personality can unfold. Here a clear enough mirroring, a good enough empathic response, allows a true enough sense of personal consciousness and will to blossom. The function of authentic unifying center can be performed by a vast variety of external and internal presences: caregivers, peers, and mentors; social, nature, and spiritual communities; and images, beliefs, values, and ideals (see chapter 3).

Like the survival unifying center discussed earlier, the authentic unifying center can be seen as having two aspects, one relating to the consciousness function of "I" ("who I feel myself to be") and the other to the will function ("what I do, how I act"). The difference here is that in the authentic unifying center these two aspects work to support and nurture a sense of "I" rather than constrict this. Although there can be many different authentic unifying centers, we will here speak of them collectively in the singular.

The first aspect of the authentic unifying center, the consciousness aspect, is a sense of intimate connection with an empathic other who sees us, knows us, and accepts us as we are. This experience may be found in the gaze of a compassionate caregiver; the respect and interest shown to us by a teacher or mentor; a rapport with a hero or heroine; a connection to a community, philosophy, or religion; or a mystical union with the Universal, the Ultimate, the Divine. All of these experiences, from the most common to the most extraordinary, are manifestations of the underlying I-Self connection.

An encounter with an authentic unifying center then gives rise to a sense of self-respect, self-acceptance, self-empathy, and having a place in a larger scheme of things. We here feel not alienated and alone, not strangers in a strange land, but fundamentally at home with ourselves and in the world. We feel valued and respected, and that existence is inherently meaningful. Experiences with this aspect of the authentic unifying center can thus be distinguished from experiences with (a) the negative unifying center: "You are inherently bad and have no right to exist"; (b) the positive unifying center: "You are perfectly good and belong not to this imperfect world, but to a higher realm"; and (c) the survival unifying center: "You are nothing but your constricted role as a member of this family/society."

While these unifying centers demand the playing of limiting roles and the disowning of important dimensions of experience, the authentic unifying center supports an engagement with a broad range of life experience. We here receive a sense of self capable of experiencing loss and pain, love and joy, isolation and union, dependence and independence. There may here be a sense of resilience, courage, and humor in the face of all life may bring.

Relating to the authentic unifying center, we would not be crippled by the tension of survival shame (e.g., low self-esteem, personal defectiveness, etc.) with its underlying threat of nonbeing. We may, however, at times experience *authentic shame*. Authentic shame arises from an awareness of the difference between our current mode of being and the possibility of a more true or authentic mode. Perhaps through loving feedback from someone we respect, or an inner sense of a greater potential in ourselves, we sense a difference between who we are and what we may be.

However unpleasant this may be, it is yet creative and life-affirming because it calls us to be more deeply who we are. Where survival shame demands stasis and conformity, authentic shame invites growth and transformation. Most essentially, authentic shame arises from a deeper encounter with Self, and may range anywhere from an aspiration towards an increased intimacy with Self and others, to a profound wonder and awe in the face of the mystery of Self.[5]

The second aspect of the authentic unifying center has to do not so much with support of consciousness as support of will—with the dimension of action, guidance, direction, and behavior. Here we feel called or invited by the empathic other to express our true selves in particular ways. We sense we are not only connected to a greater scheme of things, but also have a meaningful part to play in this scheme; we are valued actors in a greater drama, and what we do is important in how this drama unfolds. It is not only the quality of our being that has meaning here, but the concrete effects of our actions as well.

This mirroring of will supports an experience of empowerment and meaning in following our deepest sense of truth. Whether the child given greater responsibility at home or the prophet called by God, whether a team member inspired to heroic performance or the person challenged to do good in the face of evil, whether the artist passionately manifesting a vision or the political leader responding to the historical moment, there is here a sense of personal will in alignment with a greater will. This call of Self to exercise our wills can be distinguished from (a) the negative unifying center: "Whatever you do is bad; beware, punishment is imminent"; (b) the positive unifying center: "Whatever you do is needed and good"; and (c) the survival unifying center: "You must obey the rules of the family/society, however oppressive."

These unifying centers are either too active or too passive, either rigidly controlling or providing no guidance at all. Like controlling or permissive caregivers, they limit the blossoming of authentic free will and self-expression. But unlike these unifying centers, the authentic unifying center is neither rigid nor passive, and actively invites us to exercise choice, to take responsibility, to respond to the truth of the moment, and to follow particular directions in life.

This guidance aspect of the authentic unifying center is ultimately "the moral conscience that issues from the spiritual Self" (Assagioli 1965, 232). Assagioli takes care to distinguish this "spiritual morality," characterized by wisdom, love, and justice, from the rigidity and harshness of the Freudian super-ego that is "tied in with very strong affective charges of fear of consequences" (pp. 233, 232). Assagioli's two levels of moral conscience clearly reflect our discrimination between survival and authentic unifying centers.

In close agreement with Assagioli, Viktor Frankl (1948) describes well an intuitional and spiritual conscience that is an expression of the "spiritual self" (p. 39). It embodies a sense of "what ought to be" that "cannot be comprehended by any universal law" (p. 35). That is, here is not simply an abstract understanding of moral codes and ethical principles, but a direct call to action. This is a voice addressing you, personally, from the depths of your being, and your response will lead to specific choices and concrete effects in your life. In our view, this response does not even imply a particular developmental stage of moral reasoning, but rather the unique act of the individual at any developmental stage whatsoever.

Guidance from the authentic unifying center does not then generate a crippling anxiety about making a fatal mistake and so becoming a target of rage, retribution, and the threat of annihilation. In other words, there is not here the suffocating pall of survival guilt, although perhaps there may be *authentic guilt*.

Authentic guilt arises from the recognition of a dissonance between personal will and a respected greater will. But like authentic shame, authentic guilt is not a matter of blame, criticism, or self-hate. Authentic guilt is a discomfort about acting in variance with our own most valued guidance, deepest sense of truth, or most heartfelt vocation. Whether arising from current choices, or from looking at past choices with new eyes, authentic guilt is ultimately a creative dissonance calling us to act more in accord with our own values and life direction. Moreover, authentic guilt and shame both work to increase empathy—we here recognize, accept, and amend our shortcomings and thereby find compassion for the shortcomings of others.[6]

Although the authentic unifying center is clearly not formed by the wholesale introjection of rigid external rules and is more an intuitional guiding light than a set of moral dictates, neither is it devoid of particular values, ideals, and ethical principles. It may in fact carry ethical wisdom received from caregivers, the educational system, religion, and society at large. It is simply that this sense of conscience develops in such a way that it does not truncate authentic personality, but supports this.

Authenticity and Wounding

Whereas the survival unifying center inflicts wounds and then demands that they be hidden, the authentic unifying center accepts these wounds and acts to heal them. Connected to an authentic unifying center, we no longer feel the need to hide and compensate for our wounds, but can recognize and accept them as a part of our life experience.

Moreover, as wounding is recognized and accepted, it often is found to be the source of important strengths and abilities for a meaningful life. Indeed, there are many cases in which awareness of wounding is an important means of receiving vocation—a personal experience with childhood abuse, sexual harassment, the violent loss of a family member, or discrimination and prejudice may well be the very place one hears the call of Self. From her study of positive transformation after trauma, psychotherapist Mary M. Baures concludes: "In contrast to people who repress trauma and are unable to heal from it, these survivors revisited, reworked, and transformed their horrible experiences in creative projects and through helping others. Maintaining fidelity to the trauma, they charted a new life course and took risks to fulfill their highest potentials. Finding a mission or meaning in trauma is life-giving in a way that revenge and bitterness are not" (Baures 1996, 88).

Note that "maintaining fidelity to the trauma" does not imply these survivors adopted a victim stance, blamed the past for current failings, or refused to take responsibility for their lives. Rather, an acceptance of the trauma allowed the expression of their true selves. To the extent we do not recognize and accept the wounding we have all invariably suffered, authenticity will ever be beyond our grasp. Authentic personality is not unwounded personality; it is simply the accurate reflection of the truth of our lives.

So the authentic unifying center works to mirror our wounding as well as our talents and gifts. This is the healing principle operating so powerfully whenever people with similar trauma gather to share at an intimate level. In these situations an empathic other—one who knows our pain from the inside—can see us, respect us, and know us. And as we shall explore later, this empathic resonance is the essence of healing from the primal wound. Mirrored in the depths of our wounding, what was nonbeing becomes being, what was trauma becomes simply pain, what was a toxic abscess becomes a scar.

Nurturing the Authentic Unifying Center

The authentic unifying center (as the authentic personality) is not, to our knowledge, found in pure form. It is found intermixed with the survival unifying center and arises from a gradual transformation of the survival unifying center (and so too, from a transformation and integration of material from the positive and negative unifying centers). We are all works in progress, and at any point in time will be experiencing a percentage of survival mode and a percentage of authenticity. The idea is simply to move toward an increased percentage of authenticity. One of the ways authenticity may be increased is by attending to the formation and care of the authentic unifying center itself, seeking to develop it into an instrument finely tuned to our most essential values. This development might include entering into dialogue with different systems of morality and ethics; praying and meditating regularly; listening carefully to messages from nocturnal dreams; studying philosophical and scientific world views; learning about different religions and theologies; and finding a mentor, intimate friend, or community who supports our relationship to Self. All such things work to expand a sense of relationship to Self, and refine the ability to hear and respond to Self in the specifics of daily living.

In seeking to respond to Self, it can also be important to work with any distorting dynamics from the higher or lower unconscious. For example, caught up in the positive personality and positive unifying center, it is possible to feel an inflated sense of personal identity, a grandiosity vis-à-vis an apparent special call to carry out some grand mission vital to the life of the planet. In his excellent book about the whole subject of finding a life's calling, transpersonal psychotherapist Greg Bogart (1995) calls this type of messianic inflation the *shadow of vocation.*

But this shadow includes the lower unconscious as well. Dominated by the negative unifying center, we can become identified with rage and hate, and feel a paranoid messianic call to exterminate those who are supposedly subverting the goodness of the world. Or caught up in the negative personality, we may feel God wants nothing more than our own destruction. Here psychotherapy has something important to offer spiritual practice—tools by which to clear the playing field, as it were, for a free and clear hearing of call.

Authentic Personality and Unifying Center

Authentic personality and authentic unifying center are good enough reflections of the I-Self relationship, a relationship that revolves around the dependent-independent paradox (see chapter 2). Thus, Self-realization entails not a static state or a single mode of consciousness, but a functioning throughout a dynamic range between the poles of dependence and independence, noself and self, surrender and self-assertion. On one hand we can be called to risk intimacy, to be vulnerable, to let go of old ways of being, or to experience our unity with the Ground of Being. And on the other hand we can be called to make a stand, rise to life challenges, set healthy personal boundaries, and respond to a call from the Ground of Being.

A dynamic relationship to Self may at one moment call us to accept the things we cannot change and the next moment to change the things we can. In Piaget's (1973) terms we may be invited at times to *accommodation*—the transformation of personal structures by new experiences (the dependent pole)—and at other times to *assimilation*—the integration of new experiences into existing structures (the independent pole), and at still other times, to a creative blend of these two abilities. Self-realization may span the entire range of human functioning encompassed by the dependent-independent continuum.[7]

Again it is clear why it is extremely difficult to outline strict stages of Self-realization and thereby judge another's relationship with Self based on their state of consciousness or level of development. We cannot know absolutely whether any particular state of consciousness is regressive or progressive regarding Self-realization simply by the quality or content of that state, nor can we assume that a higher developmental stage is necessarily indicative of Self-realization. Since the I-Self relationship is transcendent-immanent, the dynamics of Self-realization can be found in any state or stage of being human (in theory, it is possible even in the womb).

In Self-realization, regression or progression in any experience can only be ascertained by noting whether or not the experience leads one eventually into or out of a deeper response to one's truth, into or out of a more intimate and committed relationship to Self. Both peak and abyss experiences can constitute obstacles or facilitators of this relationship, and while a therapist, spiritual director, or community can be a help in the discernment process—even by challenging our values and choices when appropriate—it is finally only the person herself or himself who can be the judge.[8]

It does seem, however, that there is often a particular by-product, though not a necessary goal, of Self-realization. During the journey of Self-realization one often develops an increasing openness to both the joy and pain of life, to both the heights and the depths of human experience—an increase in one's experiential range amounting to a healing of the split between the higher unconscious and the lower unconscious, in other words, an expansion of the middle unconscious.

EXPANSION OF THE MIDDLE UNCONSCIOUS

Having affirmed the difficulties in describing the precise nature of Self-realization, we can isolate a general indication that Self-realization may be taking place. It appears that in following our deepest sense of direction and authenticity, we receive a sense of I-amness capable of engaging whatever is brought our way—whether the joys of unitive states of consciousness or the suffering of fragmentation, loss, and limitation.

As Winnicott, Kohut, and others have told us, a sense of resilient, coherent self is precisely the function of an attuned, validating, empathic relationship. It would thus follow that as we are increasingly relating to Self via various unifying centers, our deepest sense of personhood would be increasingly supported and made manifest. In other words, an intimate I-Self relationship allows a sense of personal self to blossom which demonstrates an increased self-empathy, the ability to be present to all the dimensions of human experience—even, as we have seen, to death itself.

Another way of saying this is that Self-realization involves the image or reflection of Self—"I"—becoming a clearer and more accurate image or reflection of Self. Since Self is present throughout all the many levels of the person, the more "I" reflects Self, the more "I" too will be open to all these levels. Therefore, employing Assagioli's oval diagram, Self would be understood as distinct but not separate from the entire area mapped by figure 8.2.[9]

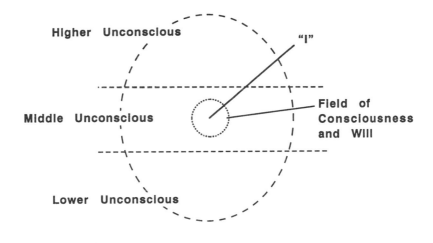

Fig. 8.2

In the above diagram, Self is not represented but is understood to pervade all the areas shown. In other words, just as "I" is transcendent-immanent within the process and content of here and now experience, so Self is transcendent-immanent within all the process and content of the psyche-soma. Thus, in developing an intimate relationship with Self, and so becoming an increasingly accurate image of Self, one may find increasing openness to the heights and depths of experience.

This increasing openness would then be illustrated in Assagioli's model as the middle unconscious expanding. That is, the band of the middle unconscious—that area of the unconscious most available to awareness and will in day-to-day living—would expand upward to include more of the higher unconscious, and downward to include more of the lower unconscious. This expansion is depicted in figure 8.3.

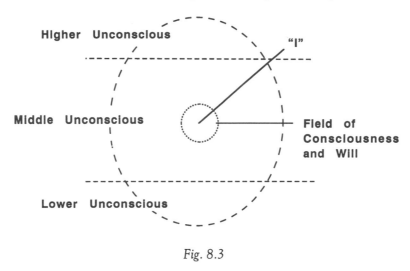

Fig. 8.3

Note that the actual field of consciousness and will is no larger in figure 8.3 than in the previous diagram. It is not that this field itself expands toward embracing the psyche-soma totality—that is the pre-rogative of Self—but that it becomes able to engage a greater variety of experiences as they may occur. A consciousness and will that embraces the totality here would be that of Self, not of "I."

This notion of a higher-lower expansion is resonant with the thinking of Washburn (1988). He outlines a spiral path of development comprising regression in the service of transcendence (lower unconscious work) and regeneration in spirit (higher unconscious work), leading towards integration. We would envision this process as an ongoing—perhaps lifelong—integration of both higher unconscious and lower unconscious material.

This expansion of the middle unconscious represents "I" as having more psyche-soma wholeness available on a daily basis. But the wholeness of an expanded middle unconscious is not necessarily a feeling of wholeness nor a harmonious integration of the personality, because this wholeness may include fragmentation and conflict as well as unity and harmony. It is a wholeness based not on a pattern of unity, but upon an openness to all experiences, even experiences of isolation, pain, and disintegration.

By this expansion of the potential range of experiencing, we would be more open to being touched by the beauty of nature or compassion for another, and more open as well to knowing our own limitations and human brokenness. We would be more self-empathic, willing to see the truth of our lives, from the mistakes to the successes, from the pains to the joys. Here, no matter what the particular type of experience, we would know: "This is my experience; this is honestly who I am in this moment." Winnicott writes of this: "The life of a healthy individual is characterized by fears, conflicting feelings, doubts, frustrations, as much as by the positive features. The main thing is that the man or woman feels he or she is living his or her own life, taking responsibility for action or inaction, and able to take credit for success and blame for failure" (Winnicott 1986, 27).

We do not necessarily here experience more harmony and beauty, but more "me-ness." For example, Joe Smith or Betty Jones become more Joe Smith or Betty Jones. Self-realization is not simply a matter of expressing transpersonal qualities or collective archetypes, but the realization of unique Joe-Smith-ness and Betty-Jones-ness within a larger context—one's unique personal expression, one's individual path or dharma, in the world.

This expansion of the middle unconscious is of course a healing of the primal split. Rather than imprisonment in the addictive dynamism between higher and lower unconscious, there is a freedom born of an ability to engage both dimensions of experience—the fears, conflicting feelings, doubts, and frustrations as much as peace, harmony, and love. Self-realization is clearly not a single experience, a dramatic breakthrough, or a particular state of consciousness; it is an ongoing journey with Self through all that life may bring.

As might be expected, one's "Yes" to Self often may involve an expansion of awareness into what was formerly unconscious—either positive or negative sectors. One may either be surprised by joy or surprised by pain as the middle unconscious begins to expand and higher and lower material becomes more available to "I."

Common elements in each expansion seem to be a surrender of the survival mode and the beginnings of a relationship to some sort of authentic power greater than ourselves. Falling deeply in love, for example, we may let go of old fears of being vulnerable and authentic, trusting a love that is "bigger than both of us." Or, falling in despair, we may find that our addictions, anxieties, or failed relationships are beyond our control; here we may come to believe that there is some greater power—a support group, nature, God—to which we can reach out for help. Surprised by either joy or pain, we disidentify from the chronic stance of survival—the domination of the being-nonbeing dialectic—and begin to trust some sort of greater relationship.

As might also be expected, both the negative and positive types of awakening imply the other: a period of higher unconscious inflow may be followed by a dark time in which lower unconscious material emerges, or the depths of despair will yield to the consolations of spiritual insight. Such oscillations of higher and lower are the warp and woof of Self-realization. While Self-realization cannot be equated with higher experiences, it can often be accompanied by this interplay of higher and lower as the middle unconscious expands and the primal split is healed. It is not that pain and suffering are obstacles to Self-realization to be worked through so that Self-realization may proceed, but that *both* higher and lower are integral parts of the whole process of relating to Self throughout a lifetime.

We need not then be surprised that, after falling in love, we find hurt and rage arising in relationship to our beloved. We need not be perplexed that our bottomless grief for the loss of a parent yields to some inexplicably serene acceptance of death, and we need not be shocked that one moment we are enjoying unitive consciousness and the next moment grieving inconsolably. In the words of a participant in a psychosynthesis group:

> In reliving my peak experience, I felt the awe and wonder of that moment again . . . actually felt it in my body. It was wonderful. Then I remembered my wife's death and felt the pain of not being able to share this with her ever again [crying]. I don't know. It's beyond me. They're both there, the pain and the joy.

Whether the individual becomes initially aware of the higher or the lower, these two dimensions of experience generally occur together over the course of Self-realization. As the I-Self relationship is healed, so the split-off dimensions of human experience begin to come together.[10]

The overall flow of therapy, too, as well as the pattern of single sessions, can be charted by these movements between the higher and lower. Such a pattern within a single psychotherapy session was described as the Down-Up-Down pattern by Vargiu (1978), and later taken up as The Cycles of a Session by Brown (1983). Work with higher and lower also can be seen in the juxtaposition of negative and positive cognitions in Francine Shapiro's (1995) innovative therapeutic procedure, "Eye Movement Desensitization and Reprocessing" (E.M.D.R.).

This juxtaposition of higher and lower is precisely what we would predict in healing the primal wound, a journey with Self in which one's transcendence-immanence is increasingly realized. We shall not here go into all the permutations of this higher-lower interplay characteristic of middle unconscious expansion. Instead, we refer you to Assagioli's (1965) excellent chapter entitled "Self-Realization and Psychological Disturbances," the most popular and widely published piece he ever wrote.

Self-realization is not then a matter of ascending the scale of being in order to achieve a special gnosis, a more advanced developmental stage, or a higher state of consciousness. Self-realization is not even necessarily attaining a balance between the personal and transpersonal dimensions or the higher and lower unconscious, because one may feel called to emphasize one or the other on this journey.

Rather, Self-realization is a matter of choosing for or against Self wherever one may be. It most fundamentally involves the business of finding one's vocation, one's individual part to play in life. Here we ask not for unitive states of consciousness nor even for an expansion of the middle unconscious (although these may be by-products), but simply that we discover that Deeper Will, that invitation in our lives to unfold our unique gifts and talents for the benefit of ourselves and the world.

However, to do so we need authentic external unifying centers capable of holding us while we attempt to respond to Self. And often part of this facilitating environment can be an empathic person who can mirror the heights and depths of our lives so that we may mend the many breaks in our relationship to Self as they emerge. This can be the task of, among other things, psychosynthesis therapy and the psychosynthesis therapist. These are the subjects of the last two chapters.

9

Psychosynthesis Therapy

Sometimes our light goes out but is blown again into flame
by an encounter with another human being.
—Albert Schweitzer

This chapter will give a brief overview of psychosynthesis therapy along with a case example. However, keep in mind that psychosynthesis therapy denotes an overall orientation to the therapeutic process and is not a particular technique or methodology. It is rather a context within which any and all appropriate methods may be employed, depending on the training of the therapist. Foreground here is not technique, but the unique person of the client. Here is Assagioli: "We use a pragmatic attitude and seek—essentially—to respond to the immediate interest of the patient, to meet him on the ground of his immediate major preoccupation . . . . So, in practice, there is no rigid system, but a responding to the actual need of the unique situation of each patient and at each stage of the patient's life" (Assagioli 1965, 86). Assagioli goes so far as to say that this focus on the unique individual demands that the therapist develop a unique approach for each person, "a different combination of the many techniques of therapy in a new *method* for each patient" (p. 4). In other words, he is advising the therapist first and foremost to seek an empathic understanding of the client, not allowing technical expertise and theoretical knowledge to stand in the way of an I-Thou relationship.

In psychosynthesis therapy the therapist functions as an empathic unifying center that allows the client to develop an internal empathic unifying center, and thus the I-Self relationship can emerge in the experience of the client. This emergence can be divided into two interpenetrating stages: the first stage, in which "I" emerges; and the second stage, in which Self emerges. Assagioli (1965) himself subdivides each of these stages into two, resulting in a scheme of four stages, but for the sake of brevity we shall stay with the two.[1]

Note that these two stages amount to the unfoldment of authentic personality. The first stage describes the blossoming of a sense of "I" which is open to a wide spectrum of experience, to both the heights and depths of the personality; while the second stage describes the developing relationship with Self, giving a sense of direction and meaning in life. As these stages are discussed remember that even though they are presented as sequential, they are most often found to overlap and intermix throughout the course of therapy.

The Emergence of "I"

The first stage of psychosynthesis therapy is based upon the understanding that "I" is a projection or reflection of Self, and that an empathic unifying center therefore will allow an increased "flow" of being from Self to "I." The psychosynthesis therapist functions as such a unifying center facilitating a connection between "I" and Self, and so allowing "I" to emerge. The therapeutic empathic relationship thus facilitates an increasingly expanding sense of human spirit, of I-amness, of personal self.

This expanding sense of self in turn allows the client to disidentify from the known sectors of the personality and begin to engage a much broader range of experience. Facilitated by empathic connection, an expanding sense of I-amness allows the many split-off sectors of one's personal universe—each beyond the reach of the unaided "I"—to be gradually contacted, explored, and transformed. Inevitably this involves unearthing primal wounding, exploring the different levels of the unconscious, working with survival personality, and so gradually dispelling the survival trance.

Assagioli is very clear that this stage of psychosynthesis includes an exploration of the higher unconscious as well as the lower unconscious. There will be the surfacing of one's authentic life story, including both the brokenness and gifts received from past relationships. Exploring the lower unconscious may yield an awareness of how past nonempathic relationships have crippled one's life, how current feelings of anxiety, rage, and low self-worth are the heritage of one's past. On the other hand, an exploration of the higher unconscious may uncover a deep gratitude for past empathic relationships that have nurtured current talents and abilities, and allow peak experiences and spiritual insights formerly prevented by a repression of the sublime. Here one begins to understand and accept the depths and heights of oneself, and can begin to act from this increased self-knowledge. This exploration and integration of higher and lower unconscious was discussed in the previous chapter as an expansion of the middle unconscious.

Note however, that psychosynthesis therapy is not an "uncovering therapy" per se. That is, the object here is not simply to access more and more material, to make the unconscious conscious by whatever means available. Rather, the empathic connection allows a natural, ordered expansion of personal selfhood guided by Self—so even in stage one of psychosynthesis therapy, stage two is operative. Here there is respect for the timing of this expansion and for the protective survival mechanisms set up to manage primal wounding. So while the empathic relationship does allow an expansion of the client's range of experience, this is a by-product of the empathic connection and not the result of a more-is-better approach to unconscious material. The therapist is not focused upon taking the person higher or deeper, not on curing or enlightening the person, but on the *person*.[2]

As a part of this stage of psychosynthesis therapy, there is a growing clarity about how the personality has developed within relationships to other people and the world at large. According to Assagioli (1965, 72), this can come from an examination of current relationships; personal history; family of origin; intergenerational history; ethnic, class, and national background; and even "the present collective psyche of humanity as a whole." Over the course of this exploration, the problematic myths, stories, and injunctions that hide the truth of these relationships are uncovered, and the family and cultural trances begin to dissolve. One also here becomes more conscious of the hidden gifts of past and current life relationships, allowing these to be solidified and nurtured.

So in this stage of therapy, clients are attempting to answer the question "Who am I?" They are owning the full range of their experience, from childhood wounding and compulsive behaviors to forgotten transformative connections to others, to transpersonal experience, to relationships with the larger contexts of their lives. And with this increased awareness, one gradually realizes that "I" am distinct but not separate from all these experiences, that "I" am the one who is conscious of these areas of experience, who can move among them, and who can take responsibility for them (i.e., the growth of personal will).

This disidentification is an emergence of the no-thingness or transcendence of "I," and yet also of immanence—one is still in seamless, intimate relationship with all these aspects of one's life and can learn to relate to them in increasingly healthy ways. Rather than being controlled and dominated by the many aspects of the personality (and so by the environment), the person begins to express via these aspects, moving from a survival mode toward an authentic being-in-the-world.

Healing and growth at this stage then amounts to an increased sense of transcendent-immanent "I," which is disidentified from, and so able to engage fully, all dimensions of one's experience. It is as if the empathic therapeutic relationship rekindles the dormant ember of "I," and "I" begins to glow in the darkness. Then, as "I" continues to glow, the radiant expression of this light once again shines through the personality. One's essential unique being, so long defended from a nonempathic world, can now begin to regain authentic expression.

THE EMERGENCE OF SELF

Just as psychosynthesis therapy mirrors "I" for the person, so too does it mirror the relationship with Self, allowing one to become more conscious of the abiding presence of Self in the therapy and in life. This second phase of therapy often begins with a natural progression from the question of the first stage, "Who am I?" to the question of the next stage: "Where am I to go?" As clients begin to awaken from the survival trance and understand the unique context of their lives, they naturally begin to pose such questions of meaning and direction in their moment-to-moment choices, in the transformation of their personalities, in everyday relationships, and in their lives generally.

Work with this question may mean anything from deciding what to address in a particular therapy session; to uncovering one's past history of responding (or not) to one's deepest truth; to a discerning of vocation, life's calling, or dharma. One may also engage different practices that support contacting inner wisdom and guidance, such as prayer and meditation, attending to important dreams and synchronistic events, or conversing with an image of a wise person or other symbol of wisdom (Assagioli 1965; Brown 1983, 1993; Ferrucci 1982; Miller 1975; Whitmore 1991).

A particularly meaningful aspect of this stage is the client's growing awareness that Self is not only acting and available in the present, but has been an abiding presence throughout her or his entire life. The person may, for example, discover that Self had been a supportive presence even during the most painful times of abuse, failure, or loss, when abandonment and betrayal seemed the only reality. Life tragedies are not ignored or explained away in such a process, but redeemed. Here the I-Self relationship is revealed as the very backbone of one's life, an unbroken axis running through all life events like the thread in a string of pearls.

This growing conscious relationship with Self may in turn involve clearing away obstacles that prevent a full response to Self and to developing abilities needed for this response to Self—work in which one will again deal with lower and higher unconscious material. For example, one may delve into lower unconscious issues of early religious abuse, fears of dependency and domination, and negative images of the Divine. Or one may again encounter the higher unconscious, perhaps struggling with idealized and overly transcendent notions of

Divinity that place the Divine completely beyond any human contact. One may also seek to contact, develop, and express desired transpersonal qualities that are valuable in responding to Self (this also may entail working through early wounds that obstruct the expression of these qualities).

So in this stage, too, there is work with primal wounding that may lead into the lower unconscious and higher unconscious and thereby allow a further expansion of the middle unconscious, a healing of the primal split. Such an expansion of I-amness illustrates the presence of stage one of psychosynthesis therapy within stage two. Again, the stages are inseparable.

There may be moments of disidentification in this second stage also, as one senses oneself not as an isolated individual but as a part of something or someone greater. Here one may perhaps have experiences in which "the sense of individual identity is dimmed and may even seem temporarily lost" (Assagioli 1973a, 128) as a profound union with deeper Self is uncovered. Such intimate moments of surrender and union can be found in peak experiences of joy and beauty, abyss experiences of loss and pain, and in communion with the contentless, imageless transcendence of Self (the Void).

One may experience this union in the depths and heights of the inner world, or via outer relationships to other people, art, music, liturgy, literature, or nature. In such moments one learns that one's authentic self-expression flows from a connection to, a union with, deeper Self. One realizes that independence is in fact fundamentally dependent upon a higher power beyond oneself.

However, remember that Self is transcendent-immanent, distinct but not separate from any particular type of experience—even from the type of intimate unitive experience just described. Beyond any type of discrete experience, however powerful and transformative it may be, this second stage of psychosynthesis therapy is fundamentally a time in which one seeks to contact and respond to Self in the concrete specifics of one's life. There is a growing conscious commitment to living a life centered in one's deepest sense of values, meaning, and direction. Here the person is not so much looking for unitive experiences or enlightenment, but attempting to live out a lifelong spiritual marriage to Self.

This commitment may eventually need an external unifying center beyond the therapeutic and psychological, a context that can sustain the ongoing living of a transformative life. Here the therapy can support a search for a religious tradition, a spiritual group, a philosophical system, or a community that can nurture a lifelong relationship to Self.

In sum, psychosynthesis therapy functions as an empathic unifying center, facilitating the connection between the client and Self. Through the therapist acting as an external authentic unifying center, the client develops an internal authentic unifying center, both of which allow the emergence of "I" and the development of an ongoing conscious and intentional relationship with Self. Overall, the emerging I-Self relationship reinstigates the unfoldment of authentic personality, that unique potential of body and soul that was broken long ago. Keeping in mind these two overlapping stages of psychosynthesis therapy, let us look at a specific case.

A Case of Psychosynthesis Therapy: David

David was an unmarried 45-year-old man who entered therapy in order to work on his relationships with women and his dissatisfaction with his career.[3] He was a successful engineer, an acknowledged leader in his company, and was well liked by friends and coworkers. In many ways, David was what Maslow called a self-actualizer, leading a generally rich and fulfilling life. David said of his early life: "I had a pretty normal childhood. It wasn't perfect, but I don't have anything to whine about."

As it developed, David's therapy focused most strongly on his highly destructive romantic relationships with women. He had a history of failed relationships in which he would become initially enthralled with a woman, then lapse into a pattern of conflict and mutual hurt feelings, and finally endure a protracted and painful dis-integration of the relationship. After each break-up, he would be plunged into a long period of despair, isolation, and grief, from which he only very slowly recovered.

David was irritated with the "wimpish" and "needy" feelings in himself that kept him so attached to women. He felt that these needs kept him in the relationship far beyond the time it had turned destruc-tive, and then made losing the relationship a miserable drama of mourning and loss. Moreover, he felt time was running out. He was now middle-aged and still unmarried, and he wanted to find a wife and have a family. But he did not know if he could face any more painful broken relationships.

Establishing the Empathic Connection

David approached his personal problems like the problems he solved at work every day: he wanted to immerse himself in the therapy, fig-ure out his difficulty, fix it, and get on with his life. His attitude toward himself was clearly not an empathic one; he was angry and impatient with himself for not yet getting what he wanted from life. He saw him-self not as a feeling subject, but as an object to be cured, as an obsta-cle to the plans he had for his life.

His anger and impatience were also apparent in the relationship with his therapist. David became irritable and moody when the ther-apist was silent too long or seemed not to grasp fully the urgency of his situation. At these times, David felt the therapist as distant and withholding, failing to quickly cure his pain and confusion.

On the other hand, the therapist felt some inadequacy in the face of David's strong expectations, leading to a subtle resentment at this pressure and then to a tendency to become passive with him. This was her own wounding from her relationship with her father surfacing within the empathic resonance with David. Having been through her own therapy, she was familiar with this wounding and was able to work with her emerging reactions on her own time.

So yes, David was responding to something actually occurring in the relationship—the therapist *was* at times withdrawn. Early in the therapy, they had the following key interaction:

> David: It feels to me like you've gone away, like you don't care about what I am saying.
> Therapist: Let me see . . . yes, I think you're right. I spaced out just then. I'm sorry. I apologize.
> David: It's okay. At least you're honest. Thanks.
> Therapist: So how did it feel when I spaced out?
> David: I got mad.
> Therapist: Uh-huh, and how did you feel just before you got mad?
> David: I don't know. I guess I felt hurt, like you didn't give a damn, like I didn't matter.
> Therapist: Is that a familiar feeling?
> David: It sure is. That's exactly how I'd feel when my father would ignore me. I'd end up feeling worthless.

The early part of this transcript illustrates an empathic failure on the part of the therapist and then the repair of that failure. Such moments can be valuable in building trust in the relationship. Here David took a risk in saying something directly about the relationship, and received an authentic response.[4]

After dealing with the here and now empathic failure, it was possible to move towards an exploration of primal wounding—feelings of low self-worth caused by the distance of his detached, critical father. This primal wound was the source of his rage at his distancing father, at his own dependency needs, and at the therapist. This rage was markedly reduced as he worked with the wounding beneath it.

Note that the therapist did not consider David's feelings to be archaic regressive displacements or projections upon the "blank screen" of the therapist. Here were not past reactions inappropriately imposed upon present reality, but wounds in his personality that were surfacing within the therapeutic relationship. Maintaining this attitude over time, the therapist was able to establish an empathic connection to this wounded and angry layer of David's personality (several subpersonalities were encountered in this process).

The Empathic Connection Deepens

Over the course of therapy, this empathic connection to the vulnerable, wounded layer within David developed and expanded. This was a gentle and slow process, and the therapist sought to respect the inherent timing of this unfoldment. In order to maintain this respect, the therapist sometimes had to struggle with her own hopelessness and impatience, thus avoiding impulses to push him or "rescue" him as this severely wounded area slowly revealed itself. Here again the therapist needed to engage her own early wounding in order to work through these reactions and so remain an empathic presence for David. In the following session David surfaced core wounding:

> David: But I *have* to find my soul mate. If I don't . . . if I don't, I really
>   don't know what I'll do.
> Therapist: How would you feel if you never found her?
> David: It's unthinkable.
> Therapist: How would you feel?
> David: I'm not sure. Humph. That would be hard. I'd feel lost, in
>   despair. It would be like when a relationship is over, only much,
>   much worse. Like a beautiful thing has been lost forever. I
>   would feel rejected by life, forsaken by God, worthless.
> Therapist: Have you ever felt that way before?
> David: Besides in a break-up? Yes. I guess the earliest was with my
>   mother. She was okay most of the time, but there were times
>   when she was pretty vicious to me.

What eventually emerged from this level was the experience of a fundamental rejection by his mother. Although David's mother had seemed nurturing and supportive, at this deeper level David experienced her as hating him for the demands that motherhood had put on her. He felt that she saw him as an encumbrance on her, as an unwanted burden forced upon her by her husband's wishes, and as symbolizing her lost potential for a career of her own. At one point David felt hated by her even in the womb.

In exploring this level of his experience, David came to recognize why it had been so hard for him to relate to his mother in his adult life. He had always been ashamed that he did not enjoy spending time with her, that keeping up the relationship was a chore, and that he had a spontaneous gut reaction to her that said "stay away from me." This had caused a distant relationship between them over the years, causing comment from her friends about David's less-than-exemplary performance as a dutiful son. His reactions and distancing had never made sense to him until he began to see the wounding he had received from her.

As David continued to uncover this hidden experience of his mother, he felt at times as if he were an ungrateful son tarnishing her good name—feelings of survival guilt and shame. David was beginning to struggle with his survival trance and survival contract. In effect, the implicit agreement had been that if he pretended he was not rejected, he could then play the role of a good son in relationship to a good mother. This contract allowed him to stay in relationship, shielded from the nonbeing wounding of the rejection. But as he now began to see through this role, he felt as though he were going back on his word and betraying a trust, and he began to feel the underlying threat of nonbeing. However, it was only by navigating these feelings of shame and guilt that the rejection and wounding could fully emerge and be healed.

During this time it was also important that the therapist validate David's sense of his mother as a nurturing presence in his life. She had in fact been there for him in a number of ways, but at the same time, at a certain fundamental level, she was rejecting of him as a human being. So while the goodness of their relationship was affirmed, this goodness no longer was allowed to mask the other, destructive side of the relationship. It seemed too that his mother had been completely oblivious of this level of her relationship with her son and would have been genuinely shocked, hurt, and disbelieving to hear about this. At one point in the therapy David did contemplate talking to his mother about all of this, but in the end decided he did not need to do so—a choice that seemed to have no adverse effect on his healing.

The Higher and Lower Unconscious

It was this traumatic aspect of David's relationship with his mother—
a wounded thread in his I-Self connection—that had been energized
in all his romantic relationships. In these relationships the initial rap-
ture of romance promised a wonderful perfect connection with the
woman, a promise that acted as a powerful addictive enthrallment.
Underpinning this pull was the desperate push from his feelings of
rejection and worthlessness. And if the romance faltered even a bit,
the rejection and worthlessness would surface, triggering withdrawal,
rage, and stormy scenes with his partner.

Eventually the relationship fell apart under the stress of the failing idealization and the surfacing of the wounding beneath it. Here
was a major higher-lower split in David, a primal split between the
higher unconscious feminine ideal and the experience of rejection
held in the lower unconscious. (Note: this attachment to the ideal is
not the result of a failure to differentiate from a supposed early archaic
state of fusion with mother; both the idealization and the enthrallment are the result of wounding.)

However, after an important dream about a beautiful angelic
woman, David began to contact the ideal of feminine perfection that
had haunted him throughout his life, experiencing this eventually as
an inner, loving presence. This angelic woman embodied his own
inner feminine (the Jungian anima) which in time he learned did not
need to be sought only in women but could be present to him directly.
As he developed an ongoing relationship with her, he found himself
increasingly immune to the pulls of highly charged romantic affairs
and much better able to see women in a clear light. He had begun to
integrate his feminine side, a part of his relationship to Self that his
mother had been unable to embody for him. The failed empathic connection with his mother had caused the feminine to be repressed in
the higher unconscious, forming an aspect of his positive unifying center and acting as an enthralling lure in his relationships with women.[5]

Hand in hand with this expansion into the higher unconscious,
the feelings of rejection, worthlessness, and emptiness from the pri-

mal wounding strongly surfaced once again. At this point David, no longer cynically critical of his vulnerability, was able to reach empathically to these aspects of himself. He was able to hold them, to be with them in a way that began to allow them to transform. He was also able to look honestly at all the things he had lost because of his early trauma, and to grieve these losses. David's compassion for these wounded aspects of himself was a complementary expansion into the lower unconscious, a bringing of light and warmth to the parts of him isolated there.

David's own empathic presence, supported by the therapist and the inner feminine, was now providing the empathic connection he had been seeking his entire life. During one session, in imagery, David held the wounded parts of himself while he in turn was held by the loving feminine presence—a beautiful image of healing between the higher unconscious and lower unconscious, a healing of the primal split. Empathy was beginning to flow in him, allowing a connection among many long lost, split-off aspects of himself.

Self-Empathy

Many different techniques were employed over the course of David's therapy: dream work, guided imagery, cognitive-behavioral techniques, abreaction, didactic discussion, the surfacing of memories, and focusing on here and now awareness. But more than anything else, the therapist's respectful empathy toward all aspects of David's experience allowed things to move forward.

The therapist acted as an external empathic unifying center that mirrored David's own potential to form an internal empathic unifying center. Feeling this empathic holding environment both within and without, David was able to adopt an empathic attitude toward the different parts of himself, toward the many deeper layers of his personality.

Adopting this stance of self-empathy, he became aware of the deeper experiential foundation of his daily functioning. He began to recognize and acknowledge the wounding he had suffered within his family, and so began to awake from the thrall of his survival trance and to understand what had been controlling him his whole life. When he was at work, with family and friends, or with women, David now was aware of his fear and isolation, his yearning for a perfect union, his tendency to idealize women, and his rage—all of which could now be transformed in the light of consciousness instead of operating unconsciously.

At one point David said it was as if he had been living his whole life in a house with no lights, bumping time and again into walls and furniture he could not see; and now he was beginning to see the walls and furniture and so was not hurting himself anymore. In terms of the ring model of the personality, David's self-empathy was allowing an awareness of the inner rings of his personality, the broader context of his present life experience.

This self-empathy was facilitated tremendously by building relationships with his inner wounded children. Here he consciously developed an ongoing empathic relationship with these young, wounded layers of his personality. He truly broke through his old habit of treating himself as an object to be fixed and was able to relate to these vulnerable and sensitive aspects of himself as living, feeling, subjects. These vulnerable subpersonalities became not problems to be fixed, not parts to be integrated, but Thou's with whom to live his life.

The Emergence of "I"

Initially this burgeoning awareness of his experiential world was disconcerting to David. He had, after all, begun therapy with a relatively stable and calm existence disrupted only by periodic tumultuous relationships with women. Did this awareness of his early wounding mean he was regressing? No indeed. He was disidentifying from a chronic survival mode of functioning, contacting the deeper layers of himself, and beginning to transform aspects of his survival personality. As he was more able to engage these wounded layers in his daily living, he could see the inner and outer behaviors these triggered, could gradually address the feelings, and could make choices relatively uncontrolled by these conditioning layers—the blossoming of personal will. In short, David was experiencing the emergence of "I."

David's gradual disidentification from survival personality and the emergence of "I" did not then immediately bring a feeling of centeredness and calm, as is sometimes supposed of disidentification. Quite the contrary, David's old sense of secure identity was disrupted as he began to experience the truth of his life. "I" is transcendent-immanent of particular contents and structures of consciousness, so the emergence of "I" does not lead necessarily to any particular state of consciousness at all, but simply to an expanded experience of oneself and world.

And the more fully David felt and understood these strata underlying his present life experience, the more aware he also became of his core values as expressed through his lifetime. His self-esteem rose as he realized the determination and strategies he had employed to maintain himself in the face of his wounding. Here was an increased empathic connection to his whole personal experience that, however traumatized, was yet his authentic experience. Through an acceptance of his brokenness and an appreciation of his struggle, he felt an increasing sense of integrity and authenticity—of I-amness.

The Emergence of Self

This healthy sense of personal identity was also supported early in the therapy by the emergence of an inner symbol of wisdom and guidance, a symbol of Self that David came to call the Wise One. As this inner relationship developed, it became an important connection to his spirituality. (This type of symbol for Self can often be introduced to the client by the therapist, but David's image appeared spontaneously one day while voicing his need for such a figure in his life.)

But David was at first typically cynical and mistrustful toward this inner figure. Further exploration revealed that he had had a spirituality as a child and had been in the habit of having conversations with God. Over the course of his life, this spirituality had faded along with the rest of his childhood, and he had become a confirmed atheist. Underlying this seemingly rational atheism, however, there was a disappointment in God for having let him down in life.

And as David began to realize the wounding that had been affecting his life so, he was not only disappointed with God, but furious as well. David was able eventually to vent his anger and disappointment toward the Wise One ("Where the hell were you when I needed you?"), then to share his pain and emptiness, and finally to build trust in this inner relationship. There was one poignant moment when David realized that the Wise One had indeed been walking with him and holding him through all the hard times in his life. He was not in fact ever alone, although his experience at the time had told him this was the case.

Faith's what you find when you're alone and find you're not.

—Terry Anderson, former hostage

The Wise One became another empathic relationship for David, and a bridge to what he believed to be God. He saw, too, that this guidance had been operating in his choice to enter therapy in the first place, although he had not realized this at the time. He recalled a moment of grace when, deep in his despair, it had occurred to him to ask God for help—a surrender of the need to solve his problem alone, an openness that had finally led him to seek therapy. As it developed, this relationship to the Wise One held no ecstatic spiritual experiences, and only few words of wisdom, but throughout David felt a strong, ongoing holding from this quiet inner presence.

Into the Wider World

As his therapy proceeded, David increasingly began seeking healthier social situations. This involved the ending of destructive relationships that he found to be unresponsive to his overtures for intimacy. As his empathic experience of himself continued to infuse his interpersonal relationships, he finally began to discover women who were similarly open to intimacy. For the first time in his life he began dating a woman with whom he had not become enthralled, but toward whom he felt a quietly growing respect and love. David did not even at first recognize the romantic nature of this relationship because it had none of the stormy drama he had come to associate with romantic involvement. He gradually came to believe that, for him, this type of less tumultuous intimate connection with a woman could be the only basis for a healthy committed relationship.

David's career issue also moved toward resolution over the course of his therapy. He began to notice that a particular aspect of his work, a formerly minor aspect, began to take on greater meaning for him. This work involved using his technical expertise in direct personal service to customers, and in it he could employ his growing ability to be empathic with himself and others. As he expanded this particular work role, he found it drawing on his whole being; it demanded he bring all his aptitudes and values into play, and also challenged him to learn and grow in new directions. Putting his heart into this new direction, he found work not something he was doing to survive, but something he was doing out of conviction and passion—a calling, a vocation, rather than a necessary evil in his life. His work in this field eventually became so successful that he received many accolades from his coworkers, management, and the public at large.

Also, after a series of significant dreams about Jesus, David began asking penetrating and serious questions about religion, Christianity, and the nature of God. In addition to working with this material psychologically, the therapist recognized that these issues where ultimately beyond the field of psychotherapy and suggested David look for a religious professional with whom to discuss these questions.[6] David subsequently sought out a priest whom he respected and entered spiritual direction with him. Here he worked on his childhood negative unifying center representation of God as a persecuting judge, which he discovered had been conditioned by the rigidity of his parochial school and by repressive religious beliefs. In other words, he discovered he was a victim of religious abuse and could now begin healing in this area. David eventually took up a meditation practice and found a community of like-minded people to support this.

We can see here David's inner development of empathic related-ness expanding to a broader network of relationships in his life. Operating both interpersonally and intrapersonally, this relatedness was working to allow the emergence of an expanded sense of "I" and of Self. And in a good example of mutual influence, his new experi-ence of himself was active in shaping these relationships, allowing him at times to change the environment around him in significant ways. His spirit had grown such that he was now responsive to, and active within, a much larger spectrum of inner and outer life experience.

In Sum

Over this course of psychosynthesis therapy, the empathic therapist entered into David's world and modeled empathic relationship. She functioned as a good enough external unifying center, using her own person to manifest the empathy of Self. In order to do this, the thera-pist had to undergo her own self-transformation, working through reactions that prevented her empathic presence to David.

This external connection allowed David to realize himself as dis-tinct but not separate from many problematic areas of his experience, and thereby to adopt an empathic attitude toward them all—the emergence of "I." This included re-owning repressed material from both the higher and lower unconscious—hidden reservoirs of joy and pain that conditioned his daily life—and so healing aspects of his pri-mal wound and primal split.

Further, he reestablished a connection with God via the positive feminine figure and the Wise One, and this led him to develop new external unifying centers in his life that could nurture this connec-tion—all indicative of the emergence of Self. The emerging I-Self connection can also be seen in his sense of vocation at work and his authenticity in interpersonal relationships. David's case demonstrates both stages of psychosynthesis therapy and thus the blossoming of authentic personality.

Of course, David's authentic personality—his true path through life—had been marked by trauma. Therefore, authenticity for him meant knowing and accepting his wounding as an important part of who he was. Again, authentic personality is not unwounded personality; it is the expression of one's core, true I-amness through time. David demonstrated that transforming survival personality and accepting the truth of one's life, however painful, can lead to a flowering of authenticity. The true acceptance that one is a victim does not lead to a passive and downtrodden "victim stance," but to fulfilling and resilient growth.

Central to this entire process was the therapist's ability to remain an empathic presence, one who could mirror not only "I" but the I-Self relationship, allowing David to develop his own inner unifying center. Let us turn now to a discussion of this crucial factor in psychosynthesis therapy, the psychosynthesis therapist.

10

The Psychosynthesis Therapist

Everyone seemed so accustomed to estimating therapeutic efficiency
in terms of applying a certain method, performing a certain
activity, that the term "just being with the patient"
was practically unthinkable.
—Helmuth Kaiser

As is clear from the last chapter, psychosynthesis therapists need to be able to connect empathically with people engaging many different levels of human experience during their path of Self-realization—from the depths of nonbeing wounding and childhood trauma to a struggle with the survival trance, addictions, and survival personality; to the peaks of spiritual and unitive experience; to the unfoldment of authentic personality and a discernment of vocation. Such therapists will of course be trained in personality theory, developmental psychology, professional ethics, abnormal psychology, spiritual traditions and practice, altered states of consciousness, and clinical technique. But more importantly, they must themselves be developing authentic personality; they must be growing in (1) their own self-empathy with the many sectors of their own personalities and in (2) their own conscious connection and response to Self.

Only this development of authentic personality can provide the therapist with the empathic wherewithal necessary to function as a good enough unifying center within psychosynthesis therapy. This development allows the therapist to connect empathically with the client no matter where the client needs to go, mirroring and facilitating the I-Self relationship over the widest possible range of experience. When such an external unifying center is provided, the client can develop an internal unifying center that, though growing and changing over the years, can support the I-Self connection indefinitely.

Most essentially, the empathic relationship between therapist and client is fundamental to psychosynthesis therapy because this is a manifestation of the empathic connection

For where two or three are gathered in my name, I am there among them.

—Matthew 18:20

with Self, which is the Ground of Being for both therapist and client and, in the end, the only healer and guide present. So the sine qua non of psychosynthesis therapy is the psychosynthesis therapist, and the sine qua non of the psychosynthesis therapist is the ability to form a deep ongoing empathic connection throughout the vast range of human experience. The following discussion of the psychosynthesis therapist will thus revolve around the empathic connection, the healing power of this connection, and the obstacles to forming this connection.

The Empathic Connection

We have seen that the personality splits into the higher and lower unconscious under the threat of nonbeing. And this threat of nonbeing arises from a disturbance in the empathic mirroring connection of true self and holding environment (Winnicott), self and selfobject (Kohut), ego and object (object relations), ego and archetype (analytical psychology), or personality and unifying center (psychosynthesis)—all of which are reflective of the I-Self relationship. From this, it seems clear that a primary task of therapy is to offer the client a new empathic unifying center that can serve to facilitate a new sense of personal self, a sense of self that can engage nonbeing wounding and thereby become free of the polarity of higher and lower unconscious.

Empathy

Winnicott states that therapy is precisely such a mirroring of the client, the same process in which the infant discovers a sense of self by seeing that self reflected within the maternal relationship: "This glimpse of the baby's and child's seeing the self in the mother's face, and afterwards in a mirror, gives a way of looking at analysis and at the psychotherapeutic task. Psychotherapy is not making clever and apt interpretations [nor the application of any other technique]; by and large it is a long-term giving the patient back what the patient brings. It is a complex derivative of the face that reflects what is there to be seen" (Winnicott 1988b, 137). The good enough therapist, as Winnicott's good enough mother, will allow the other person in the relationship to experience this: "When I look I am seen, so I exist." Such mirroring implies an empathic connection to the client, one in which the therapist attempts to sense the client's experience from the inside—a manifestation of the empathy of deeper Self.

According to Kohut, empathy is vicarious introspection, a method of inquiring into the subjective experience of another, seeking to see things from the experiential point of view of the other. He goes so far as to say that empathy does not necessarily imply love or compassion (Kohut 1985, 222). For Kohut, empathy is simply a method of understanding others from within their own perspective and, indeed, empathy can be used for good or ill. In our usage, however, empathy implies a *benevolent* vicarious introspection, because it is founded ultimately in the mutual Ground of Being that is supraordinate to both client and therapist—Self. Thus empathy in this latter sense includes what Carl Rogers called the "acceptance, or caring, or prizing" of the client, or "unconditional positive regard" (Rogers 1980, 116).

Assagioli (1973a) approaches the issue of empathy via the distinction made by William James between "knowledge about," or knowing facts about someone, and "acquaintance with," meaning empathic understanding. Assagioli states that "acquaintance with" is necessary for understanding the unique individual, and quotes Gordon Allport's description of this: "To be truly acquainted with a person means to be able to take his point of view, to think within his frame of reference, to reason from his premises. Acquaintance leads us to realize that the existence of the other [is] rationally consistent from his standpoint, however disjointed it may appear to be from ours" (Assagioli 1973a, 259).

For Assagioli, such an intimate connection is not fundamentally a function of having particular positive feelings or thoughts about the other. It is, rather, a choice, a manifestation of what he calls good will: "[Empathy] can be achieved by actively arousing, or letting oneself be pervaded by, an absorbing human interest in the person one *wills to understand.* It means approaching him or her with sympathy, with respect, even with wonder, as a 'Thou' and thus establishing a deeper inner relationship" (p. 89). Empathy is then perhaps most centrally an act of will that, as we shall see shortly, begins with the will to transform oneself in order to function as an empathic other. Empathy does not imply a feeling of love or affection, but rather a connection distinct but not separate from particular feelings and thoughts, a transcendent-immanent connection. For example, empathy is quite different from any sort of gushing, idealistic validation of the other, and from a passive "everything is okay" stance (both of which are manifestations of the positive unifying center). Empathy is an attitude that may be expressed in disagreement as well as accord, in receptivity as well as action.

Empathy also can be distinguished from intuitive or psychic impressions of the other. That is, one may sense intuitively that another person is feeling fear and anger, but this is not yet empathy as understood here. Empathy allows not simply insight into the inner world of the other, but into the person's relationship to the inner world, into the precise stance of "I" vis-à-vis the inner world. For example, one will not only sense the other's fear and anger, but sense that the person is identified with the fear and unconscious of the anger. One thus will be able to respect this identification—the person's subjective perspective—and not increase the fear by disregarding it to move directly toward the anger. Empathy is not simply information, but a function of a connection between "I" and "I," between "I" and Thou, founded in Self.[1]

Finally, remembering the principles of I-Self relationship, we know that empathic relationship does not involve a fusion of self and other, but a communion that preserves boundaries. Ergo, empathy does not involve an identification with the client such that the therapist's own point of view is obscured. Empathic connection is not identification, enmeshment, or any other blurring of the self-other distinction. Empathy implies relationship, and relationship is impossible without what Gestalt therapists call the *contact boundary*, a healthy boundary that allows the participants to interact as distinct individuals. There is in empathy a mysterious synthesis of "I" and "We," of individuality and unity—a reflection of the underlying I-Self union. But how exactly then does empathy facilitate the therapeutic process?

Empathic Resonance

As an empathic connection forms between two people, a resonance develops between the two personalities. Such an empathic resonance is fundamental to any intimate relationship, a fact we recognize by saying we are in tune or on the same wavelength with another person. Empathic resonance is quite like the principle in physics known as sympathetic resonance.[2]

Sympathetic resonance is illustrated when one sounds a tone loudly near a silent piano, thereby causing that same tone to sound from the corresponding string within the piano. Vibration at one frequency will evoke that same frequency from the other, causing the other to resonate in simpatico, *en rapport*.

Furthermore, an intimate empathic relationship will develop a resonance with many, if not all, of the different ages within the person. In Kohut's words, "when the adult experiences the self-sustaining effects of a maturely chosen selfobject, the selfobject experiences of all the preceding stages of his life reverberate unconsciously" (Kohut 1984, 49–50). In such an empathic reverberation all the many psychological ages within us may be called into play. Using the ring model of the person, empathic resonance between two intimates might be diagrammed as in figure 10.1.

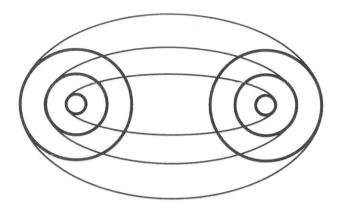

Empathic resonance

Fig. 10.1

This diagram illustrates two people who are experiencing a resonance among the many layers of themselves (infant, child, adolescent,
adult, etc.). This is deep intimacy, a connection among all the many
inner levels or ages (the word intimacy comes from a root word meaning "within"). This type of conscious empathic resonance would
mean, for example, that the two people would be able to play with
each other in childlike ways, or to be a child in relationship to the
adult of the other, or for them both to go off together seeking adventure like two adolescents, or for them to be adults together sharing
adult responsibilities. In other words, all the many levels are brought
to the relationship, making for an infinitely rich and ever-new relationship.

An intimate relationship will find all the personality layers from
the different ages of life taking part in this empathic field between the
two people. All intimate relationships exhibit such a multifaceted and
transgenerational character, because they engage these many depths
of the personality. At a minimum, each is open to all the levels in the
other. In our terms, such intimacy is a meeting of two authentic personalities.

Empathic resonance ultimately derives, of course, from the shared source and Ground of Being, Self. "Such empathy is made possible by the fact of the essential unity of human nature existing beneath, and in spite of, all individual and group diversities"(Assagioli 1973a, 89).

What Empathy Does

Therefore, when empathic intimacy is offered in therapy, the wounded layers within the personality will become energized and active—thereby illuminating the trauma of broken empathic connections that exist in the present and have roots in the past. The therapeutic connection amounts to a new energetic flow in the intimate I-Self relationship, a flow that will reveal the breaks in that relationship. To use a very rough analogy, establishing an empathic connection is like running water in a pipeline that will find the breaks in the line.

For example, think of the client who exhibits strong irritation at the most subtle inaccuracies in the therapist's understanding of his or her words or process. The client feels overt or covert rage at not being heard precisely, at not being mirrored accurately—revealing a relational wounding in an earlier level of the personality. Or think of the client who continually questions the shape and direction of the therapy, wanting reassurance about the holding environment every step of the way—here is distrust of being held, a broken trust in relationship perhaps at the level of infancy. Finally, consider the client who expects the therapist to provide a magical cure. Here the therapist feels the pressure of a desperate plea to "save me" or "fix me," fueled by underlying pain and rage—the client is looking for the empathic other who never came, a wound from another early level of the personality.

Such reactions derive from experienced disruptions in the I-Self connection at various ages. And these patterns will become active as the whole, empathic, therapeutic relationship grows. To put it another way, as the new unifying center encourages a new continuity of being, any *discontinuities* in being will be energized and revealed.

This heating up of broken patterns of relationship by empathic resonance is not limited to therapy, but can be observed in any ongoing, intensely intimate relationship such as marriage, a close friendship, or an intentional community. For example, one may be surprised and shocked to find one's new spouse suddenly turn cold and unreceptive sexually, as the feelings from past sexual abuse emerge within the relationship. Or one's friend may suddenly become mysteriously quiet and moody, having heard the slightly critical tone in your well-intentioned comments. Or the committed spiritual group may find itself awash in the emerging childhood hopelessness and rage of its members.

But such emergence of relational wounds—of wounds ultimately in the I-Self connection—is a natural outcome of any intensification in intimacy. The "breaks in the water line" are being revealed by the increased "flow." It is then understandable why people often resist intimacy, empathy, and connection—these energize past moments in which connections were nonexistent, broken, or betrayed: "If I let in your love, I will realize how much I have not been loved in my life; it is almost better not to let your love in." Empathy energizes the primal split, revealing the primal nonbeing wounds. The acceptance of, and working with, such reactions in clients is an essential task of the psychosynthesis therapist.

At this level, the level of the I-Self relationship, the therapeutic endeavor is not concerned with technique or content, but is essentially an exercise in connection. The task of the client is to negotiate the wounded strands of connection as they emerge in relationship. The task of the therapist is to maintain an empathic stance and continually process her or his own wounded strands of connection as they emerge in relationship. These two tasks take place in what are traditionally called the client's *transference* and the therapist's *countertransference*. These are the twin poles by which problematic twists in the I-Self relationship are revealed and healed in psychotherapy. Let us examine transference and countertransference in turn. (Remember that this level of work does not eliminate the need for therapeutic techniques, but provides the deeper context for these.)

TRANSFERENCE

We might be well advised to leave behind the older notions of trans-ference, and adopt the clear definition given by psychoanalyst and professor of psychiatry, Karen J. Maroda: "For this discussion, transfer-ence is defined as the conscious and unconscious responses—both affective and cognitive—of the patient to the therapist" (Maroda 1991, 66). In these terms, transference is not simply the supposed dis-torting projection of past issues onto the present, nor a supposed regression to archaic or infantile responses. Rather, transference is the expression of the many different layers of the client's personality as they are surfaced by an intimate empathic relationship (cf. the ring model of the personality).

Any deep empathic relationship will draw upon many, if not all, of the different ages comprising the personality. Such an ongoing rela-tionship will find the personality layers of infancy, childhood, adoles-cence, and adulthood all in some way taking part in the empathic field between the two people (this does not mean every layer is actually expressed in the relationship). All intimate relationships exhibit such a multifaceted and transgenerational character because they engage these many depths of the personality.

And as these various ages are accepted and included, so will the woundings to these ages. This also is to be expected, but it does not mean that an intimate relationship is a regressive movement back in time. It is instead a deeper awareness of the present, a full experience of the many layers of the personality that exist now. Early wounding emerging within the transference is therefore not the opposite of gen-uine relationship, but the opposite of *superficial* relationship. Psychotherapy is simply a particular type of intimate relationship in which one may focus upon healing these wounds as they reveal them-selves.

As Kohut (1984) points out, transference is not simply a function of the past, but has a basis in the here and now reality of the thera-peutic relationship. For example, the client who is so sensitive about being misunderstood *is* in fact being misunderstood at some level. And it is nonempathic to sidestep culpability here, claiming the client is simply projecting the infantile past and is therefore overly sensitive or is misperceiving reality. When this type of interpretation is made, the therapist takes on an authoritarian role vis-à-vis the client. The therapist, and the therapist alone, presumes to possess the objective truth about the relationship—clearly a nonempathic stance.

However, empathic response demands that therapists understand their client's experience, which means therapists must understand their empathic failures vis-à-vis their clients and take responsibility for these failures (as did David's therapist in the previous chapter). Whether or not therapists are aware of something in them that is triggering the client's reaction, it is important to acknowledge the client's experience and to acknowledge the possibility that something the therapist said or did may have triggered the reaction. Therapists must honestly scan their own experience for the source of the client transference reactions, however small and insignificant this source may seem.

As self psychology tells us, the processing of empathic failures between client and therapist is a major way of healing. An example of this is a client in group therapy who uncovered a tremendous amount of childhood pain in an experiential group exercise. He reacted with anger toward the therapist leading the group because he felt not sufficiently warned by her that the exercise might bring up such material. The challenge for the therapist was to avoid becoming defensive and instead to maintain authentic empathy: "Yes, I didn't explain the exercise fully enough for you, and could have. I apologize. I see you are angry about it." To deny the empathic failure is to deny the experience of the client, and to deny the client's experience would have prevented repair to the broken relationship.

Neither did the therapist attempt to avoid the issue by interpreting the client's reaction as anger toward the childhood abusers, nor even by leading the client into an exploration of his feelings. Both interventions would have been motivated by the therapist's avoidance of her own authentic guilt. There was instead a simple, honest acknowledgment of the empathic failure. By maintaining an empathic stance, she was able to remain available to the client as he struggled with the break in connection. Held by such acceptance, the client was gradually able to see for himself that the anger about the exercise was mixed with anger about the past abuse that he had just uncovered (although there still remained some amount of anger belonging to the current event). A problematic strand in the I-Self relationship had been surfaced successfully and could now became a part of the client's ongoing healing.

If this group leader had lost her empathic stance and become caught in an attempt to defend her exercise, she and the client would have entered an impasse. The therapist's reality would have been at war with the client's reality. But if psychological healing constitutes healing in the empathic connection, neither will take place if the client merely yields to the therapist's supposedly superior, objective, and more mature view of reality. This merely creates a "pseudoalliance based on the patient's compliant identification with the analyst's point of view in order to safeguard the therapeutic relationship" (Stolorow, Brandchaft, and Atwood 1987, 11).

In other words, the client would in this impasse either have to (a) give up his experience in order to form survival personality, a false-self pseudoalliance or (b) leave the relationship. These are precisely the options given a child in a nonempathic early environment. Choosing the first alternative means that the client's survival personality has been incorporated seamlessly into the therapeutic relationship, and thus will most likely never be addressed within the therapy. Indeed, one can proceed for a very long time in therapy, uncovering deeply unconscious material and yet still have the therapy guided by this ultimate context of inauthenticity. Choosing the second alternative involves finding a new therapeutic milieu, one that can connect empathically with the wounds of broken connections made by empathic failures, however covert and inadvertent.

But good enough therapy avoids both of these outcomes, offering a third alternative to the dilemma. Such therapy negotiates a new relationship that fully acknowledges the empathic failure and thus can bridge to the person experiencing disconnection. The I-Self rela-

tionship begins to be healed by including even the breaks in that connection—a new sense of being is derived from confronting and overcoming nonbeing. This is the essence of working with the
transference.

And does an empathic stance then imply that the therapist is to
become passively responsive to anything the client wants? Of course
not. Remember, empathic connection is not to be confused with an
identification or merging with the other; it does not imply a passive
giving up of individuality by the therapist, nor an idealizing gush of
positive feelings. Recall Winnicott's analogy of therapy as a holding
environment—the empathic relationship with the caregiver conditions all aspects of infant care and, ipso facto, must include active
interventions and self assertion on the part of the caregiver.

We know of no method of parenting that does not include—with
no necessary loss of empathic connection—actions such as parental
initiative, confrontation, and limit-setting. This is not to say that
therapy is to be cast in a parent-child mode, but simply that relationship is informed by mutual influence and will be limited by passivity
on the part of either party. As Stolorow, Brandchaft, and Atwood
(1987) point out, both client and therapist function as selfobjects for
each other at different times. In our terms, both parties function as
external unifying centers at different times. In fact, passive compliance is not empathic connection at all, but a *lack* of connection.

COUNTERTRANSFERENCE

From the above group therapy example, it is clear how central the
therapist's experience is to the therapeutic situation. Just as the
client's vulnerabilities emerge in the newly energized I-Self relationship, so too do those of the therapist. So let us now consider the matter of countertransference. Again, we can turn to Maroda for our
definition: "In parallel fashion [to transference], the countertransference is defined as the conscious and unconscious responses of the therapist to the patient" (Maroda 1991, 66). Or here is Michael Kahn in
his excellent text used by graduate psychology students: "We will

adopt what is now, I believe, the most common usage and consider countertransference to include all feelings and attitudes about the client that occur in the therapist" (Kahn 1991, 118).

Countertransference is simply the therapist's aspect of the empathic field vis-à-vis the client and, as with the client, can include responses from any and all layers of the entire personality. Again, this is simply the nature of an intimate relationship. Countertransference is not the opposite of a genuine relationship—*all* of the therapist's responses are a part of the genuine relationship. Problems can arise, however, when the therapist's own emerging wounds begin to control the relationship unconsciously.

Emerging Wounds

Consider the situation in which a client begins to see through survival personality to encounter a lifelong feeling of eternal despair and grief, a sector of the lower unconscious. Here perhaps is the experience of the abused child who, with a limited sense of chronological time, feels the abuse is endless.

Such a profound despair may trigger the therapist's own childhood feelings of despair—the therapist's lower unconscious—in what psychiatrist Judith Herman has called *traumatic countertransference*, meaning that "hearing the patient's trauma story is bound to revive any personal traumatic experience that the therapist may have suffered in the past" (Herman 1992, 140). This plunges the therapist towards the negative personality position, his or her own abused inner child.

And these emerging feelings then may challenge inwardly the therapist's own survival trance, because to acknowledge the feelings means the end of the therapist's beliefs: "I had mostly a happy childhood, and am mostly okay" or "I've done my own personal work already; I'm done with that." The threat posed by the surfacing feelings may in turn motivate an attempt by the therapist to make the client feel better, to alter the client's experience. "After all," the therapist rationalizes inwardly, "this despair can't *really* be endless; it's not *that* bad."

But interventions motivated by such sentiments minimize the client's experience, and so break the empathic connection, retraumatizing the client and derailing the therapy. Here, in response to an emergence of the client's negative personality position, the therapist is drawn into the positive unifying center position—"Just listen to me. I know. It's not as bad as you think"—in an attempt to drag the client into the positive personality position, i.e., to feel better (this may work, but only for a while).

Or perhaps the abject helplessness emerging in the client throws the therapist into her or his own helplessness, threatening even the therapist's professional self-confidence. Here is Herman again:

> The therapist also empathically shares the patient's experience of helplessness. This may lead the therapist to underestimate the value of her own knowledge and skill or to lose sight of the patient's strengths and resources. Under the sway of countertransference helplessness, the therapist may also lose confidence in the power of the psychotherapy relationship. It is not uncommon for experienced therapists to feel suddenly incompetent and hopeless in the face of a traumatized patient. (P. 141)

As Herman points out further, since the therapist does not trust the patient's process of healing or the healing power of psychotherapy, he or she may revert to rescuing behavior. Therapists may thus take on the role of savior, disempowering clients and violating the boundaries of the therapy. Ultimately this can lead the therapist into "a stance of grandiose specialness or omnipotence" (p. 143), an inflated sense of self from which one may feel free to break the rules and operate outside therapeutic boundaries.

In psychosynthesis terms, this is the therapist becoming identified with structures conditioned by the positive personality and positive unifying center, an identification that avoids the helplessness and despair of the negative personality. In the worse cases the therapist draws the client into a joint acting-out, as in sexual relations, romantic involvement, or a sham guru-devotee relationship. Here, both therapist and client are caught up in the momentary security of higher unconscious identifications, enjoying an unethical and ill-fated flight from the primal wounds of nonbeing.

The Negative Unifying Center

In other cases of countertransference, the therapist may not be dominated by the positive unifying center but by the negative unifying center. As Herman writes, "She [the therapist] comes to identify not only with the feelings of the victim but also with those of the perpetrator" (p. 144). Here perhaps a response of rage in the therapist manifests as a judgmental attitude toward emerging vulnerability in the client—the therapist comes under the sway of the negative unifying center. The therapist may become critical of supposed whining from the client, begin hating the client and minimizing the client's pain, make the client feel guilty for not appreciating all the good things in his or her life, or perhaps adopt a coldly impassive stance that tells the client covertly, "You are weak to feel this way." Terms such as *archaic*, *primitive*, and *infantile* are ready-made to support this nonempathic stance vis-à-vis the client.

This type of countertransference too may become sexualized and, in Herman's words, involve "voyeuristic excitement, fascination, and even sexual arousal" (p. 145) on the part of the therapist. In confronting these types of countertransference, one must be able to acknowledge one's own personal potential for evil—a sometimes daunting challenge for the therapist attached to a self-image as a compassionate and dedicated healer.

On the other hand, the therapist uncomfortable with the power and grandeur of the higher unconscious may become dominated by the negative unifying center as a client begins to have transpersonal experiences. Faced with the heights of ecstatic or unitive experience, the therapist may be thrust toward his or her own early wounding related to these types of experience. Here the criticism and rage of the therapist's negative unifying center may arise to defend against those wounds and so block any empathic response to the client. The therapist may, for example, frame the client's profound experience as a wish-fulfilling fantasy, as a regression to the infantile "oceanic feeling," or even as psychotic process. In any case, the joy, wisdom, and beauty of the glimpsed transpersonal potential will certainly not be mirrored, and the client will find no help in integrating these higher states of consciousness.

Misuse of Techniques

Faced with their own emerging primal wounds, therapists may employ any technique to change the client's experience: interpretation, hypnosis, guided imagery, free drawing, catharsis, affirmation, pedagogy, even going deeper into the feeling—anything will do. Both client and therapist are hereby saved from the emerging material as they become engrossed in technique. The use of techniques in this way can evolve into an actual technique-driven therapy that prevents nonbeing material from emerging at all. In such therapy, the client begins to look to the therapist's clever use of the latest psychotherapeutic technology to attain salvation, and the therapist, wanting to appear as a technically proficient professional, cooperates by employing powerful techniques to surface memories, abreact feelings, and change behavior.

However, what is not developing in this hypertechnological orientation is an authentic, intimate, empathic relationship from which can emerge the relational wounds of nonbeing. Techniques are here a means by which both therapist and client avoid relating to each other, and in effect treat therapy and themselves as objects—precisely the behavior that created the wounding in the first place. Psychological work here becomes simply an aspect of survival personality, operating upon this covert assumption: "If we just keep using these techniques, the threatening feelings will finally go away." This endless and futile process can be seen in Winnicott's (1987) description of interminable analysis caused by working with an unrecognized false self.

But any intervention motivated by the avoidance of primal wounds that are emerging in the client—whether the intervention appears therapeutic or not—will break the empathic bond. The therapist no longer is connected to the existential reality of the client but is unconsciously attempting to direct the client away from an experience that is threatening for the therapist.

Traumatic Resonance

These transference-countertransference dynamics can be pictured by employing the ring model of the personality (see figure 10.2). It is as if activity within the client's inner strata is causing a resonance in the therapist's inner strata. The client's traumatic despair energizes the therapist's traumatic despair; energy passes from the client to the therapist, making the therapist feel her or his own nonbeing feelings.

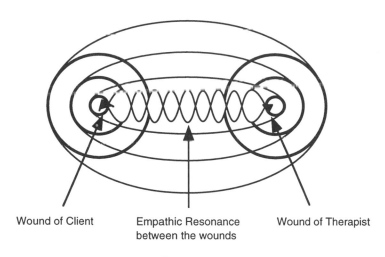

Wound of Client   Empathic Resonance   Wound of Therapist
                       between the wounds

Fig. 10.2

The therapist in this situation who has not come to terms with the particular wounding emerging in the empathic field will find this resonance highly disturbing. This emergence of the therapist's wounding may lead in turn to the type of avoidance strategies listed earlier, including a focus on technique, changing the subject, inwardly spacing out, or even sending a message with subtle body language. In an infinite number of ways the therapist can invalidate, and so avoid, the client's experience. By so doing, the resonance will be broken, allowing both client and therapist to move away from the experienced threat of nonbeing. Again, any intervention will do. Sometimes merely remaining silent will do the trick.

And this nonempathic intervention (or silent nonintervention) will break the mirroring connection because the client looks in the mirror and sees not a reflection of self, but a demand or enticement to become something for the therapist. This constitutes a retraumatization of the client—"When I look I am not seen, so I do not exist." Then, in reaction to that threat of nonbeing from the therapist, the client is led to become something for the therapist, to further develop survival personality. In this way nonempathic interventions—however brilliant, powerful, and even mood-altering for the client—simply continue to support the primal split.[3]

Countertransference then is not simply a function of projection—the client's issue has not been projected onto the "blank screen" of the therapist. Rather, the client's issue has evoked an issue in the therapist. This is not projection, but evocation. It is not that something foreign has entered into the therapist from the outside (except perhaps the subjective impact of the client's process), but that the therapist's *own* hidden wounds and survival mechanisms are being revealed by the empathic resonance.

Thus the major job for therapists here—far more important than any technique, theory, or intervention—is to recognize and deal with the aspects of themselves that are revealed in the countertransference. Therapy for the client cannot be separated from therapy for the therapist; both have to tread their own paths over the course of the work. As Walsh and Vaughan write of the transpersonal therapist, "Indeed, working with one's own consciousness becomes a primary responsibility, for the growth of one participant is seen as facilitating that of the other" (Walsh and Vaughan 1980b, 20).

Given the nature of countertransference outlined above, it seems axiomatic that good enough therapists need ongoing work with their own lower and higher unconscious so they might sustain consciousness of the primal split in themselves. Therapists do well to remain in therapy or spiritual direction, find supervisory contexts, and join support groups that allow them to process their emerging material in an ongoing way.

THE DEVELOPMENT OF THE PSYCHOSYNTHESIS THERAPIST

The prime tasks of a psychosynthesis therapist, then, are (1) consciously developing a relationship to Self in an ongoing way, engaging one's own path of Self-realization, and (2) developing an increasing empathic connection with all the sectors of one's own personality, undertaking a continuous psychosynthesis of the ages. In other words, a good enough therapist is developing good enough authentic personality.

This does not mean, of course, that the therapist need work completely through all primal wounding, nor have awareness of the personality as a whole, nor be living a perfect Self-realization (whatever that might be). Rather, the therapist must have engaged these two areas with integrity, explored them at some depth, and have some sort of lifestyle and practice that supports working with them in a continual manner.

Unless there is such an ongoing cultivation of authentic personality, the therapist will ever remain an ineffective mirror. The rejected areas of experience will constitute blind spots in the ability to function as an empathic unifying center that can facilitate the I-Self relationship at all levels. One cannot form an empathic connection to the many levels of another unless one has established an empathic connection to those levels in oneself.

Note this does not mean one must have had the exact same depth or content of experience as the client. Drawing upon the model of empathic resonance above, one might say that the therapist must be open to the same wavelength or tone set by the client's experience. For example, to be with someone in their despair, joy, or unitive experience entails an openness to one's own personal experiences of despair, joy, and unitive experience. Similarly, to be with someone's struggle with Self-realization—with direction, vocation, or dharma—demands an openness to one's own personal experience of Self-realization.

This openness to all levels of experience allows the therapist to form an empathic resonance with the client, even though the specific content and intensity of the client's experience may be dissimilar. In other words, the therapist must be willing to go to the same "depth," "altitude," or "frequency" as the client.[4]

Barriers to Empathy

As trainers and supervisors, we have seen psychotherapy students struggle valiantly with many inner barriers to empathic connection and resonance. Perhaps a major one of these barriers is the resistance to accepting and allowing the client's early primal wounding to reveal fully its reality. Here therapists may be challenged, for example, to accept a world in which intentional methodical evil was done to a helpless child, without softening this reality in any way; or to allow the unmitigated hatred of a wounded inner child toward the care-givers, without rushing to forgiveness; or to accept that a pleasant-looking childhood (like the therapist's own, perhaps) was rife with neglect and abuse, without deflecting the client's dawning recognition of this.

Empathy with early nonbeing wounding also demands forgoing the adult perspective in which one sides with those adults responsible for the wounding (for simplicity of discussion, we shall refer to these adults as the caregivers). For example, interventions that heavily stress the caregivers' difficulties in their own lives or overemphasize the caregivers' essential goodness have no place in an empathic connection to trauma suffered at the hands of the caregivers. Here is that strong advocate of the inner and outer child, Alice Miller: "If we permit him [the patient] instead to see in us an advocate, whose concern is not to defend and protect the father [and mother] but to stand by the patient, then our imagination and empathy will help him experience his early feelings of abandonment, loneliness, anxiety, powerlessness, and rage without having to protect his parents from them, because with our aid he will realize that feelings do not kill" (Miller 1984b, 171).

The childhood levels within the adult do not include an adult understanding of the caregivers' plight, nor should they be forced to do so. The client should instead be allowed the rightful pain and outrage of a dependent, small person who has been betrayed. This has nothing to do with blaming the caregivers for all of one's difficulties in life; it is simply connecting to the experiential truth of one's childhood roots, discovering one's life story, and recontacting the direction of one's authentic personality.

The therapist also can mirror the adult aspect of the client in relation to emerging childhood wounding. However, while validating this adult perspective, the therapist yet must ask that the child be allowed the full, unhampered experience from the child's own point of view. This intervention allows the unfoldment of the child's experience, and models for the adult how to connect empathically with the child so that healing can take place.

Empathy for early wounding also entails avoiding the temptation to romanticize the wounding. It is not useful, for example, to maintain that one chose a traumatizing environment for some sort of spiritual or karmic reason. Such metaphysical notions place the blame squarely on the victim, anchoring the survival shame and guilt already produced by the wounding itself and deflecting the authentic pain and outrage of a child betrayed. This can lead to a further abandonment of the child and the development of a spiritual survival personality. Again, the point is not to blame other people but to connect empathically to the deeper layers of one's personality and so to move toward wholeness, taking responsibility for one's healing and growth.

In any case, there is no ultimate explanation for primal wounding, no technique that can completely remove it, no act of forgiveness that can totally erase it—one can never in fact live that period of life over again. While wounds can be healed, there will always be scars based upon the irreversiblity of time. There are truly losses to be grieved. At bottom, one is facing the ancient mystery of evil, a mystery left unresolved by the best minds of the ages. But what is most important here is not logic or technique, but the actual experience of the unique individual human being in that moment of personal annihilation. One does not solve the problem of human suffering so much as one enters into it. One must connect empathically with the sufferer.

Only the therapist willing to undertake an ongoing exploration of this pit of nonbeing with the client can hope to heal the break in the continuity of being. The therapist thereby forges an empathic connection, a lifeline, to the spirit buried in seeming nonexistence. This allows that sense of self to gradually reemerge, wounded but resilient. In these moments the authentic experience of the client is that of nonbeing, and this experience—in both client and therapist—must be accepted in order for a new sense of being to be born.

Furthermore, it is crucial to realize that not only has the childhood level of the personality been wounded, but so too has the client's empathic connection to these levels. There has been a disconnection from childhood experience, from one's unique life story, through splitting, repression, and other defenses. And healing this wounded self-empathy may be one of the biggest tasks faced in therapy. The emphasis may not be so much upon "healing the wounded child," because this can lead to treating the child as an object to be fixed—a nonempathic stance. Instead, the emphasis may be upon healing the broken *relationship* with the wounded child. We stop trying to change the wounded child and begin to find a place in our lives for him or her. Here we begin to relate to ourselves as a Thou, to develop self-empathy for our life path, and to respect where this path leads in the future.[5]

Through the empathic external unifying center of the therapist and the developing internal unifying center, this type of compassionate self-empathy blossoms. Here the primal wound that separates us from our heights and depths is healed, and we move toward bridging the primal split. Here we find the reactivation of authentic personality, scarred but resilient, and begin to walk our path of Self-realization in a much more conscious and intentional way.

Didactic Psychosynthesis

It now seems abundantly clear why therapists must have a good enough openness to their own personalities and an intimate, ongoing relationship with Self. Psychosynthesis therapy challenges both client and therapist alike to surface and heal the many forgotten, wounded strands in the I-Self relationship. Assagioli therefore strongly emphasizes the facilitation of one's own transformation as an integral part of any training in psychosynthesis: "Such a self-psychosynthesis should be practiced, or at least seriously attempted, by every therapist, social worker and educator (including parents). Of course, great help can be given by didactic psychosynthesis; it is therefore advisable, and I strongly recommend such a didactic training—as is done in psychoanalysis" (Assagioli 1965, 9).

Assagioli's didactic psychosynthesis is analogous to the training analysis in which prospective psychoanalysts undergo their own personal analysis. Note that he is here implying that anyone seeking to practice psychosynthesis—*in whatever field, including parenting*—should undergo a serious program of self-exploration and self-transformation within a psychosynthesis context, preferably with a trained psychosynthesis counselor or therapist. In this way practitioners cultivate an intimate empathy with themselves and others and so become facilitators of the I-Self connection within their particular field of application.

In sum, psychosynthesis therapists must not only be competent in clinical theory and method, and students of spiritual traditions and practices, but they also must be engaging their own healing and transformation. Only in this way can they hope to function as a mirroring presence throughout the broad terrain of human experience which may be traversed in Self-realization.

Healing the Human Spirit

We have in this book attempted to fill out some of the areas of psychosynthesis that Assagioli outlined in his original thinking, drawing on the work of others who have been addressing these areas in related fields. We hope this has been of use to students and professionals within the fields of psychosynthesis, transpersonal psychology, psychotherapy, and to the interested public as well.

In closing, we would like to emphasize that this rekindling of the human spirit and unfoldment of authentic personality is, of course, not only a function of the therapeutic relationship, but of all the relationships in our lives. Healing the human spirit cannot be separated from the healing of the many relationships in which we are held, such as those with:

- Family, friends, and colleagues (living and dead)
- The human family, extending back to our dim origins and forward to future generations
- Plants and animals, favorite and sacred places, and the natural environment in general
- Treasured possessions, from a bicycle, teddy bear, and blanket, to an article of clothing or a home
- The poor, homeless, and marginalized both within ourselves and in the outer world
- Conscience, beliefs, ideals, and images of the Divine
- Body, feelings, thoughts, images, and intuition
- Religious, spiritual, and self-help groups
- Those heroes and heroines—living, dead, and imaginary—with whom we feel connected
- The local, national, and global social-political communities
- The planet as a whole, living system
- Contentless and ineffable experiences of the Divine, God, Universal Spirit, Tao, etc.

All these relationships, and more, comprise the crucible of Self-realization. No relationship can be considered insignificant, and we may find life-changing issues embedded in even the most seemingly commonplace of them. The personal transformation involved in coming to right relationship within all these levels can be profound indeed, both in and out of therapy, because it is here that we meet and respond to deepest Self. It is here we find—or lose—our true sense of personal identity, meaning, and life direction.

Notes

Introduction

1. For descriptions and documentation of this epidemic of abuse and neglect, see Herman 1992, Higgins 1994, and Whitfield 1995, and for a close look at the pervasive effects of psychic trauma see Terr 1990, 1994.

2. The emergence of this wounding may also lead to a temporary rise in child abuse and neglect, addictions, and violence in general. These are understandable reactions to an increased collective sensitivity to wounding. As the wounding emerges, so too does the violent rage and desperate compulsions by which we attempt to obliterate this growing collective realization of what has happened to us.

Chapter One: An Addiction/Abuse Workshop

1. It may appear from the model of wounding presented here and elsewhere in the book that the treatment for addictions lies solely in a depth psychotherapy which would reach to the primal wounding. However, a major addiction takes on its own momentum, establishing strong patterns of thought, behavior, and biochemistry that must be addressed on their own terms before the deeper wounding can be worked through. This is often said informally as "recovering before uncovering." See, for example, Whitfield's (1991) stages leading from active addiction (Stage Zero) through the establishment of an ongoing recovery program (Stage One) through working on childhood wounding (Stage Two) to an increasing focus on spirituality (Stage Three).

2. The perspective on being throughout this book would then be an aspect of what Abraham Maslow (1962) called a "psychology of being."

Chapter Two: The Source of Human Spirit

1. The connection between this view of infancy and an insensitivity to the infant may be seen in the following quotation from a marriage and family text book:

For the most part, the neonate is blankly unemotional, although he may smile when contented, whether he is awake or asleep. There is no indication that the neonate feels affection toward anybody or anything, although such affection develops quickly in the first few months.

The neonate is also relatively insensitive to pain, but his sensitivity picks up rapidly in the first few days. *Circumcision can be performed a few days after birth with no anesthetic* and with apparently very little discomfort. (*The Individual, Marriage, and the Family,* (1968) Belmont, California: Wadsworth Publishing, p. 426, quoted in Romberg, 1985, 277, emphasis added)

2. As Joseph Chilton Pearce (1979) has observed, modern technological birth procedures traumatize the infant into a state of shock—one wonders how many indications of so-called "primary narcissism" are a result of this virtually universal early trauma.

3. Some Jungian thought emphasizes this interpersonal manifestation of self as a function of the projection of the self of the individual onto the outer reality. However, the work of Neumann (1989) and Robert Aziz (1990) supports the notion that the self (e. g., Neumann's "self-field") includes both an intrapsychic and extrapsychic function, representing a unitive reality which includes both the subjective and objective, the inner and outer.

4. Following psychosynthesis usage, we throughout the book will consider self (lowercase "s"), personal self, and "I" as equivalent terms, while Self (capital "S") will be used to indicate the Higher Self or Transpersonal Self. When addressing Jung's notion of self, we will generally follow his convention of a lowercase "s," although some Jungian authors capitalize the term.

5. Assagioli's notion of Self is also different from Jung's self in important ways. For example, Assagioli remains extremely clear that Self is distinct but not separate from the totality of the personality, while Jung at times identifies self with this totality. In a similar way, Assagioli's "I" is different from Jung's "ego." The latter is "a complex of ideas which constitutes the centre of my field of consciousness" (Jung 1971, 425), while for Assagioli "I" is a center of consciousness and will that is distinct but not separate from all psychological content such as "ideas."

6. Of course, as in any relationship, this "thou-ness" may include a state in which one is not for the moment conscious of the thou-ness, but only of intimate union. This can be seen in moments of ecstasy in which one feels united to the other beyond any distinction of I-Thou. However, one is still in an I-Thou relationship here, even though the focus of the relationship at that moment is "we" rather than "me and you." As we shall see, the I-Thou relationship with Self can include experiences of such unity, as well as experiences of the "nothingness" of personal individuality.

Chapter Three: The Human Spirit

1. We use the word *transcendence* to indicate a distinction from particular phenomena. Transcendence should not be confused with concepts such as *far away, totality, other worldly*, or *movement upwards*. The complementary term, *immanence*, implies a presence within particular phenomena. Note that *immanence* should not be confused with *eminence*, meaning *superior or important*, nor with *imminent* meaning *about to occur*. Therefore the complete term, *transcendence-immanence*, indicates both a distinction from, and a presence within, particular phenomena (see Firman 1991).

2. Although throughout this chapter we are speaking of disidentification as a somewhat simple discrete event, this can be somewhat misleading. We are here attempting to express the essence of the experience, ignoring all the complexities sometimes encountered in this process. Disidentification from a major personality pattern, for example, is often only attained through much self-exploration, psychological work, and spiritual practice.

3. This freedom of will also includes the ability to choose to identify fully with any particular mode of being as well. This is a conscious act that can be consciously undone—very different from becoming unconsciously identified with something. In the words of psychosynthesis writer Betsie Carter-Haar: "It [disidentification] gives us the freedom to choose at any moment to become fully identified with any part of ourselves—an emotion or habit pattern or subpersonality—to be involved in it and experience it deeply" (Carter-Haar 1975, 78).

4. This insubstantiality of "I" describes a phenomenological reality embedded in the world's great spiritual traditions. This insight seems consistent with the Buddhist concept/experience of "noself" (*anatman* or *anatta*). In the Jewish tradition, one thinks of the idea that to see the face of God means death (see Exodus 33:20), or in the Christian tradition, God's words to St. Catherine of Siena: "You are she who is not, and I am Who Is" (Raymond of Capua 1980, 85). Religious traditions have expressed this no-thingness of "I" in practices such as insight meditation and contemplative prayer which open us to our insubstantiality vis-à-vis Ultimate Reality, and also in offering moral principles that encourage us to live out this Reality in the practical challenges of day-to-day life.

5. Such a trichotomy, as distinguished from the dichotomous model comprising only body and soul, has ancient roots in Western thought dating back to the Hebrew Scriptures, the Stoics, and St. Paul (Ferm 1945), and has appeared in recent psychology in the work of Viktor Frankl (1967) and James Hillman (1975). Indeed, Aldous Huxley views the trichotomy as a central element in what he calls the Perennial Philosophy, which he sees as underlying all the world's great spiritual traditions: "All the exponents of the Perennial Philosophy make, in one form or another, the affirmation that man is a kind of trinity composed of body, psyche and spirit" (Huxley 1945, 38).

6. Here Stolorow and Atwood describe their two major categories of psyche-soma splitting: "(1) those reflecting an initial failure to achieve the sense of psychosomatic indwelling, a failure that leaves the person vulnerable to states of severe depersonalization and mind-body disintegration...and, (2) those reflecting active disidentification with the body in order to protect oneself from dangers and conflicts associated with continuing embodied existence" (Stolorow and Atwood 1992, 47). (Their use of the term *disidentification* differs from the usage in psychosynthesis, and would be termed *dissociation*.)

Stolorow and Atwood go on to describe less extreme forms of mind-body splitting: a sense that the mind is somehow floating outside or above the body; states in which the mind is localized in the person's head; and identification with some external, usually critical viewpoint on the self. They also elucidate psychosomatic disorders, conversion symptoms, sexual enactments, and hypochondriacal fantasies as based on a lack of psyche-soma cohesion.

7. Western psychology has implicitly recognized this transcendent-immanent nature of "I" in terms such as Freud's (1965, 52) *ego splitting*; Anna Freud's (1946) *endopsychic perception*; Richard Sterba's (1934) *therapeutic dissociation*; Assagioli's *disidentification*; and more recently Arthur Deikman's (1982) the *observing self* and the psychoanalytic usage *decentering* (Stolorow, Brandchaft, and Atwood 1987). All such understandings carry the assumption—usually unspoken—that we are not identical to any particular content or state of consciousness, but are in some way distinct from these.

8. This concept of a transcendent-immanent "I" seems quite akin to psychiatrist Gordon Globus's (1980) notion of an analytical singularity. Such a singularity is neither illusory nor does it imply some sort of supposedly "transcendent" order, but instead it represents a point at which "the ordinary rules governing the domain no longer apply." Globus's concept and the notion of the transcendent-immanent "I" have been discussed elsewhere (Firman 1991).

Chapter Four: The Development of Spirit

1. This dependence of human beings on nature has been called the *biophilia hypothesis* in the book by that name: "The biophilia hypothesis proclaims a human dependence on nature that extends far beyond the simple issues of material and physical sustenance to encompass as well the human craving for aesthetic, intellectual, cognitive, and even spiritual meaning and satisfaction" (Kellert and Wilson 1993, 20).

2. Throughout this discussion, we are speaking to the "nurture" side of the nature-and-nurture dichotomy. However, there are unifying centers that are founded more in the psyche-soma endowment than in the outer environment, e.g., inborn patterns of physical, emotional, and mental development. As did Neumann (1973)

in his concept of the *body-Self*, we posit an operation of Self throughout this more "automorphic" development as well.

3. As Piaget and Inhelder have shown, even the child's conception of objects in space is not a passive taking-in of the perceived object, but is based upon actively relating to the object in some way: "It will therefore be seen that spatial concepts are internalized actions and not merely mental images of external things or events . . . " (Piaget and Inhelder 1967, 454).

4. The term *mutual influence* comes from the work of Beebe and Lachmann (1988), and has been discussed as *mutual influence theory* by Lee and Martin (1991).

Chapter Five: The Primal Wound

1. Communications theorist Neil Postman (1994) points to a counterforce to this evolution of empathy, a force working toward the erasure of childhood once again: the violation of today's children via mass media rife with adult images of sex and violence. He sees this as a blurring of the boundary between childhood and adulthood—a good definition of child abuse.

2. While not using the word *trauma*, Winnicott maintains that the fetus may be impinged upon by the "mother's rigidity and unadaptability (due to her anxiety or her depression mood)" (1988a, 128). R. D. Laing also believes it likely that intrauterine experience from conception to birth may be mapped onto natal and postnatal experience; he states that even the implantation of the fertilized egg in the uterine wall may in some cases be a traumatic event, giving rise to feeling "frantic, helpless, impotent" (1976, 45). The work of M. Lietaert Peerbolte (1975) is also in accord with Laing, describing many different types of prenatal trauma as represented in the dreams of psychoanalytic patients, and there are many excellent studies of prenatal trauma documented in the *Pre- and Perinatal Psychology Journal* (see especially Emerson 1989). Finally, the copious research of Stanislav Grof strongly indicates that human beings universally experience wounding within the womb. He states that feelings such as "separation, alienation, metaphysical loneliness, helplessness, hopelessness, inferiority, and guilt" are integral to a stage of the intrauterine experience and "appear to have a primary quality intrinsic to human nature" (1975, 118, 119). We would say yes, that this trauma is ubiquitous, but it is not intrinsic.

3. R. D. Laing (1976) also suggests a connection between mythology and intrauterine experience.

4. We are here ignoring the many different specifics of this split as elaborated by various thinkers mentioned earlier, remaining focused on the essence of positive-negative splitting. This is not the time, for example, to discuss Klein's distinction between the good object and the idealized object (her good object is akin to what we call later the *survival unifying center*).

5. We therefore disagree in part with Guntrip's statement just quoted (and with Fairbairn, whose ideas Guntrip is discussing in the quotation). While there does seem to be a compensating balance between the negative and positive, and the negative is repressed, the caregivers cannot carry the full idealization needed to compensate for the negative system. It would seem that most caregivers—no matter how much the child may ignore their destructive side—cannot completely fulfill the pattern of perfection needed to balance the heavy weight of nonbeing wounding. Perhaps an idealized inner fantasy world or an idealized image of Divinity can support such a bond, but the actual human parent cannot but eventually fail here. Thus a significant part, perhaps most, of the positive must also be repressed along with the wounding, amounting to a "repression of the sublime" (Haronian 1974).

6. Psychosynthesis hereby may begin to offer a point of view that not only includes the splitting found in the general population, but that recognized in more severe disturbances such as psychoses, narcissistic and borderline disorders, mood disorders, anxiety disorders, and substance abuse. For example, narcissistic disorders would relate to the positive personality and positive unifying center of the higher unconscious; depression, rage, and anxiety to the negative personality and negative unifying center of the lower unconscious; and borderline and bipolar disorder to an inability to form any stability between the higher and lower.

Chapter Six: The Higher and Lower Unconscious

1. In psychotheological terms, the lower unconscious would not constitute hell, nor would the higher unconscious constitute heaven. Hell would be a personal choice for nonrelationship with one's deepest authenticity or truth, and both the higher and lower unconscious may be used to this end. One may be in hell—that is, choosing non-relationship with deepest Self—just as much in the higher unconscious as in the lower unconscious. Similarly, a true heaven would imply a good relationship with Self and the concomitant right relationships with one's personality, other people, and the world.

2. Winnicott (1963) points out a most striking example of this preference for negative being over nonbeing when he maintains that even the chaos and fragmentation of psychosis is a defense—a defense against a deeper primitive agony that we would trace to primal wounding.

Chapter Seven: Personalities and Subpersonalities

1. Note then that Fairbairn, Winnicott, and Kohut all point to the normality of splitting—more testimony to the ubiquitous nature of primal wounding.

2. For an excellent example of the development of, and recovery from, such a

survival personality, see Ingo Hasselbach's (Hasselbach and Reiss 1996) story of his experience as a neo-Nazi.

3. This energetic model of shame and guilt is analogous to the psychoanalytic notion that guilt is a tension between the ego and superego, while shame is a tension between the ego and ego-ideal (Piers and Singer 1971).

4. We are indebted here to the discussions of R. Shor's (Shor and Orne 1965) study of hypnosis in both Deikman (1982) and Tart (1987). Shor describes very much this same process in his analysis of hypnotic trance: a constriction of one's "generalized reality orientation," the assuming of a role, and a dependency on the hypnotist. Of course, good hypnotherapy respects and supports the free will of the subject.

5. For an excellent short essay illustrating the power of the family trance, see Calof 1994.

Chapter Eight: Self-Realization

1. Assagioli at times tended to confuse the terms *transpersonal psychosynthesis* and *Self-realization*. As will become clear, we use transpersonal psychosynthesis to refer to the integration of higher unconscious, unitive, and mystical experiences, and Self-realization to refer to the I-Self relationship which can operate with or without any such experiences (see Firman and Russell 1993, Firman 1996).

2. The mystic, Hindu monk, and social scientist Agehananda Bharati writes from his own experience in India and elsewhere: "On the other hand, I have witnessed, with much initial dismay, that some of the best mystics were the greatest stinkers among men. Self-righteous, smug, anti-women, anti-men, politically fascist, stubborn, irrational" (Bharati 1976, 91).

3. Here is the Buddhist monk Ajahn Amaro speaking to this same dynamic: "Of course, if you go on retreats for 20 years you can create tremendous inner space. But it can become almost like a police state. You just clear the streets of all the unruly inhabitants of your mind. And while you may get them off the streets, the guerillas will still be active underground. So when you leave the retreat, you begin to experience your ordinary life as difficult and turbulent. Then you can't wait to get to the next retreat" (Amaro 1995, 4).

And here is Jack Kornfield speaking of his return to the United States after five years in Asia practicing as a Buddhist monk: "What I found upon my return is that there are compartments in the mind. Although I worked well in certain compartments, when I got into an intimate relationship again, I was back exactly where I had left off: I was saying and doing the same old things. What was horrifying and interesting was that I could see it very clearly. Things that had been themes in my life—loneliness, fear of abandonment—were very, very visible. The same issues and fears not only remained but came back in spades" (Simpkinson 1993, 37).

4. More recently, this concept of call as a relationship between the individual and Self has been addressed well in the work of Greg Bogart (Bogart 1994; Bogart 1995), a transpersonal therapist who has researched the phenomenon of finding a life's calling. Bogart's own call to be a psychotherapist came via a nocturnal dream, an ecstatic moment, and an obscene phone call!

5. For a discussion of the connection between shame and a sense of the sacred and holy, see Schneider 1977.

6. This type of distinction between healthy and unhealthy guilt and shame is made by Maslow (1962, 114) in his concepts of real guilt and neurotic guilt, by Buber (1988) in distinguishing existential guilt from guilt having to do with repressed childhood dynamics, and by Bradshaw's (1988b) distinction between toxic shame and healthy shame.

7. It is interesting that these two principles operate together at conception: the dependent-receptive position of the ovum and the independent-active position of the sperm, the fertilized egg a product of the two. These two positions of sperm and egg have been reported as important in working with traumas of conception (cf. Emerson 1989, Farrant 1985). It would also seem possible to see sperm and egg each manifesting both principles at different times (e.g., the selectivity of the ovum, the dissolution of the sperm).

8. This does not of course preclude society's right to set standards of acceptable behavior and enforce them. We are talking here about the individual's relationship to her or his own truth.

9. This is a modification of Assagioli's original diagram that represented Self in the higher unconscious. Depicting Self in the higher unconscious has supported a confusion between the integration of higher unconscious contents (what we are calling the transpersonal dimension) and Self-realization—it gave the impression that one must move into the higher unconscious in Self-realization. However, Assagioli was otherwise extremely clear that higher unconscious experiences—peak experiences, mystical experiences, and spiritual awakening—were quite distinct from the process of Self-realization. This modified diagram has been employed by Molly Young Brown and Tom Yeomans (Brown 1993, 229), and by Ann Gila and myself (Firman and Russell 1993).

10. Here is Dwight Judy clearly describing this same interplay of light and dark: "The Christian mystical tradition has spoken of the process of ensouling as initially quite traumatic, during which there are alternations between periods of illumination and of purification. In fact, this initial stage is often called 'purgation' (Underhill 1961). I suggest that the natural response of the soul to an infusion of energy or insight from the causal realms or simply from the relaxation of egoic tensions is to dredge up repressed material from the childhood mythic mind. These monsters of the deep contain within themselves the clues to unlock the pathologies of our bodies as well as of our emotions" (Judy 1991, 52).

Chapter Nine: Psychosynthesis Therapy

1. Assagioli's (1965) four stages are (1) thorough knowledge of one's personality, (2) control of the various elements of the personality, (3) realization of one's true self—the discovery or creation of a unifying center, and (4) psychosynthesis: the formation or reconstruction of the personality around the new center.

2. For descriptions of the empathic approach employed successfully even in serious cases of psychopathology see Stolorow, Brandchaft, and Atwood (1987), Stolorow and Atwood (1992), and Stolorow, Brandchaft, and Atwood (1994).

3. David's story is based on an actual case, but has been disguised in order to guard the identity of the client. David is of course not his true name, the gender of client and therapist may or may not be correct, there are elements of the case that have been borrowed from other cases (again in disguised forms), and quoted dialogues are loose paraphrases of the originals. David's case thus represents an authentic pattern of psychosynthesis therapy while providing anonymity for therapist and client.

4. Kohut (1971) goes so far as to say that empathic failure can constitute *optimal frustration* and become a main way of building a sense of self. However, we would say that building and maintaining the empathic connection is what nurtures self, and that such failures and their repair are simply part of this larger process. Stolorow (Stolorow, Brandchaft, and Atwood 1987) agrees with our view, replacing Kohut's notion of optimal frustration with his concept of *optimal empathy*.

Also, the reader will note here that the therapist did not report her deeper responses of inadequacy and resentment beneath the spacing out. She did not feel that David was asking for this type of self-revelation from her, but only a validation of the particular interaction. However, the sharing of such responses is quite appropriate when the client is asking to go to that depth or the therapist thinks it essential to the emerging issue (see Maroda 1991). But as always, interventions must always be held within and be judged in relationship to the empathic connection to the client.

5. Had David not had this dream, the higher unconscious could have been approached eventually with interventions that ask, "What is the ideal situation you would create in your life if there were no limitations?" This type of question moves toward the higher unconscious, just as a question like, "What would it be like *not* to get what you want out of life?" moves toward the lower unconscious. Both lines of inquiry are useful in exploring, transforming, and integrating unconscious material in the overall expansion of the middle unconscious.

6. This type of religious referral is an ethical responsibility for any therapist, quite the same as refering matters of physical illness to a physician or legal issues to a lawyer. If the therapist does not recognize this need for a religious or spiritual unifying center, there may be confusion between a spiritual psychology and a religious

tradition or spiritual path. If this occurs, the client (and therapist) may be tempted to use psychology to meet needs for community, tradition, and scripture. The dangers of not recognizing the client's burgeoning need for a larger spiritual-moral context beyond the therapeutic setting have been discussed elsewhere (Firman 1991).

Chapter Ten: The Psychosynthesis Therapist

1. Howard Book speaks of this distinction between information and empathy as that between "empathy" and "being empathic." For Book, empathy is an "experiencing of the patient's conscious and unconscious emotional states," while being empathic uses this information to "voice comments about this patient's internal state, which results in the patient's feeling understood and soothed" (Book 1988, 421).

2. The notion of sympathetic resonance was first introduced to psychosynthesis theory by Vargiu (1977) in describing the relationship between the higher unconscious and the personality as a whole. According to Rowan (1990, 151), this concept has also been employed by John Watkins (1978) in describing the resonance between ego-states in psychotherapy.

3. It seems countertransference reactions are a major dynamic behind child abuse and neglect. When a child expresses a type of experience that resonates to the caretaker's own repressed wounding, the caretaker will be mobilized to change the child's experience at all costs. The caretaker may not, for instance, be able to tolerate the desperate expression of the infant's pain because this energizes the desperation of the caretaker's own pain. One study reported that 80 percent of parents interviewed said that excessive infant crying was the reason for the battering (Check 1989). The caretaker may actually feel that the child is *creating* these terrible feelings in the caretaker, rather than energizing latent feelings already present. In such a case, the infant's pain may trigger physical violence or cold withdrawal because the caretaker must keep this raw nonbeing state repressed both within and without. It seems clear that the healing of our own primal wounding is perhaps the greatest gift we can give children.

4. In the early 1970s Tom Yeomans simply called this openness *presence*, and it has remained an aspect of psychosynthesis clinical theory since then (see Brown 1983, Whitmore 1991).

5. For an outline of inner child work and recovering authentic personality, see Firman and Russell 1994.

Bibliography

Allport, G. 1961. *Pattern and Growth in Personality*. New York: Holt, Rinehart, and Winston.

Amaro, A. 1995. "The Happy Monk." *Inquiring Mind* 12, no. 1:4–13.

Ariès, P. 1962. *Centuries of Childhood: A Social History of Family Life*. Translated by R. Baldick. New York: Vintage Books.

Armstrong, T. 1985. *The Radiant Child*. Wheaton, Ill.: Quest; London: The Theosophical Publishing House.

Assagioli, R. 1965. *Psychosynthesis: A Manual of Principles and Techniques*. New York: Viking.

———. 1973a. *The Act of Will*. New York: Penguin.

———. 1973b. *The Conflict Between the Generations and the Psychosynthesis of the Human Ages*. Vol. 31. New York: Psychosynthesis Research Foundation.

———. 1973c. Audiotape.

Aziz, R. 1990. *C. G. Jung's Psychology of Religion and Synchronicity*. Albany: State University of New York Press.

Balint, M. 1968. *The Basic Fault: Therapeutic Aspects of Regression*. London and New York: Tavistock/Routledge.

Baures, M. M. 1996. "Letting Go of Bitterness and Hate." *Journal of Humanistic Psychology* 36, no. 1:75–90.

Beebe, B., and F. Lachmann. 1988. "Mother-Infant Mutual Influence and Precursors of Self and Object Representations." In *Frontiers in Self Psychology: Progress in Self Psychology*, edited by A. Goldberg. Vol. 3. Hillsdale, N.J.: The Analytic Press.

Bharati, A. 1976. *The Light at the Center: Context and Pretest of Modern Mysticism*. Santa Barbara, Calif.: Ross-Erikson.

Binswanger, L. 1958. "The Existential Analysis School of Thought." In *Existence: A New Dimension in Psychiatry and Psychology*, edited by R. May, E. Angel, and H. Ellenberger. New York: Basic Books.

Blakney, R., ed. 1941. *Meister Eckhart*. New York: Harper & Row.

Bogart, G. 1994. "Finding a Life's Calling." *Journal of Humanistic Psychology* 34, no. 4:6–37.

———. 1995. *Finding Your Life's Calling: Spiritual Dimensions of Vocational Choice.* Berkeley, Calif.: Dawn Mountain Press.

Bollas, C. 1987. *The Shadow of the Object: Psychoanalysis of the Unthought Known.* London: Free Association Books.

Book, H. E. 1988. "Empathy: Misconceptions and Misuses in Psychotherapy." *American Journal of Psychiatry* 145, no. 4:420–24.

Boorstin, D. J. 1983. *The Discoverers.* New York: Vintage.

Bowlby, J. 1973. *Separation: Anxiety and Anger.* New York: Basic Books.

Bradshaw, J. 1988a. *Bradshaw on: The Family.* Deerfield Beach, Fla.: Health Communications.

———. 1988b. *Healing the Shame that Binds You.* Deerfield Beach, Fla.: Health Communications.

Brown, M. 1983. *The Unfolding Self.* Los Angeles: Psychosynthesis Press.

———. 1993. *Growing Whole: Self-realization on an Endangered Planet.* A Hazelden Book. New York: Harper Collins.

Brownell, B. 1950. *The Human Community: Its Philosophy and Practice for a Time of Crisis.* New York: Harper and Brothers.

Buber, M. 1958. *I and Thou.* Translated by R. G. Smith. New York: Charles Scribner's Sons.

———. 1988. *The Knowledge of Man.* Translated by M. Friedman and R. G. Smith. Edited by M. Friedman. Atlantic Highlands, N.J.: Humanities Press International.

Bucke, R. 1967. *Cosmic Consciousness.* Reprint, New York: E. P. Dutton. Originally published in 1901.

Calof, D. L. 1994. "False Reality." *Common Boundary* 12, no. 5 (September/October): 57–61.

Carter-Haar, B. 1975. "Identity and Personal Freedom." *Synthesis* 2:56–91.

Chamberlain, D. 1988. *Babies Remember Birth.* Los Angeles: Jeremy P. Tarcher.

———. 1994. "The Sentient Prenate: What Every Parent Should Know." *Pre- and Perinatal Psychology Journal* 9, no. 1:9–31.

Check, W. A. 1989. *Child Abuse.* New York and Philadelphia: Chelsea House.

Couliano, I. P. 1992. *The Tree of Gnosis: Gnostic Mythology from Early Christianity to Modern Nihilism.* San Francisco: HarperSan Francisco.

Deikman, A. 1982. *The Observing Self.* Boston: Beacon Press.

deMause, L., ed. 1974. *The History of Childhood: The Untold Story of Child Abuse.* New York: Peter Bedrick Books.

DeRopp, R. 1968. *The Master Game.* New York: Delacorte Press.

Desoille, R. 1945. *Le Rêve Éveillé en Psychotherapie.* Paris: Presses Universitaires de France.

Dowd, A. 1992. "Making Room for the Recovery Boom." *Library Journal*, 1 May, 49–52.

Edinger, E. 1972. *Ego and Archetype*. New York: Penguin.

Emerson, W. R. 1989. "Psychotherapy with Infants and Children." *Pre- and Post-Natal Psychology* 3, no. 3:190–217.

Fairbairn, W. R. D. 1986. *Psychoanalytic Studies of the Personality*. London and Boston: Routledge & Kegan Paul.

Farrant, G. 1985. "Cellular Consciousness: From Preconception to Fertilization." Paper delivered at the Pre- and Perinatal Psychology Congress. Sponsored by the Association for Pre- and Perinatal Psychology and Health. San Diego, Calif.

Ferm, V. 1945. "Soul." In *An Encyclopedia of Religion*, edited by V. Ferm. New York: The Philosophical Library.

Ferrucci, P. 1982. *What We May Be*. Los Angeles: Jeremy P. Tarcher.

Firestone, R. W. 1987. *The Fantasy Bond*. New York: Human Sciences Press.

Firman, J. 1991. *"I" and Self: Re-visioning Psychosynthesis*. Palo Alto, Calif.: Psychosynthesis Palo Alto.

———. 1996. *Self and Self-Realization*. Palo Alto, Calif.: Psychosynthesis Palo Alto.

Firman, J., and A. Russell. 1993. *What is Psychosynthesis?* 2d ed. Palo Alto, Calif.: Psychosynthesis Palo Alto.

———. 1994. *Opening to the Inner Child: Recovering Authentic Personality*. Palo Alto, Calif.: Psychosynthesis Palo Alto.

Firman, J., and J. Vargiu. 1977. "Dimensions of Growth." *Synthesis* 3/4:60–120.

———. 1980. "Personal and Transpersonal Growth: The Perspective of Psychosynthesis." In *Transpersonal Psychotherapy*, edited by S. Boorstein. Palo Alto, Calif.: Science and Behavior Books.

Frankl, V. E. 1967. *Psychotherapy and Existentialism*. New York: Washington Square Press.

———. 1975. *The Unconscious God*. Reprint, New York: Pocket Books. Originally published in 1948.

Franz, R. 1963. "Pattern Vision in Newborn Infants." *Science* 140:296–97.

Freud, A. 1946. *The Ego and the Mechanisms of Defense*. New York: International Universities Press.

Freud, S. 1961. *Civilization and Its Discontents*. Reprinted in *The Standard Edition of the Complete Psychological Works of Sigmund Freud*, edited by J. Strachey. Vol. 21. New York: W. W. Norton. Originally published in 1930.

———. 1965. *New Introductory Lectures on Psychoanalysis*. New York: W.W. Norton.

———. 1981a. "Family Romances." Reprinted in *The Standard Edition of the Complete Works of Sigmund Freud*, edited by J. Strachey. Vol. 9. London: The Hogarth Press and the Institute of Psycho-analysis. Originally published in 1909.

————. 1981b. "On the Sexual Theories of Children." Reprinted in *The Standard Edition of the Complete Psychological Works of Sigmund Freud*, edited by J. Strachey. Vol. 9. London: The Hogarth Press and the Institute of Psycho-analysis. Originally published in 1908.

————. 1981c. "An Outline of Psycho-Analysis." Reprinted in *The Standard Edition of the Complete Psychological Works of Sigmund Freud*, edited by J. Strachey. Vol. 23. London: The Hogarth Press and the Institute of Psycho-analysis. Originally published in 1940.

————. 1981d. "Splitting of the Ego in the Process of Defence." Reprinted in *The Standard Edition of the Complete Psychological Works of Sigmund Freud*, edited by J. Strachey. Vol. 23. London: The Hogarth Press and the Institute of Psychoanalysis. Originally published in 1940.

Friedlander, B. Z. 1970. "Receptive Language Development in Infancy." *Merril-Palmer Quarterly* 16:7–15.

Galatzer-Levy, R. M., and B. J. Cohler. 1993. *The Essential Other*. New York: Basic Books.

Globus, G. 1980. "On 'I': The Conceptual Foundations of Responsibility." *American Journal of Psychiatry* 137, no. 4:417–22.

Grof, C. 1993. *The Thirst for Wholeness: Attachment, Addiction, and the Spiritual Path*. New York: Harper San Francisco.

Grof, S. 1975. *Realms of the Human Unconscious: Observations from LSD Research*. New York: Viking.

Grotstein, J. S. 1986. *Splitting and Projective Identification*. Northvale, N.J.: Jason Aronson.

Guntrip, H. 1961. *Personality Structure and Human Interaction*. New York: International Universities Press.

————. 1971. *Psychoanalytic Theory, Therapy, and the Self*. New York: Basic Books.

Haronian, F. 1974. "The Repression of the Sublime." *Synthesis* 1:125–36.

Hasselbach, I., and T. Reiss. 1996. "How Nazis are Made." *The New Yorker* 71, no. 43 (8 January): 36–56.

Heidegger, M. 1949. *Existence and Being*. Translated by Werner Block. Chicago: Henry Regnery.

Herman, J. L. 1992. *Trauma and Recovery*. New York: Basic Books.

Higgins, G. O. 1994. *Resilient Adults: Overcoming a Cruel Past*. San Francisco: Jossey-Bass.

Hillman, J. 1975. *Re-Visioning Psychology*. New York: Harper & Row.

Huxley, A. 1945. *The Perennial Philosophy*. New York: Harper & Brothers.

Jacobi, J. 1967. *The Way of Individuation*. Meridian, N.Y.: New American Library.

James, W. 1961. *The Varieties of Religious Experience*. New York: Collier Books. Originally published in 1902.

Jonas, H. 1963. *The Gnostic Religion*. Boston: Beacon Press.

Judy, D. H. 1991. *Christian Meditation and Inner Healing.* New York: Crossroad.

Jung, C. G. 1976. *The Development of Personality.* In *The Collected Works of C. G. Jung.* Vol. 17. Princeton: Princeton University Press.

———. 1972. *Two Essays on Analytical Psychology.* In *The Collected Works of C. G. Jung.* Vol. 7. Princeton: Princeton University Press.

———. 1979. *Aion.* In *The Collected Works of C. G. Jung.* Vol. 9, pt. 2. Princeton: Princeton University Press.

———. 1969. *Psychology and Religion: West and East.* 2nd ed. In *The Collected Works of C. G. Jung.* Vol. 11. Princeton: Princeton University Press.

———. 1960. *The Structure and Dynamics of the Psyche.* 2d ed. In *The Collected Works of C. G. Jung.* Vol. 8. Princeton: Princeton University Press.

———. 1971. *Psychological Types.* In *The Collected Works of C. G. Jung.* Vol. 6. Princeton: Princeton University Press.

Kahn, M. 1991. *Between Therapist and Client: The New Relationship.* New York: W. H. Freeman.

Kaiser, H. 1965. *Effective Psychotherapy.* New York: The Free Press.

Kellert, S., and E. O. Wilson, eds. 1993. *The Biophilia Hypothesis.* Washington D.C.: Island Press.

Kernberg, O. 1992. *Borderline Conditions and Pathological Narcissism.* Northvale, N.J.: Jason Aronson.

Kierkegaard, S. 1954. *The Sickness Unto Death.* Translated by Walter Lowrie. New York: Doubleday.

Klein, M. 1975. *Envy and Gratitude and Other Works, 1946–1963.* New York: Dell.

Kohut, H. 1971. *The Analysis of the Self.* Vol. 4 of *The Psychoanalytic Study of the Child.* Madison, Conn.: International Universities Press.

———. 1977. *The Restoration of the Self.* Madison, Conn.: International Universities Press.

———. 1978. *The Search for the Self: Selected Writings of Heinz Kohut, 1950–1978.* Vol. 1. Madison, Conn.: International Universities Press.

———. 1984. *How Does Analysis Cure?* Edited by A. Goldberg. Chicago: The University of Chicago Press.

———. 1985. *Self Psychology and the Humanities.* New York: W. W. Norton.

Kritsberg, W. 1985. *The Adult Children of Alcoholics Syndrome.* New York: Bantam Books.

Laing, R. D. 1976. *The Facts of Life: An Essay in Feelings, Facts, and Fantasy.* New York: Pantheon.

Laski, M. 1968. *Ecstasy: A Study of Some Secular and Religious Experiences.* New York: Greenwood Press.

Lee, R. R., and J. C. Martin. 1991. *Psychotherapy after Kohut.* Hillsdale, N.J.: The Analytic Press.

Lewis, C. S. 1955. *Surprised by Joy.* New York: Harcourt Brace Jovanovich.

Lichtenberg, J. D. 1983. *Psychoanalysis and Infant Research.* Hillsdale, N.J.: The Analytic Press.

MacFarlane, J. 1975. "Olfaction in the Development of Social Preferences in the Human Neonate." In *Parent-Infant Interaction,* edited by M. Hofer. Amsterdam: Elsevier.

Maddi, S. R. 1967. "The Existential Neurosis." *Journal of Abnormal Psychology* 72:311–25.

Mahler, M. S., F. Pine, and A. Bergman. 1975. *The Psychological Birth of the Human Infant.* New York: Basic Books.

Maroda, K. J. 1991. *The Power of Countertransference: Innovations in Analytic Technique.* Edited by F. Epting, B. Strickland, and J. Allen. Wiley Series on Psychotherapy and Counselling. New York: John Wiley & Sons.

Maslow, A. 1962. *Toward a Psychology of Being.* Princeton, N.J.: D. Van Nostrand.

———. 1971. *The Farther Reaches of Human Nature.* New York: Viking.

Masson, J. M. 1984. *The Assault on Truth: Freud's Suppression of the Seduction Theory.* New York: Farrar, Straus, & Giroux.

———. 1990. *Final Analysis.* New York: Harper Collins.

Masterson, J. F. 1981. *The Narcissistic and Borderline Disorders.* New York: Brunner/Mazel.

May, R. 1977. *The Meaning of Anxiety.* New York: Pocket Books.

May, R,. E. Angel, and H. Ellenberger, eds. 1958. *Existence: A New Dimension in Psychiatry and Psychology.* New York: Basic Books.

Mellody, P. 1992. *Facing Love Addiction: Giving Yourself the Power to Change the Way You Love.* San Francisco: HarperSan Francisco.

Meriam, C. W. 1994. *Digging up the Past: Object Relations and Subpersonalities.* Palo Alto, Calif.: Psychosynthesis Palo Alto.

Miller, A. 1981. *The Drama of the Gifted Child.* New York: Basic Books.

———. 1984a. *For Your Own Good: Hidden Cruelty in Child-Rearing and the Roots of Violence.* Translated by H. and H. Hannum. New York: Farrar, Straus, & Giroux.

———. 1984b. *Thou Shalt Not Be Aware: Society's Betrayal of the Child.* Translated by H. and H. Hannum. New York: New American Library.

———. 1991. *Breaking Down the Wall of Silence.* New York: E. P. Dutton.

Miller, S. 1975. "Dialogue with the Higher Self." *Synthesis* 2:122–39.

Neumann, E. 1973. *The Child.* Translated by R. Manheim. London: Maresfield Library.

———. 1989. *The Place of Creation.* Translated by H. Nagel, E. Rolfe, J. van Heurck, and K. Winston. Bollingen Series. Princeton: Princeton University Press.

Nigg, W. 1962. *The Heretics.* Translated by R. and C. Winston. New York: Dorset Press.

Pearce, J. C. 1979. *Magical Child: Recovering Nature's Plan for Our Children.* New York: Paladin.

Peerbolte, M. L. 1975. *Psychic Energy in Prenatal Dynamics, Parapsychology, Peak-Experiences.* Wassenaar, The Netherlands: Servire Publishers.

Piaget, J. 1973. *The Child and Reality: Problems of Genetic Psychology.* Translated by A. Rosin. New York: Penguin Books.

Piaget, J. and B. Inhelder. 1967. *The Child's Conception of Space.* Translated by F. J. Langdon and J. L. Lunzer. The Norton Library. Reprint, New York: W. W. Norton. Originally published in 1948.

Piers, G., and M. B. Singer. 1971. *Shame and Guilt: A Psychoanalytic and a Cultural Study.* New York: W. W. Norton.

Polster, E. 1995. *A Population of Selves: A Therapeutic Exploration of Personal Diversity.* San Francisco: Jossey-Bass.

Postman, N. 1994. *The Disappearance of Childhood.* New York: Vintage.

Ram Dass. 1980. "Relative Realities." In *Beyond Ego: Transpersonal Dimensions in Psychology,* edited by R. Walsh and F. Vaughan. Los Angeles: Jeremy P. Tarcher.

Rank, O. 1990. "The Myth of the Birth of the Hero." In *In Quest of the Hero,* edited by R. A. Segal. Reprint, Princeton: Princeton University Press. Originally published in 1909.

Raymond of Capua. 1980. *The Life of Catherine of Sienna.* Reprint, Wilmington, Del.: Michael Glazier. Originally published in 1395.

Richards, D. G. 1990. "Dissociation and Transformation." *Journal of Humanistic Psychology* 30, no. 3:54–83.

Riordan, K. 1975. "Gurdjieff." In *Transpersonal Psychologies,* edited by C. Tart. New York: Harper & Row.

Robinson, J. 1983. *The Original Vision: A Study of the Religious Experience of Childhood.* New York: The Seabury Press.

Rogers, C. R. 1980. *A Way of Being.* Boston: Houghton Mifflin.

Romberg, R. 1985. *Circumcision: The Painful Dilemma.* South Hadley, Mass.: Bergin & Garvey.

Rowan, J. 1990. *Subpersonalities: The People Inside Us.* New York: Routledge.

Russell, A. 1977. "Integrating Transpersonal Experiences." *Synthesis* 3/4:129–34.

———. 1990. "Healing as Self-Acceptance: Living Authentically and Fully through our Woundedness." Keynote address at Moving Beyond Survival Conference. Three Rivers Center, Menlo Park, Calif.

Schneider, C. D. 1977. *Shame, Exposure, and Privacy.* Boston: Beacon Press.

Schumacher, E. F. 1977. *A Guide for the Perplexed.* New York: Harper & Row.

Shane, E., and M. Shane. 1990. "Object Loss and Selfobject Loss." In *The Annual of Psychoanalysis.* Vol. 18. Hillsdale, N.J.: The Analytic Press.

Shapiro, F. 1995. *Eye Movement Desensitization and Reprocessing: Basic Principles, Protocols, and Procedures.* New York: Guilford Press.

Shor, R., and M. Orne, eds. 1965. *The Nature of Hypnosis*. New York: Holt, Rinehart, and Winston.

Simpkinson, A. A. 1993. "Mindful Living." *Common Boundary* 11, no. 4:34–40.

Sterba, R. 1934. "The Fate of the Ego in Analytic Therapy." *The International Journal of Psycho-analysis* 15:116–26.

Stern, D. 1985. *The Interpersonal World of the Infant*. New York: Basic Books.

Stevens, A. 1982. *Archetype: A Natural History of the Self*. London: Routledge.

Stolorow, R. D., and G. E. Atwood. 1992. *Contexts of Being: The Intersubjective Foundations of Psychological Life*. Hillsdale, N.J.: The Analytic Press.

Stolorow, R. D., B. Brandchaft, and G. E. Atwood. 1987. *Psychoanalytic Treatment: An Intersubjective Approach*. Hillsdale, N.J.: The Analytic Press.

Stolorow, R. D., G. E. Atwood, and B. Brandchaft, eds. 1994. *The Intersubjective Perspective*. Northvale, N.J.: Jason Aronson.

Tackett, V. 1988. "Treating Mental and Emotional Abuse." In *Readings in Psychosynthesis: Theory, Process, and Practice*, edited by J. Weiser and T. Yeomans. Vol. 2. Toronto: The Department of Applied Psychology/The Ontario Institute for Studies in Education.

Tart, C. 1987. *Waking Up*. Boston: Shambhala.

Terr, L. 1990. *Too Scared to Cry*. New York: Harper & Row.

———. 1994. *Unchained Memories: True Stories of Traumatic Memoires, Lost and Found*. New York: Basic Books.

Tillich, P. 1952. *The Courage To Be*. New Haven: Yale University Press.

Trungpa, C. 1973. *Cutting Through Spiritual Materialism*. Edited by J. Baker and M. Casper. The Clear Light Series. Berkeley, Calif.: Shambhala.

"Transpersonal Qualities." 1970[?]. Redwood City, Calif.: Psychosynthesis Institute.

Tuchman, B. W. 1978. *A Distant Mirror*. New York: Ballantine Books.

Underhill, E. 1961. *Mysticism*. New York: E. P. Dutton.

Vargiu, J. 1974. "Subpersonalities." *Synthesis* 1:52–90.

———. 1977. "Creativity." *Synthesis* 3/4:17–53.

———. 1978. "Courses at Synthesis Graduate School." San Francisco: Synthesis Graduate School.

Vaughan, F. 1985. *The Inward Arc*. New Science Library. Boston: Shambhala.

Verny, T., and J. Kelly. 1981. *The Secret Life of the Unborn Child*. New York: Dell.

Walsh, R. N., and F. Vaughan, eds. 1980a. *Beyond Ego: Transpersonal Dimensions in Psychology*. Los Angeles: Jeremy P. Tarcher.

———. 1980b. "Comparative Models: Of the Person and Psychotherapy." In *Transpersonal Psychotherapy*, edited by S. Boorstein. Palo Alto, Calif.: Science and Behavior Books.

Washburn, M. 1988. *The Ego and the Dynamic Ground*. Albany: State University of New York Press.

———. 1994. *Transpersonal Psychology in Psychoanalytic Perspective*. Philosophy of Psychology. Albany: State University of New York Press.

Watkins, J. G. 1978. *The Therapeutic Self*. New York: Human Sciences Press.

Whitfield, C. L. 1991. *Co-dependence: Healing the Human Condition*. Deerfield Beach, Fla.: Health Communications.

———. 1995. *Memory and Abuse: Remembering and Healing the Effects of Trauma*. Deerfield Beach, Fla.: Health Communications.

Whitmore, D. 1991. *Psychosynthesis Counselling in Action*. London: Sage.

Wilber, K. 1980. *The Atman Project*. Wheaton, Ill.: The Theosophical Publishing House.

———. 1983. *Eye to Eye: The Quest for the New Paradigm*. Garden City, N.Y.: Anchor Books.

Wilber, K., J. Engler., and D. Brown. 1986. *Transformations of Consciousness*. Boston: Shambhala.

Winnicott, D. W. 1963. "Fear of Breakdown." In *Psycho-Analytic Explorations*, edited by C. Winnicott, R. Shepherd, and M. Davis. Cambridge: Harvard University Press, 1989.

———. 1986. *Home is Where We Start From: Essays by a Psychoanalyst*. London: Penguin.

———. 1987. *The Maturational Processes and the Facilitating Environment*. London: The Hogarth Press and the Institute of Psycho-Analysis.

———. 1988a. *Human Nature*. New York: Schocken Books.

———. 1988b. *Playing and Reality*. London: Penguin.

Wu, J. 1975. *The Golden Age of Zen*. Taipei: United Publishing Center.

Yeomans, T. 1992. *Occasional Note (February)*. Concord, Mass.: Concord Institute.

Yoder, B. 1990. *The Recovery Resource Book*. New York: Simon & Schuster.

Zweig, C., and J. Abrams, eds. 1990. *Meeting the Shadow: The Hidden Power of the Dark Side of Human Nature*. Los Angeles: Jeremy P. Tarcher.

Index

Italicized numerals refer to pages with illustrations.